CRACKING *the* TECH CAREER

CRACKING *the* TECH CAREER

Insider Advice on Landing a Job at Google, Microsoft, Apple, or Any Top Tech Company

GAYLE LAAKMANN MCDOWELL

WILEY

Cover image: © iStock.com/min6939

Cover design: Wiley

Published by John Wiley & Sons, Inc., Hoboken, New Jersey.

Published simultaneously in Canada.

For general information about our other products and services, please contact our Customer Care Department within the United States at (800) 762-2974, outside the United States at (317) 572-3993 or fax (317) 572-4002.

Wiley publishes in a variety of print and electronic formats and by print-on-demand. Some material included with standard print versions of this book may not be included in e-books or in print-on-demand. If this book refers to media such as a CD or DVD that is not included in the version you purchased, you may download this material at http://booksupport.wiley.com. For more information about Wiley products, visit www.wiley.com.

ISBN: 978-1-118-96808-6 (pbk.)

ISBN: 978-1-118-96809-3 (ebk)

ISBN: 978-1-118-96895-6 (ebk)

Printed in the United States of America

10 9 8 7 6 5 4 3 2 1

Contents

1 Life at the World's Greatest Tech Companies

Everything you've heard is true. Almost.

Tech companies are known for brightly colored walls, ball pits in the office, free food (organic and gluten-free, of course), and shuttles transporting you to and from work. They're engaged in a constant game of one-upmanship, the latest and greatest company taking what its predecessor does and morphing it into something even better.

With an obvious focus on technology, their engineering divisions are presumed to be filled with nerds who eat, sleep, and breathe code. Some started coding early in life and some not until much later—but nearly all are passionate about technology. It's not just a job to them; it's something they love.

Outside of engineering—and in fact most employees at tech companies are not coders—intelligence is still prized. The focus on academics is hotly debated; some companies value elite institutions, while others recognize that many of the most brilliant people never finished college. After all, the founders of many of these companies dropped out of college.

Landing a spot at these companies can be challenging for some people, but it's absolutely doable.

Job seekers who attended strong universities are fairly technical (even if they don't want to be programmers), have strong and demonstrable skills in their chosen profession, communicate well, have solid work experience, have a strong network, and can pull this all into a nice resume—they'll probably find it not terribly difficult to land a job at a prestigious firm. They might still get rejected by their top choice, but there will be other options.

That's the ideal candidate, but most successful candidates aren't ideal. You're likely missing several of those attributes. Don't count yourself out—there's still a path in to these hot companies.

Life at Infinite Loop and Microsoft Way

Even their addresses are suggestive of company stereotypes. Microsoft, at One Microsoft Way, screams big and mammoth. Google's 1600 Amphitheatre Parkway address is understated, like its user interfaces. Apple, of course, takes the bold "think different" step with One Infinite Loop—a play on words that could come back to bite a less beloved company.

Youthful

Despite the little eccentricities of each company, these companies are much more alike than they are different. Software companies are youthful—at heart, if not in actuality. They scorn the stuffy suit-and-tie atmosphere of their predecessors and elect to wear just jeans and a T-shirt. In fact, this casual attitude is so potent that it's pervaded even the social scenes of tech hubs; only a handful of restaurants in Seattle and San Francisco would request anything beyond jeans.

Perks

Desperate to attract and retain the best and the brightest, tech firms shower their employees with perks. Microsoft offers free drinks, a heavily discounted membership to a deluxe gym, and a multitude of extracurricular sports teams. Google matched and then one-upped Microsoft on almost all of these. Free sodas? Try free breakfast, lunch, and dinner. Free gym membership? Use the on-site gym and pool. Facebook cloned many of Google's perks and added a few of their own, such as an on-site bank.

Cynics argue that there's another side to this. They argue that the perks are just there to ensure that you'll stay at the office longer, and to infantilize employees to the point where they no longer feel self-sufficient and able to quit.

That might be a nasty spin on things, but there's some truth to it. When you get your dining and daily errands done on campus, you spend less time off campus and more time working.

Work/Life Balance

Despite rumors to the contrary, the biggest tech companies generally offer a pretty reasonable work/life balance. It's not a 9-to-5 job—in fact, the office is relatively quiet at 9 a.m.—but few people work more than 45 to 50 hours per week on a regular basis. Many people work around 40 and are considered strong employees.

Hours are flexible, too. Come in early or come in late—it doesn't matter, so long as you get your work done and are there for meetings.

To a large extent, the flexibility and the work/life balance is a reaction to the difficulties these companies have in finding talented engineers. There's a shortage of great engineers in the United States. If a tech company overworked them, the company would have even more trouble hiring engineers.

The exception, as in most jobs, is during crunch times. Software releases will be stressful on any team.

Moving Up: Individual Contributors

Although other industries push high-performing employees into management roles, technology companies tend to be more open to the individual contributor role. Many companies have promotion tracks that offer a great salary and more individual responsibility without becoming a manager. After all, great engineers do not necessarily make the best managers.

An employee, particularly in engineering, can continue to get promotions and increased technical responsibilities, without becoming a people manager. Eventually, this employee can grow into an architect or a distinguished engineer, earning one of the most respected positions within the company. It's perhaps not as glamorous as being a VP, but for some people, this is just right.

The Differences

Cultural differences between companies can often be traced back to the company's roots.

- **Amazon**, many would argue, is more of a retail company than a software company. It faced extremely hard times during the dot-com crash and continues to battle profit margins that are levels of magnitude lower than those of a core software company. Amazon is consequently extremely frugal, and refrains from providing the lavish perks that other software companies might. Additionally, some employees have suggested that the company does not value technical innovation for its own sake, and instead looks for an immediate and causal link to profits. But, do not let that deter you too much; indeed, Amazon is leading in multiple industries (retail, cloud computing, etc.) largely because of its technical innovation. The company moves at a rapid pace and pending deadlines often mean late nights.
- **Apple** is just as secretive inside as it is outside. When your innovation lies so heavily in your look and feel, and your market share depends on beautifully orchestrated hype, it's no wonder. The company can't afford to let its secrets slip. Employees are die-hard fans, just as one would expect, but rarely know what coworkers from other teams are working on.
- **Microsoft** has dabbled with search and the web, but a large chunk of its earnings come from Windows and Office. Live patches to these products are expensive, so the company tends to operate on longer, multiyear release schedules. This means moving slower, taking fewer risks, and making sure to get everything right the first time. The bright side is that the company tends to have a good work/life balance, as ship dates are relatively infrequent. Many former employees say that though they loved the company, its mammoth size could stifle innovation and risk taking. However, individual team cultures are all over the map, and some may be more innovative than others.
- **Google** is the nerdiest of the nerdy. Founded by two former Stanford PhDs, the company still prizes engineers above nonengineers. The company moves quickly, shipping products weekly, and can value technical innovation even to a fault. As a web-based company, it can afford to take some risks on products; after all, shipping a new application to the web is so much easier than boxing up and mailing software. Google values its flat hierarchy, but there's a downside as well. Your manager may have too many people under her to fuss about the progress of your career, and moving up can be a challenge.

- **Facebook** has learned from Google's example and modeled much of its culture after it—with a few differences. Whereas Google tends to be more science-y and academic, Facebook prioritizes getting things done. Its original mantra—"move fast and break things"—speaks volumes about the attitude of the company. It doesn't want to let an opportunity go by because it moved too slowly or was scared of taking risks. It looks for this sort of attitude in its employees. As the company has grown, it has seen the value in getting more things right the first time, but it still retains hacker culture.

While these generalizations are fairly consistent, some companies have a great deal of variance across teams. For example, Microsoft and Amazon tend to be fairly team based and therefore less consistent in their cultures. Always investigate both your company's culture and your team's culture.

Big versus Little: Is a Start-Up Right for You?

Go to almost any business school and you'll find that there are about three times as many people who claim to be interested in start-ups than people who actually end up pursuing this career path. Why? Because start-ups are sexy.

Newspapers splash stories about start-ups that made it big, or crashed and burned, and we always think we can do that or we can do better. Start-ups are a high-stakes game, and you're gambling with your time as well as your money.

For the right person with the right opportunity, however, a start-up environment can be fantastic.

The Good

Many say that for true start-up people, this high-risk career is just in their nature. They get that entrepreneurial itch, either in college or at some big company, and know they need to be somewhere much, much smaller. And their new career path offers a ton of value to them in return:

- **Diversity of skills.** Whereas big companies have designated marketing and finance people, start-ups never have enough people to fill every role. And the smaller the company, the more hats you have to wear. Unless you are truly narrowly focused on just one field (in which case you should avoid start-ups), this can be a great thing.

You'll get to develop a more diverse skill set, which will help you in your future job search.

- **Leadership opportunities.** When—or if—your start-up grows, you'll be in a great place to lead your own team. Many people join a company and find that within months they're expected to manage several new hires. You'd have to be at a bigger company for years to get such an opportunity.
- **Control and influence.** Would you rather have a tiny influence on the error reporting tool at Microsoft, or drive a major pivot for an obscure start-up? Both are valid answers, but some might lean toward the latter. They'd rather have big, meaty things to show for their work even if their employer is unheard of. At a start-up, you are not only shaping the company in how you perform your immediate responsibilities, but you're also offering feedback on all aspects of the business. Think the newsletter should have some content about related tools and plug-ins? It's your job to speak up, and everyone will listen. You always know the decision makers in any department.
- **Rapid results.** You won't have to wait years to see your work out in the real world; it'll happen within months. That holds true for any decisions you make as well. For better or worse, the outcome is visible within months, enabling you to learn from your mistakes (and successes) much faster.
- **High reward.** Hey, we don't take on all this risk for nothing. Start-ups can make you very, very rich if you get very lucky. Of course, it could just as well do absolutely nothing for you financially—and usually that's the case.

Some people love start-ups. The speed. The innovation. The risk. The learning as you go. The impact. For as much as start-ups are glorified though, it's also reasonable to decide that they're not for you, or to at least have mixed feelings.

The Bad

Start-up burnout is a very real thing. Sure, you may be passionate about your new social-location-group-buying-thingy-dot-com, but things change and passions die. The following stresses tend to wear on people the most.

- **Long hours.** With the amount of money and careers depending on a start-up's success, long hours are critical. Those who do the bare minimum don't last long, and start-ups don't have the fear of firing underperformers that bigger companies do.

- **Unclear job description.** You were hired in to be a tester, and now you're helping look for office space. Well, tough. Someone's got to do it. Start-ups don't have the time and money to hire a specialist for each and every task, so employees are expected to chip in on projects that are outside of their roles. That may mean you spend less time doing what you love and more time doing what the company wants you to do.
- **Lower pay.** With very few exceptions, start-ups tend to pay below-industry salary and compensate for the difference with stock options. If the company fails (which it usually does), your stock options are worth nothing. Unfortunately, it's difficult to understand the worth of stock options.
- **Limited credibility.** The earliest employees of Google and Facebook have lots of credibility, but let's face it—what are the odds? You may join a start-up, only to have it fail in six months. And all of a sudden you're back on the job market with some no-name company on your resume.
- **Less mentorship.** Big companies have invested time and money in understanding how to train new employees; start-ups lack both of those things. They probably won't invest in growing you into a great leader in three years because they'll be lucky if they make it that long. Big companies can teach you a structured way of solving problems, under the guidance of more experienced professionals, while those at start-ups are learning on the go. And if your coworkers have never spent time at a big company, they may have never been taught how "real" companies do things.
- **Instability.** Start-ups are inherently unstable; it comes with the risk. If it's easy for you to find a job, you might not be too worried about job stability—yes. What happens, though, when you go through four jobs in five years? At some point, you might just want to settle down.

Interestingly, many ex-employees of big companies find that the lack of credibility was the hardest for them to deal with. They spent years where the name of their company meant something to anyone on the street. Now, they're in the same grouping as everyone else fighting for credibility and reputation.

The Ugly

In Ryan's first four years after leaving Amazon for the start-up scene, he'd worked for four different companies. He left one company because of a personality mismatch between him and the CEO. Words were exchanged.

It wasn't pretty. The next start-up folded. The third one started to veer in the wrong direction, and he decided to get out before it was too late. Lucky number four is a company he started himself.

Whenever you join a start-up, you're rolling the dice. Things tend to get messy.

- **Broken promises.** "As soon as we raise our next round of funding," one start-up CEO promises, "you'll get a promotion." It's a familiar story. The CEO likely means well. Perhaps he's being overly optimistic, but he's probably not lying. But, very often, the promotion—or the assistant, or the team, or the project—is never a reality.
- **Bad management.** Many start-up CEOs and managers are first-time managers. Sometimes they're fairly fresh out of college and barely even have work experience. They're going to screw up—a lot.
- **Working for kids.** Are you prepared to have a 25-year-old as your manager? It's unlikely at a bigger company, but it could happen at a rapidly growing start-up. This can be a problem not only in terms of the aforementioned management issues, but it can also be a blow to someone's ego to have someone so much younger manage him.
- **Lost work.** Projects getting canceled before or after launch is just part of the tech industry. It'll happen at big companies, too, but it's especially common at start-ups. A start-up might need to make a rapid change in direction and cut everything you poured your time and effort into. In fact, it's not unusual to meet someone with 20 years of experience and *zero* "surviving" projects. You typically won't get laid off if it's just a project change. The bigger concern is the effect on company morale.

It's going to be a bumpy ride. People joining start-ups should be mentally prepared for this constant change.

The Job Title: What Do You Want to Be When You Grow Up?

The question every kid is asked over and over again: "What do you want to be when you grow up?" We answer definitively as kids, but as we get older, many start to think *I really don't know.*

Few, especially outside of engineering roles, have a laser focus on their long-term career goals. That's okay. Talk to people, research positions, and start figuring out what's important to you. Ask yourself the following questions to start understanding what career path makes sense.

What Do You Need?

Our society contradicts itself every day. On one hand, we are told over and over again, "Money doesn't buy happiness," and we have the disastrous lives of celebrities to drill this into us. On the other hand, we're also told that we really do need that new jacket. Let go of what you think should matter, and be honest with yourself. How much do the following matter to you?

- **Money.** Money may not buy happiness, but it does buy your kid's college tuition. And a house in a nice neighborhood. Or maybe just a nice bottle of wine after a hard week. Does that matter to you? Be careful with looking too heavily at money. While you can be fairly confident that your teaching dream will never bring in the big bucks, you can't be as certain about many other career paths. Passionate, driven people can earn a good living in unexpected ways.
- **Recognition and respect.** Many people who shun the spotlight still desperately crave the admiration of their fellow people. How much do you care about what others think of you? Would you be okay with people giving just a courtesy smile when you share your profession?
- **Work/life balance.** There is nothing wrong with wanting a nice, stable, 9-to-5 (or in the tech world, 10-to-6) job. You want to be able to enjoy a nice day out on the boat during the summer, and that's fine. You don't have to decide to prioritize your career above everything else.

If you find your answers leaning away from a job for some reason, ask yourself why. Is there something you need from the job that you wouldn't get?

How Do You Enjoy Working?

Job seekers think so much about their project, responsibilities, company, and other factors. Few think about the actual *style* of work though. How do you enjoy working?

- **Teamwork versus independent work.** Everyone loves to say, "Teamwork is the best!" but deep down, you see the problems. Coworkers letting you down or just getting in the way. Needing a consensus just to make a decision. Managing everyone's emotions and expectations. Is this really something you enjoy?

- **Creating versus maintaining.** While software development is creating a new product, testing is maintaining it. There are no tangible results of your work; it's more like pulling the plug in a sink while the water's still running. It'll just keep coming and coming. How important is it to feel that you built something? Remember that even "maintenance" jobs (like being a surgeon) can have huge impacts on the world.
- **Leading versus joining.** Leading is great, but it's the joiners who get their hands dirty. Do you want to lead, with all the joys and responsibilities that come from that? Or would you rather relax a bit more and join someone else to accomplish a task?

What Are You Good At?

Even if you don't know what field you want to go into, you probably have an instinct as to what your skill set is. Which of the following are your strengths?

- **Numbers.** Numbers come more easily to some than to others. Are you the kind of person who can understand real-world word problems and whip up a spreadsheet to demonstrate?
- **Writing and communication.** Don't worry about prose and poetry; it's rarely relevant to the professional world. It's more important to be able to communicate effectively, both in speaking and in writing.
- **Creativity.** Creativity stretches beyond artistic skills; it's also about how you solve problems. When faced with an issue of releasing a software product in China, can you brainstorm other revenue streams to dodge the nearly 100 percent piracy rate?
- **People skills.** Being good with people is more than just being likable (though that's certainly part of it). It's also about reading people, knowing how to encourage them, and knowing when you might be pushing them too hard. Those who are especially good with people may find themselves well suited for management positions.

Most people's college majors have little to do with their eventual career path, so don't feel constrained by your major. Your skill set is so much more than your raw factual knowledge. Analyze your success and failures. Think through actual projects or jobs where you've been particularly happy or unhappy. What was it that made the difference? The answers to these questions will help point you in the right direction.

It's Not for Everyone

For many people, technology is the best field they could possibly be in. They love the culture, the world impact, the hard problems, and the fast pace.

But tech isn't universally the best, and it's not for everyone.

Some people decide to take their job, pack up their San Francisco home, and move away from the tech industry entirely—literally and figuratively. They were sick of what they felt was a college mentality. They were frustrated by constantly working under 25-year-old kids. They were turned off by an assumption that the world revolves around these tech firms. Or, perhaps they just didn't want to live in Silicon Valley anymore, where the majority of big tech companies are.

Tech is a wonderful place for the right type of person. If you think this is you, then read on . . .

2 Advanced Positioning and Preparation

Landing a job at a tech company may start with an interview, but to land an interview, you need be thinking months or years in advance. Waking up one morning and saying, "You know what? I'd like to work for Google," doesn't work—not if you haven't already done the right things.

In this case, doing the right thing means establishing, ideally, all four parts of a framework:

1. Relevant skills
2. Prestige/credibility
3. A technical connection
4. Something special

Let's talk about each of those—and how to obtain them.

A Positioning Framework

The exceptional candidate has coverage of all four areas: skills, credibility, technical connection, and something special. A typical *successful* candidate, however, has only two or three of these—but is hopefully exceptional in one of these areas. You can compensate for weaknesses in one with strength in the others.

Relevant Skills

If you want to be a software developer, you need software development skills. If you want to be a marketer, you need marketing skills. These skills can come from your college work, volunteering, launching your own business or side project, or your professional life.

These skills can include the following:

- **Field-specific skills.** You'll position yourself best for these companies if you develop a specific, tangible skill. If you want to be a marketer, learn about marketing. If you want to be in sales, help a local organization raise money. Without a tangible skill, you'll likely blend in with everyone else—everyone else who's waiting at the door to be let in.
- **Numerical/quantitative skills.** Quantitative skills can be important by themselves, but they can also be important because people think *good with numbers* equals *smart.* You can leverage this assumption. Take some classes, either at your school or online, that require math: engineering, calculus, statistics, economics, and so on.
- **Communication skills.** Communication, whether written or oral, is vitally important to your career success. If you aren't comfortable with public speaking, get practice with it. If your writing is weak, take a writing course or start a blog to get more practice. You don't need to be able to do dramatic readings or write elegant prose, but you do need to be able to write in a way that is clean and professional.
- **Initiative.** Initiative is shown through starting things, so start something. This can be a new club at school, running a meet-up on SEO (search engine optimization) skills, or launching a new project at your current job.
- **Accomplishment.** Develop a track record of achievement. Recruiters want to see that you have a pattern of setting ambitious goals and accomplishing them. Your successes could be in academics, project work, volunteer work, employment, or athletics.
- **Leadership.** You don't need to be the president of a club or the manager of your team (though those are nice, of course), but find something you can lead. Kevin, now a Google employee, led the fund-raising process for a local entrepreneurship club. His team of three raised 17 percent more money than they did the year before!

Think broadly about which skills and attributes makes someone good at this role, and then find activities to match them.

Don't spread yourself too thin though; depth is more important than breadth. You don't need to play sports *and* sing *and* volunteer *and* teach classes. Pick something and throw yourself into it. You will have much more to show for an activity when you have the time to really pursue it.

Prestige/Credibility

You don't have to have attended an Ivy League. In fact, most applicants did not attend an exceptional university. However, it sure helps.

Finding a way to associate yourself with something prestigious can offer you credibility.

- Attending a great university
- Working for a well-known company
- Working for a start-up funded by a well-known venture capital firm
- Working for a company with prestigious clients
- Winning an award
- Creating a successful side project

Sometimes, candidates actually have prestige but don't do a great job showing it. Did you mention how selective that award you won was? Did you specify that you managed the sales account for the top three finance companies?

Prestige is often the hardest for candidates to establish. It is not strictly necessary—most candidates do not have prestige—but it dramatically helps your chances. Do the best you can here.

Technical Connection

Marketing skills are great (for marketers), but if your whole resume is about health care marketing, you're not in the best position. Your resume will blend in with all the other people who just don't seem like the right fit.

It's important to establish some relevance to technology. If this isn't immediately obvious from your background, you can start building a connection:

- Attend start-up weekends.
- Take some online classes.
- Build a project on the side (outsource if you need to).
- Start a blog or website about technology.
- Learn to code.

Your goal is to help someone envision you as a person
breathes technology. You want to show passion, knowledge, and
about technology.

If you don't know much about technology, now is a great time to start reading websites like TechCrunch and CNET, as well as company-specific blogs. Think about what the major topics are—social networking, mobile applications, cloud computing—and ask yourself, who are the leaders in this field, and why? In what ways are these fields changing technology, and therefore the world?

Something Special

Ah, the "something special" part!

Finding a way to be unique can be valuable, particularly when establishing skills are less quantifiable. In other words, being unique as a software developer is less important; there are clear, established ways to prove your software development skills (and there's a severe shortage of qualified software developers). If your specialty is marketing, though, establishing your skills can be more complex. This is where having something special on your resume comes in.

Ideally, this "something special" will relate back to a skill, even if indirectly.

- "Completed 60 miles of a 100-mile marathon, after being injured at mile 30." Shows extreme persistence and eagerness to tackle hard challenges.
- "Founder and lead singer of rock band. Wrote all songs and performed in 20 concerts annually." Shows charisma, initiative, leadership, creativity, and public speaking.
- "Teaching online class on marketing and published five articles in major media websites (Forbes, CNBC, and AOL)." Shows marketing skills, written communication skills, and initiative.

Far too many candidates brush off that "extracurricular" activity, assuming that it's irrelevant. If there's something you do that your friends think is cool, there's a good chance an employer will, too—if you word it the right way.

If you don't have this "something special," find it. Sometimes it's as easy as saying yes to the right opportunity.

University

Academia is merely one way to distinguish yourself, and there are plenty of other ways. So if your GPA or your school doesn't stand out, look for additional avenues. Besides, you'll need to excel in multiple areas to get your resume selected.

Elite Schools: What's in a Name?

A degree from an elite college doesn't get you in the door, but it does make it easier for you to get noticed. If you go to a smaller or lesser known school, there are still plenty of avenues.

Ben, a student at a small liberal arts school in Indiana, got recommended for a Microsoft internship through his professor. Once he was in the door, his college name stopped mattering, and it all came down to his interview—and his internship. "After I finished my internship, they worked hard to recruit me for a full-time position," Ben says. His coworkers couldn't care less about what college name was on his diploma.

If your school isn't nationally known with the prestige of a Harvard or MIT, reach out to your professors or your college's alumni network for connections. Or, you can try to build those connections yourself by seeking out mentors or advice from people in the field.

Majors

Although some well-meaning people will advise you to find a major that you love, that isn't the best career advice.

If you want to get a job at a top tech company, some majors will simply make it easier to get in. The more directly applicable your major is, the better. Computer science, marketing, finance, and accounting majors will have a much easier time getting their resume noticed than, say, a history major. After all, they have academic experience, and possibly other work experience, that lends itself to a specific role.

Even majors that aren't necessarily directly applicable (like mathematics, in most cases) can still show rigor.

But there are all kinds. Paul landed an internship at Microsoft as a music major from Berkelee College of Music. Not a dual computer science and music—just a plain old music major. And even he had a directly applicable role: making sound effects for Xbox. He spent his days using ordinary household objects to mimic sounds like a golf ball hitting the grass.

Minors

If you choose to major in something less applicable, like history, your minor is your opportunity to add an applicable skill to your resume. Seek out a relevant minor that complements your path, whether that's finance, marketing, computer science, or one of several other career majors.

A minor is also a great place to prove that you're quantitative. A minor in math or engineering will do that, but so will a minor in economics, finance, or accounting. Whether fair or not, many techies associate the ability to work with numbers as a sign of intelligence (as well as an important job skill), and a minor is your chance to show that.

Learn to Code

Learning to code is, of course, essential for software development roles, but it's *valuable* for far more than that. After all, this is what software firms are all about: writing software.

Learning to code has a number of benefits for the noncoder:

- It shows that you can communicate with developers.
- It shows that you understand technology, including what's hard and what's easy.
- It shows rigor and persistence—and even intelligence, to some people.
- It shows a passion for technology.

You can learn to code through a major or minor in computer science, but it's not the only avenue. There are plenty of tools online that will let you start writing your first lines of code within minutes.

Get Project Experience

Project-heavy courses are an excellent way to add tangible accomplishments to your resume, even before you have the credentials to get real work experience. While other students are trying to dodge these rigorous courses, you should seek them out. You should cherish them for all the grueling, pizza-and-coffee-filled late nights that they bring.

Peter Bailey, a software engineer from Denver advises:

> Remember the projects you work on. Understand them. Deconstruct them. Save samples of particularly tough problems you've solved. Improve them, even if only on your own machine and on your own time. Because in the future, interviewers will ask you many, many questions about the projects you've worked on. They don't want to know that you're smart. They don't want to know that you can figure out anything with 30 seconds of Google time. They want to know that you can solve problems and produce results—sometime before Christmas. And this holds true whether you're fresh out of college or a 20-year IT veteran.

Grade Point Average: Does It Matter and What Can You Do?

Of all companies, Google is perhaps the most renowned for being GPA snobs. Hysteria surrounds the recruiting process, screaming that Google takes only candidates with at least a 3.7. Like most myths, there's some truth to it, but it's mostly just hot air.

The top companies look for the top candidates—people with a track record of success. Your GPA is one point on that graph. But there are other points, too, and you can recover from any low point, whether that's your GPA, your college degree (or lack thereof), or even work experience.

Here is how two candidates with unusually low GPAs scored offers with top companies:

John

John applied to Microsoft with a mere 2.55/4.0 GPA, placing him around the bottom 9th percentile in his class at Dartmouth. Though brilliant, he was never terribly interested in his classes. They were dry and too removed from practicality; he liked to get his hands dirty.

His junior year, John discovered that the robotics team was the perfect fit for his nerdy-yet-practical side. He led the Robotics Club the next year and came in second in a robotics competition. He showed that he was, in fact, a high achiever, even if homework and tests weren't his thing.

He came off to his interviewers as your classic tuned-out geek, who finally found his passion in building things—or taking them apart. His robotics and other projects gave him plenty to talk about in interviews, and he knew the intricacies of nearly any gadget.

Though he got rejected from more by-the-books consulting companies, Microsoft was thrilled to offer him a position as a program manager.

Beth

Beth started off strong in Berkeley's computer science program, getting As or Bs in every course, until family issues derailed that. Her grades sank, but before that happened, she got a position as a teaching assistant (TA) for one of the toughest computer science courses.

Her low-to-mediocre GPA was offset by other successes: president of her sorority, a bachelor's and master's degree in just four years, serious project work beyond the bounds of her required courses, several TA positions. On top of all that, she got a personal referral to Google, Amazon, and Microsoft from friends who graduated before her.

Between the referrals and her other experiences, Beth had no problem landing a phone screen and then a full round of on-site interviews. Her interviewers gave her the usual range of software engineering questions, and never gave her GPA a second look. Google, Microsoft, and Amazon were all practically begging for her to join them.

Though their reasons for the low GPA may differ, as well as their compensation strategies, Beth and John found that their GPA really only mattered in the resume selection process. They were both able to compensate for poor academic performance by excelling in other areas. Companies care about what you can actually do, and your interview performance is generally considered a better indication of that than some silly number.

Doctor Who? Getting to Know Professors

Getting to know professors can help you in so many ways. They can help you navigate the school's bureaucracy and help you bend—or break—the rules. They can give you advice on the best classes and professors. They can give you opportunities for research positions, sometimes even leading to publications. And they often have hundreds of prior students whom they can connect you with when needed.

Despite what many students assume, excellent grades are neither necessary nor sufficient to establish a close relationship with a professor. The truth is that regardless of how much professors emphasize studying, few professors will be impressed by academics alone.

To get to know professors, you need to go above and beyond.

- **Get involved in their research.** Professors usually welcome assistance with their research projects. For freshmen and sophomores, research positions can also be a great way to get a bit of experience before the biggies like Facebook and Google will open their doors to you.
- **Ask them for help.** If you're doing something on the side—whether it's building a software application or researching a new market—your professors' research may intersect your project. Asking them for guidance is a win-win; you get expert advice, and they get to geek out on a novel application of their favorite topic.
- **Become a teaching assistant.** Not only do you (usually) get paid for this, but your professor gets to see you in action. This makes for a much stronger letter of recommendation if you need one down the road.
- **Take advantage of lunch, coffee, or office hours.** Many universities offer some sort of take your professor to lunch program. If yours doesn't, you can seek your professor's suggestions on course selection or career direction over coffee or during office hours.

Your relationship with professors can be immensely valuable. If possible, select one professor each semester to try to connect with. Some of those will naturally fizzle out, but by graduation you should have two of three strong relationships. Maintain those.

Graduate School

Whether we long for the days of beer pong or for the (potentially less memorable) intellectual stimulation, many of us dream of going back to school. The grueling schedule of three hours of class four or five days per week no longer seems so bad after years of 40- or 50-hour workweeks. What's harder to stomach, however, is the cost: $40,000 of tuition for a typical private university, plus another $100,000 or more perhaps in lost salary.

Still, it tempts us. Maybe we can switch careers. Maybe we can move up in our current career. Maybe it'll give us the credibility that we need. Maybe, maybe, maybe.

The choice is complex because we never know exactly what we'll gain or give up by going back to school.

The True Cost of Graduate School

Costs for graduate school range widely, but the important thing to remember is that your tuition is only a fraction of the true cost. The full costs include:

- **Tuition.** Tuition varies based on whether a school is public or private; if public, whether you are in state or out of state; and what the field of study is. Tuition can be anywhere from $10,000 to $60,000 per year.
- **Lost salary.** Every year that you're in grad school is salary that you could be getting but aren't. Depending on your previous job and the length of your graduate program, that might be $200,000 or more. This is usually the biggest factor of the costs.
- **Lost promotions.** In addition to lost salary while you were getting your master's degree, you also lost two years of experience. That's two years of lost promotions and lost raises.

By this math, a typical two-year master's degree could cost effectively $300,000 ($100,000 in tuition and $200,000 in lost salary).

You do get a small salary bump for a master's degree, but it's usually less than $10,000. A master's degree is generally only worth it if it opens up a career option that you couldn't have obtained with two years of work experience.

Career Graduate Degrees

Career graduate programs, such as in statistics or marketing, offer you the ability to either switch into a new field or obtain a specialty in your existing field. They are often intensely academic programs, where students are often expected to juggle multiple graduate courses while doing additional research.

As rigorous as these programs can be, they can offer you a leg up on your (future) coworkers. You're no longer just any other entry-level employee; you have a specialty. You have unique knowledge that you can offer that relatively few people can compete with. That knowledge can offer the ability to contribute in a way that other people cannot and to therefore get ahead faster.

The flip side of this is that you may not want this specialty anymore once you've invested two or more years studying in it. In fact, this is exactly what many PhDs find; after five years researching a tiny aspect of their field, the last thing they want to do is work in that one, narrow aspect.

Before enrolling in your master's or PhD program, ask yourself the following:

- Do you want to work in this field afterward? If you don't plan on directly using the knowledge from your graduate studies, it may not be worth it.
- Is the pay worth it? Look up your desired postschool jobs. How much do they pay? Is the cost of graduate studies compensated for by your expected salary?
- Are there other ways you can get this experience? If all you want is some additional knowledge in a field, there may be more affordable and efficient ways to get it. You could, for example, just enter at a lower level and hope to move up.

Preparing Now

Positioning yourself for acceptance differs based on which graduate program you are enrolling in and what your background is. If you're applying to a computer science program with only an electrical engineering degree, you may need to refocus your professional work on coding or enroll in additional courses. Other people may already have the right background and can get accepted whenever they apply. Regardless, analyze the following four areas:

1. **Academics.** If you're still in college, focus on keeping your grades high. If you have already graduated but have low grades, you might consider taking some classes part time at your local university and really, really focus on getting good grades. This will help show that you can indeed perform well academically.
2. **Professional.** The more closely your professional experience matches your graduate field, the better off you'll be. Seek out graduate students in your field and talk to them about what they did before.
3. **Extracurriculars.** Extracurriculars can be a great way to set yourself apart and prove that you're exceptional. Some activities will carry more weight than others, so check with students and professors about what might boost your chances.
4. **Graduate Record Examinations (GREs).** A great GRE score may not ensure your admission, but a poor one can certainly make it much harder to get admitted. Get books, take prep classes, whatever you need to do to ensure that you're in the expected range for the schools you want to go to.

The earlier you can do this preparation the better.

The MBA

The tech community, and in particular Silicon Valley, has a love/hate relationship with the MBA. On one hand, big firms and some smaller companies do actively recruit MBAs, particularly from the top schools. On the other hand, many hiring managers complain that MBA applicants are useless, arrogant, and a myriad of other broad generalizations.

What's an MBA Worth?

Even Harvard and Stanford MBAs are not "shoo-ins" for tech jobs. Certainly, they stand a better chance than MBAs from less prestigious schools, and they do receive value from their MBAs, but they received these at significant cost.

Benefits:

- **Prestige and credibility.** If you attend a strong MBA program, you will associate yourself with a good name. Many—but not all—people assume that MBAs from great schools are smart and relatively competent.

- **Educational breadth.** An MBA gives you broad exposure to many of the core aspects of business, such as accounting, finance, and marketing. It probably won't teach you enough to actually take on these jobs (without some additional on-the-job training), but it will teach you enough so that you know what you don't know. It will make you a bit more well-rounded.
- **Network.** You can build a good network in the real world, too, but an MBA network is different. A network built through your professional life is filled with people like you—in your job function, related job functions, and your company. That's very valuable. However, when you need to contact people outside these focuses, you might be stuck. Your MBA network is much more diverse: many countries (at many schools, up to 40 percent of people at top U.S. MBA programs are international), many industries, and many roles. And, the network extends not just to people you know, but also to past and future graduates.
- **Experience.** MBA students run clubs, play on sports teams, meet with renowned business leaders, and get exposed to a ton of interesting and educational situations. This isn't just enjoyable, but it's also educational. In fact, many MBA students report learning more from their classmates than from their classes.
- **Recruiting and career switching.** An MBA program attracts employers nationwide to recruit their students, offering more exposure than some students could otherwise get. This is especially true for students from nontraditional backgrounds.

Costs:

- **Opportunity cost.** As with most full-time graduate programs, you are giving up two years of time. This means two years of salary, two years of work experience, and two years of promotions.
- **Stigma.** Many MBA grads report facing stigma due to their degree, to the point where they essentially hide the fact that they received it.

The benefits of an MBA increase with the quality of the program. Your network will be stronger, you'll have more recruiting opportunities, and so on. The costs, however, stay relatively fixed.

Should You Get an MBA?

If you've read the benefits and costs of an MBA and think you still want to go ahead with this, proceed with caution. Specifically, you should be aware of the following:

- **You will not learn how to manage people.** The best way to learn how to manage people is to actually do it, and you won't get that experience in an MBA program. You might take one or two classes on the *theory* of management, but you could replicate this through your own research.
- **It is not a place to figure out what you want to do.** Two years might seem like a long time, but it's not. Students start applying for internships about three months into their first year—which means they need to start thinking about where to apply even earlier than that. To get value from your MBA, you need to know what you want to do from the beginning.
- **Be sure this is a higher step, not just a step.** If you get an MBA, do it because you got into the *best* program for you, not just any program. Some people get an MBA from their local university because it's close, when they could have gotten into a much better program. When the costs of an MBA are so high, it's often not worth it to go to anything less than the best program for you.
- **Don't go for the education.** You will indeed get a good education on a bunch of different topics, but there are many ways to learn. You can read books, study independently, listen to talks from business leaders, and so on. If you're focused and motivated, you can replicate much of the MBA education on your own. An MBA is too expensive to justify exclusively or primarily on the grounds of education.

With all this said, many people receive a lot of value from their MBAs.

Preparing Now

MBA programs want people who will be leaders and will make an impact on the world. You need to have shown that you already are a leader, whether it's through starting your own company or through leading projects at work. They want people who have shown success in the following areas:

- **Academics.** Your undergraduate grades are a predictor of your graduate grades, as well as your work ethic and intelligence. You don't have to get straight As, but it'll certainly help if you do. Extremely poor grades can be a deal breaker without something major to compensate for this. If your grades are low, you will need to take extra care that you perform well on the Graduate Management Admission Test (GMAT).

- **Professional.** Find ways to demonstrate leadership and business accomplishments in your professional work. If you're a software engineer, MBA programs won't care about the fancy algorithm you wrote; they will, however, care about the projects you led and the challenges you faced. Working for a big name company also goes a long way.
- **Extracurriculars.** Unless you have an extremely demanding job, top MBA programs will expect that you have gotten involved outside of work, and preferably at a leadership level. Handing out soup in the soup kitchen won't count for much, but being the president of a major help-the-homeless group will.
- **GMAT.** Business school's standardized test, called the GMAT, is a test of your grammatical, analytical, and mathematical ability. You don't need to get a perfect 800 on the test, even for admission to Harvard, but a score below 650 may hurt you. Schools publish their 25 percent to 75 percent range, so make sure you don't fall below that.

The earlier you can plan for pursuing your MBA, the better. Many candidates started planning their business school applications two years in advance.

Your "Story"

In addition to proving yourself in multiple areas, your experiences must fit into a coherent story about why you want an MBA, what you'll get out of it, and what your short-term and long-term goals are.

Here's one sample story:

> I am passionate about technology and hope to become a VP or CEO at a major technology company in the consumer products space. I have previously worked as a program manager at Microsoft, where I have had the opportunity to lead the development of several features. I maintain a blog about the newest gadgets, which has offered me the ability to share my insights and receive feedback on them. I hope to double major in marketing and strategy at your MBA program, which will help me to better understand the direction of a company. After graduation, I plan to join Bain, BCG, or McKinsey as a consultant, where I will get to see a

wide variety of business problems in a short amount of time. I will then join a medium-sized tech company and work up to a VP or CEO role.

Many MBA students admit that their short-term and long-term goals (as expressed in their application) might not have been completely accurate. MBA programs want to know that you understand exactly what you want to want to do in life, and that has encouraged some people to fib a bit with their goals. The best stories, however, tend to be the truest ones.

Part-Time Graduate Programs

The idea of part-time graduate programs is enticing to many. Rather than scrimping to get by for two years while paying tuition and forgoing salary, you get to keep your current salary while just taking a few classes on the side. This is a great option for many, but you should make sure that you know what you're getting into.

- **It's really, really hard.** You know how stressed out you get about work? Double it. Your professors won't care that you have a major project due at work; it's not their business. Likewise, your manager doesn't care that you have a big essay due. Both will assess you based on what you are contributing to them, and that can leave you being pulled in different directions.
- **There goes your social life.** Many people find that after juggling work and school, they have little time and energy left for friends. You might be able to make it out on the weekends, but grabbing dinner with friends any night of the week is probably shot.
- **You may get less out of it.** The networking and recruiting opportunities are a key value of many graduate programs (especially MBA programs). If you're working full time, you're less likely to get to know your classmates. Additionally, part-time graduate programs typically have fewer recruiting opportunities, since many students are obligated to stay at their current company for a period of time. Even if you are not obligated, fewer companies will recruit from your school if many of your classmates are.
- **You significantly restrict your options.** If you're attending school part time, you are probably not relocating. That means that you are restricted to schools in your area that allow part-time students. Rather than attending the very best school that you can get into, you are restricting yourself to a small set of schools.
- **It's much longer.** Rather than getting graduate school over in one fell swoop, you will likely drag it out over four or more years.

Are you prepared to deal with the time, stress, and cost of a graduate program for this long? You might also have difficulty switching roles while you're studying, and this might mean making worse career decisions.

On the bright side, you'll have your salary to live off of, and your company may even help pay for your tuition.

Work Experience

While we may hope that our bosses are our best advocates, we need to face facts: our bosses have their own agenda. That's casting it in a very negative light, of course. Many bosses will be unselfish and help you move up in the company, or out to a better position. After all, the vast majority of MBAs had bosses who wrote them great letters of recommendation that ultimately led to their departure from the company.

Nonetheless, while you can usually trust your boss with having the best intentions, there are limits to this. You are your own best advocate, and you—not your boss—must map out your career from day one.

Make an Impact

A good employee does everything that's assigned to her; a great employee asks for more. Perhaps the best thing you can do to get a great next job is to do a great job in your current one:

- **Think broadly.** If you're in an engineering role at a web-based company, is there additional debug information you can log? You probably (or hopefully) work with testers; how can you make their lives easier? The more people that you impact, the better your peer reviews will be and the more the company will value you.
- **Solicit feedback proactively.** Don't wait until your midyear review to solicit feedback. At that point, your manager may be so overwhelmed that she writes your feedback hastily, at best. Asking for feedback early and frequently will demonstrate maturity, while also ensuring that you are able to quickly correct any issues.
- **Learn about other teams.** Understanding the broader context of the company's roles will be useful when you want a more senior position; for example, if you're a developer, learn about what program managers do. If you're in sales, learn about marketing. Even a little bit of exposure will help you a lot. It'll show you what other roles are doing and how they all fit together.

Obviously, being really good at what you do is important, too. This doesn't mean that you have to double your time at work. Perhaps it's merely a matter of shutting off other distractions or finding ways to emulate the leaders of your organization.

Become a [Half a] Generalist

The best product managers, the best marketers, and the best developers have something in common: they each understand the others' roles. The marketers are figuring how to position and price a product, while the product manager designs user specifications and passes them down to the developer. It's all interconnected in the great circle of product development.

Start from your role and work outward: Who (outside of your own position) do you interact with on a regular basis? Make a point of grabbing lunch with them to understand their roles. How do they make decisions? What do they do on a day-to-day basis (you know, when they're not with you)? Understanding the roles around you will enable you to perform better at your own job by offering greater context, while also offering you transferable skills.

Size Matters: Quantify Your Impact

No matter how happy you are in your current job, with any luck, this role will wind up as a stepping-stone to a new position or to a new company. Suddenly, all your years of work get mashed into a tiny five-bullet box on your resume and you picture yourself with a T-shirt saying, "I slaved away for five years and all I got were these lousy bullets."

Your five-bullet box should be planned while you're working, not after you leave. Seek out measurable, tangible accomplishments. Build something, create something, lead something. If you've tackled a major issue for your company, can you quantify its impact in terms of dollars, hours, or reduced sales calls? Seek out this information when it happens to ensure that you can get the most precise, accurate data.

Part-Time Jobs and Internships

Some students lift boxes at the university mailroom during the year and bus tables during the summer; others go do something a little more interesting. If at all possible, find a way to do the interesting work.

If you can find something relevant to your desired profession, that's ideal. For example, if you are looking for a job in sales eventually, you might be able to get a part-time job doing fundraising for the school.

If you can't find something directly relevant, then seek a professional role—something as close to business as possible. There are lots of interesting jobs you can take—paid, unpaid, and, well, underpaid. Whether you're looking for a part-time position during the school year or for a summer job, you can get an interesting, resume-building position through the following:

- **Help a professor out with research.** Many freshmen and sophomores can land research assistantships with professors, where you might code (if you're a computer science major) or do other field-specific jobs.
- **Contact a start-up.** There's nothing a young start-up loves more than a bit of free labor. One start-up I talked to had 30 interns—and only 12 employees! Offering to help out a start-up for free can give you fantastic experience. If you really need the money, you can always split time between a start-up and a paid-but-boring job like waiting tables.
- **Volunteer for a nonprofit.** Like start-ups, nonprofits are usually cash strapped and desperate for help. See if you can help them out with something, whether it's coding, fund-raising, or advertising. You'll not only learn marketable skills, but you'll meet other volunteers who may have full-time jobs—jobs at companies who could, one day, hire you.

The earlier you can do this the better since experience differentiates you from your classmates. When you have a professional job your first year of college, you're in a much better position than your classmates. This can lead to you being first pick for interviews the next year. Your path to getting your dream internship junior year starts freshman year, or even before.

Extracurriculars

Not all extracurriculars are created equal. Some show more intelligence, some show more creativity, and some show more leadership. What's right for you depends on your background and, of course, what you enjoy. This section will focus solely on the resume-building aspects of extracurriculars; it's up to you to mesh those with your happiness and other preferences.

Volunteering

Much like I won't delve into selecting activities based on enjoyment (which should absolutely be a factor), I won't discuss selecting volunteer activities based on the value-add to the world. If you choose to volunteer, the way in which the nonprofit or volunteer activity contributes to the world is no doubt important. You can make your own determination on this matter.

With that giant disclaimer in mind, allow me to offer this resume-specific advice: don't serve soup in a soup kitchen. Don't sort clothes for homeless people. And don't pick up roadside trash. While these may be great activities to do for other reasons, no employer will look at your resume and say, "So, just how many ladles of soup did you say you could do per hour? We've needed a Senior Soup Ladler around here for a while, and I think you're just the right fit!"

These activities will certainly help in some ways. They'll show that you are eager to help and that you can juggle multiple responsibilities. They can help fill employment gaps, and they can expand your network. They won't, however, go the extra mile.

To get the most mileage out of your community service hours, focus on activities that will build your skills, let you explore career tracks, or get initial experience in a field.

- **Sales positions.** Consider helping raise money for a homeless shelter through cold calls and other connections.
- **Marketing positions.** Help a local minority entrepreneurship group figure out how to target their advertising and promotion materials.
- **Software engineering/design.** Ever seen a nonprofit's website? They could probably use your help. Or what about getting involved with an open source project?

Almost any role that you wish to break into at a tech company probably takes place at a nonprofit as well, so you are sure to find something that adds a little extra oomph! to your resume.

Start Something

Volunteering is great, but *launching* a new initiative is even better. It's one of the best things you can do to boost your odds.

David, a Microsoft program manager, launched a consulting firm whose clients included Fortune 500 companies. He worked nights and weekends for them, which boosted his resume and refreshed his coding skills. Although program managers often have trouble getting considered for software engineering roles, David landed interviews with both Amazon and Google. Amazon loved his passion and commitment, and offered him a job as a software engineer.

Provided you have the dedication and time to follow through, starting something can be a great way to make your resume leap. It shows initiative, creativity, and a commitment to go above and beyond. And, if your background lacks in particular areas, whether that's leadership, coding, or marketing, launching a business or a website can be a great way to fill that gap.

If you've got some time to spare, consider pursuing the following paths:

- **Launch a business.** Lots of us have ideas floating around in our heads—why not pursue one of them? If you're a coder, this is a great way to learn something beyond the relatively narrow field of your work experience. If you're not, this can be a great way to boost your tech or field background. You can hire developers or other skilled workers to implement your project from websites like Odesk.com and Elance.com.
- **Write a blog.** Writing a blog is a great way to show that you have great writing skills, to increase your net presence (making it easier for recruiters to find you), and demonstrate your interest in a field such as technology, media, or gaming. Your blog should be updated at least every week or two, so be sure that you have the diligence to post regularly. This can prove much harder than many people expect.
- **Start a club or organization.** You don't want to form clubs just for the sake of forming clubs, but if there's a genuine gap in your area, you may want to create an organization to fill it. Doing so can build your leadership experience, expand your network, and show a proven interest in a new field.

But, be warned: If you don't follow through on your project, it can demonstrate flakiness and potentially burn bridges. Make sure that you are excited and committed to your plans.

Questions and Answers

Well, There Go the College Hires

I'm a senior in college and as such, you can find pictures on my Facebook profile dating all the way back to my junior prom. This means plenty of pictures of illegal underage drinking, keg stands, toga parties, and so on.

My parents, of course, are mortified and insist that I take down these irresponsible pictures. Better safe than sorry, they say. And then they tell me all sorts of stories about their friend's son or daughter who didn't get a job because of one picture ("Just one! And you have so many!"). I'm going to get rejected by Microsoft! The world will end! Aaah!

I think this is all crazy talk. Times have changed, right?

Yes and no. But mostly yes.

Your Facebook profile is a pretty good reflection of who you are, and employers want to learn about you. Drunken party pictures tell them that you drink. Will that be an issue for your employer? Most likely, no. Tech companies are fairly open-minded and are unlikely to care that you drink, even if you were underage at the time. After all, they'd have a very difficult time hiring college students if they did care about this.

In fact (and parents everywhere will hate me for saying this), it could even help you. Tech companies ideally want people with good interpersonal skills and many people assume *not* drinking is an indication of poor sociability.

I should qualify my statements a bit. There is a chance that your Facebook profile will hurt you, for example, if

1. You're doing something offensive. Overtly racist or sexist statements are an excellent reason for a company to reject you.
2. You're doing something illegal, dangerous, or outright stupid. That is, really illegal—not something relatively common like

(*continued*)

(*continued*)

underage drinking. If you're shooting heroin, or beating someone up, that will give them a real, legitimate cause to be concerned.

3. Your interviewers think like your parents. Your parents think drunken pictures are unprofessional. There are other people who think like your parents. Therefore, your interviewer might think drunken pictures are unprofessional. Hey, stranger things have happened. But then again, such interviewers probably aren't going around Facebook stalking people, and if they were, they'd realize that what you're doing is completely normal.

That said, it's still good practice to play it safe and keep your profile picture relatively nonembarrassing and then secure your settings to only show to your friends.

If there *is* truly offensive content—which I sincerely hope there isn't—considering removing it entirely. It's a liability.

Will Code for Food

I'm a freshman in college and I know I need some real work experience. The problem is that I also need money to pay for basic expenses. Is there any chance of getting a paying, career-building job for the summer?

It can be tricky to do this, but it's well worth the effort. If you can do something career building now, it will help you tremendously in the future. Find a way!

First, assess your skills and resources. What can you contribute? Do you have any connections? Use everything you have. You'll need to be aggressive here. Anything that is more *career* than *job* will go a long way, even if it's not really related to your ultimate goal.

Second, if at all possible, try to find a way out to the San Francisco area or (less ideally) to another tech hub. I know this is hard for most people, but there are a lot more options there.

Third, if you can't get a local job, try outsourcing *yourself* on a site like Odesk.com. Outsourcing does not just mean shipping projects off to India or the Philippines. People outsource stuff within their own country, too. Build up your professional reputation by taking on writing or research tasks, or anything related. You'll even get paid for this.

Fourth, if you can't get paid enough for this work, then you might need to take a more boring summer job and then do a project on the side. Perhaps you could spend your summer learning to code? It's a great skill to have if you want to work at a tech company.

Remember that the first priority is to gather some business experience, even if it's not directly related.

The Un-manager

I'm currently working at large software company in Southern California. Things aren't going so well at the company (layoffs, etc.), so it doesn't look like a management position is in reach anytime soon. That's okay, though, sort of. I'll likely be leaving the company in a year and relocating to Northern California, where there are more career opportunities.

Even if I switch companies, though, will I be able to get a management position without prior experience?

It depends. What do you call *prior experience*?

It's certainly much easier to get a new position when you've already held that title. Otherwise, you need to prove not only your value to the company, but also your ability to accomplish something new.

(*continued*)

(continued)

However, you may be able to get much of the experience you need, even if you can't win the title. Ask your current manager for more leadership responsibilities. You can even take advantage of the poor situation—explain that you recognize the company and the team are under some stress, and you'd like to help out by leading a subteam to do X. You won't get the title for that, but you'll get the experience. And ultimately, that's more important.

When it comes to applying for new jobs, you can't lie about your title, but you can tweak things to show what you really did. Your cover letter is a great place to emphasize the management-like responsibilities you took on, while the bullets under the job should focus on your leadership-related accomplishments.

3 Getting in the Door

Think companies like Microsoft, Amazon, Facebook, and Google are getting tons of great applicants? Think again. "Hiring managers at Amazon are spending so much time recruiting these days that they barely have time to actually, well, *manage*," one technical program manager at Amazon told me. Employees from other top companies echoed similar concerns:

- "There aren't enough good engineers in the United States. Period. We're like vultures fighting over what little there is to eat." (Apple employee)
- "We're always hiring great talent. Always." (Google employee)
- "It's not that we don't get enough good candidates. It's that we just don't know who they are." (Facebook employee)

It's true. While you're banging down their door to get in, recruiters are running around trying to find you.

You might be able to just stand still, dutifully submitting your resume online. With a bit of luck and an outstanding resume, they just might bump into you and ring you up. Most candidates, however, find that they must get a bit more creative.

The Black Hole: Online Job Submission

Candidates call it a black hole for a reason. You drop your resume in and it essentially disappears, never to be heard from again. Normally.

But it happens. Kari, a financial analyst at Amazon, applied through Amazon's website and promptly received one of those e-mails—"Blah, blah, blah . . . we'll keep your resume on file." And they did, and later offered her a job. Philip got his job at Bloomberg LP through applying on Monster.com. I got my internship at Apple by applying online.

Companies do recruit from their online job applications, but there are so many candidates in there that it's difficult to stand out from the crowd. That's true even if you're a strong candidate.

As random as the process is, you can do something to shift the odds just a bit more in your favor.

Making the Best of the Black Hole

To increase your chances of getting a call, make sure you follow every instruction. Needle, haystack: you do the math. With so many applicants to wade through, recruiters and hiring managers may look for any excuse to toss your resume. If they want your transcript, submit your transcript. If they want your top three desired teams, answer their question. Little mistakes can be fatal.

Second, if the job opening is fresh, apply quickly. Waiting three days to think things over just increases the size of the haystack. Companies may even stop looking after a certain point so that they can make decisions on the early birds.

Third, put yourself in the shoes of the hiring manager. If she does a search through the Applicant Tracking System, what keywords will she use? Make sure to list these on your resume. For example, if the role encourages an MBA, you'll want to make sure that you have "MBA" written on your resume rather than just "Master of Business Administration." You may want to list your education as "Master of Business Administration (MBA), 2010" to make sure your resume gets picked up by both searches.

Fourth, remember that just because you discover the opening through a job website doesn't mean you have to apply through it. "If the application mentions the recruiter's or hiring manager's name, you might be able to track down his name to send a personalized note," advises Barry Kwok, a former Google recruiter.

Getting a Personal Referral

Sure, Kari, Philip, and I wiggled our way out of the black hole, but all of our other jobs? Referrals. The same goes for almost everyone I know (with the notable exception of those who came through college recruiting).

Personal referrals are, hands down, the best way to get a job. Not only will a company be more likely to consider someone who's been referred, but you'll also be more likely to find a position that matches your skills and interests. It's a win-win.

The following techniques can help you get that internal referral:

- **Use your friends of friends.** You have many more friends of friends than you do friends. *These* are the people you want to reach. Be open and specific to your friends about what sort of person you want to talk to, and ask for their help in connecting you with such a person.
- **Build connections with strangers.** If you don't personally know anyone who works at your desired company, you can certainly find someone online. Establish a relationship with some employees via responding to their tweets on Twitter, commenting on their blog, or interacting with them through another medium. Be helpful and positive. Your goal is to get them to know your name and to get them to like you. The super famous employees will be harder to get to know; target, instead, the less known people.
- **Make their work easy.** When you do reach out to them via e-mail, look at the situation through their eyes. Make it as easy as possible for them to get your resume. Find a specific job posting and give them the link to it. Attach your resume in the initial e-mail (don't ask, "May I send you my resume?"). Write your first letter to them as a cover letter, with concrete reasons why you're a good fit. Reducing the friction on their side will dramatically increase your chances of the referral.

Doing these things will also help you with building a network, and that will be valuable through your life.

The Informational Interview

The informational interview is an informal discussion with a company that is conducted before the recruiting process has even begun. Usually, you approach an employee of a prospective company and seek his advice about the role or company. Though it's called an informational interview, don't mention the word *interview* when you talk to the employee.

Part of the value of the informational interview is that it's low pressure. An employee can meet with you and offer advice, regardless of whether the company is hiring. She gets to vet you a bit, and you get to evaluate her and her company.

These informational interviews are very common across tech companies, both for external applicants and for internal candidates wishing to transfer teams.

Make sure to come with good, well-researched questions. The person will not be evaluating your skills extensively, but he will evaluate your personality, communication, and interest. Make sure to write a note thanking him for his time.

After this conversation, the person may invite you to apply to her company and even offer to refer you. If not, you can follow up after the interview and ask her the best way to apply or to get in touch with a recruiter. If she doesn't respond with an offer to help, then she is probably not comfortable doing so for whatever reason. You will simply need to use alternative avenues to apply for the position.

Reach Out to Recruiters

It's not hard to find recruiter's e-mail addresses. After all, their job is to reach out to candidates.

A quick Internet search with a query like <recruiter *@adobe.com> will turn up recruiters from virtually every major company. Which recruiter would you like to talk to? Microsoft? Google? Amazon? You name it, you got it.

Don't e-mail your resume yet, though—that's just the first step. "Recruiters can tell if they're being spammed," Kwok reminds us. "It's quality, not quantity. A sincere, well-researched letter that's tailored to our company will go much further than a generic one."

You should always try to contact the most relevant recruiter you can. If you can't find someone who recruits for your desired position, state what position you're interested in and ask the recruiter to put you in touch with the appropriate person. If you know the name of the person you need to speak with or the exact position, even better. The less of a burden you are to the recruiter, the more likely he is to help you.

Alumni Network and Beyond

Personal referrals may also be found in alumni networks or other official groups. If you're a student or recent graduate, your school's career services office may be able to help you with searching the alumni directory for a connection.

Other groups might include relevant industry groups, many of which can be found on Meetup.com. Get out there—you never know whom you might meet!

Career Fairs

Before talking to Microsoft at the career fairs, students in the know would watch the line for a few minutes. Each employee had his own system. Some would put a little mark (which was at times as obvious as a smiley face) to indicate his invite/don't invite decision. Others separated resumes into good and bad piles. Either way, an observant person could learn the system. It didn't do the student any good, of course, but it sure was nice to know the decision earlier.

Some candidates walk up with their elevator pitch all prepared: here's who I am, here's what I've done, here's what I'm good at, and here's what I'd like to do.

Other candidates walk up, hand a recruiter their resume, and just wait for the recruiter to ask them questions. When asked what they want to do, they shrug. "Well, what kind of jobs do you have for my major?"

"When a candidate can't tell me what they want to do, or what they even like doing, that's when there's not a good fit," Raquel Garcia, a senior Microsoft recruiter, says. "Basically it's like I'm giving you a ticket to go anywhere in the world, and you can't even tell me what continent you want to go to."

To maximize your chances of getting an interview invitation, follow these suggestions:

- **Do your homework.** Research the companies you're interested in and know which roles you'd be a good fit for. What do they look for in candidates? How can you address those skills in your conversation with a recruiter?
- **Prepare questions.** Part of your job at a career fair is to show your passion for the company and the job. You should prepare a few open-

ended questions to ask the company. This will facilitate conversation, as well as offer both you and the recruiter the chance to discover if there's a good fit.

- **Prepare answers.** A company might ask you basic questions about your background. You should be able to talk intelligently about your biggest accomplishments and challenges.
- **Practice your elevator pitch.** The first 30 seconds with the staff at a career fair is your opportunity to impress. A strong candidate will be able to succinctly communicate her value-add.
- **Tailor your resume.** There's no rule that says you can bring only one copy of your resume to a career fair. If you're applying for different types of positions, create tailored resumes for each position.
- **Dress appropriately.** The tech world is generally not into suits and ties, but being extremely sloppy is also bad. Jeans and a nice top are generally appropriate for most techie roles. For very businessy roles, slacks might be safest. Your attire at a career fair should be more or less the same as what you would wear to an interview.
- **Follow up.** If possible, get the business card or e-mail address from the person you talk to, and follow up immediately after the career fair. You should reiterate your interest in the company, explain what you'd bring to the company, and attach a copy of your resume.

After speaking with hundreds of candidates at career fairs, recruiters find that most blend together in a giant mix of resumes. Sometimes, however, one candidate stands out: in this case, Alex, a precocious sophomore who brought a portfolio of his project work with him. On two additional sheets of paper, he provided screenshots of his four biggest projects, with lengthier explanations that would head off some of the recruiters' questions: How did he build it? What did he enjoy? What did he learn? What was the hardest part?

Raquel Garcia loves it when younger students like Alex approach her. "Whenever a freshman comes up to talk to me, I always thank them for doing so. They showed guts in talking to me, and I appreciate that. And they get early feedback on how they can start shaping their career so that, in a year or two, they're ready for Microsoft."

Professional Recruiters

Though usually not open to recent graduates, professional recruiting agencies (a.k.a. headhunters) can assist a more experienced hire in connecting and landing jobs with the right firms. They can add value in five key ways:

1. **Connections.** A good recruiter will have relationships with many companies. This will mean not only that the recruiter can convince someone to pick up your resume, but he may also know about unadvertised job openings. Before hiring a recruiter, you should assess which companies he works with. Where have his recent candidates gotten offers?
2. **Matching you.** A good recruiter will understand your background and interests, as well as the culture and expectations of her client companies. She may do a better job matching you with a good fit than you could do yourself.
3. **Feedback.** A good recruiter will be able to assess where your weaknesses are with respect to each individual job. By knowing this in advance, you can be better prepared to reassure the company of your qualifications. They can also help you prepare by suggesting questions you should or telling you what questions to avoid.
4. **Handling issues.** Once you land the offer, your recruiter can help you with anything from understanding if an offer is fair to actually helping you negotiate your offer. Because recruiters get a percentage bonus of your salary (from the company, not you), they have a strong incentive to help you get the best offer you can.
5. **Reopening a door.** Sometimes rejections don't mean that you weren't a good fit for the company; you just may not have been a good fit for the position. "A professional recruiter can sometimes reopen a door in these cases," says BJ Bigley from Big Kind Games.

Like any other profession, some recruiters are great and some are not. Make sure you've found a good one.

When Things Get Ugly: What to Watch Out For

While professional recruiters can be enormously helpful, they can also be a waste of time or actually detrimental.

Divya discovered this firsthand when her current manager stumbled across her resume, sent to him by Divya's own headhunter. "I was considering moving to a smaller company, so I signed up with a recruiting agency. I figured this would be a good way to save myself some time, while increasing the number of opportunities. A week later, my manager called me to his office and passed me a print-out of an e-mail. It had a short note from my own recruiter saying, 'Here's a candidate you should check out,' and my resume was attached. He didn't know that I was looking for a new job, and this was not how I wanted him to find out." Divya was able to smooth things over with her manager, but things were never quite the same once he knew she was on the way out.

Katy Haddix from VonChurch advises candidates to "beware of any recruiter who won't tell you the name of the company. It's a sign that your resume will be fired off at random." You should always maintain complete control of where your resume goes.

Additional Avenues

If you go to a small school in Oklahoma, you may not have the connections—or the job fairs—to give you a helping hand. Hope isn't lost, though. You can still get someone to pick up your resume, but you may have to work a bit smarter, or harder.

Start Elsewhere

"How do you get into Google? Work for Microsoft," Jason, a Microsoft program manager, jokes. As much as this comment may have been said in jest, it has some truth to it. The best way into a company or role may be an indirect path.

In addition to joining one company so that you can eventually transfer to another, you may want to consider joining your dream company in a less-than-dream job. Technical recruiter Barry Kwok points out that a role like an office manager at a start-up can be an easier avenue into the tech world for those who lack specific qualifications. "At a start-up, office managers do everything under the sun," Kwok explains. "As the company grows, you can begin to specialize in an area like HR. Couple that with an additional night course or two in HR, and all of a sudden you're the perfect candidate for a full-time HR position."

Contract Roles

Companies like Microsoft hire hordes of contractors every year to do everything from testing to development to, yes, even program or product management. If you're having trouble proving that you have what it takes to earn a full-time position, a larger company might be willing to hire you on a contract basis. Because the company can terminate you much easier, it takes on much less risk.

So what's the catch? The catch is that you're treated as a second-class citizen. No employee stock purchase plan. No health club membership. You don't even get invited to the morale events. And at Microsoft and some other companies, you can only work there nine months per year. Even if the lack of perks doesn't hurt you, the unfortunate attitude of your so-called teammates might. You're not a "real" Microsoftie, you see.

In fairness to these companies, it's not their fault that they have this attitude. Believe it or not, they're legally obligated to treat you differently. Microsoft lost a lawsuit years ago because it treated its contractors too much like regular employees, and no company wants to repeat that experience. So that's life.

That said, a contract role can be a wonderful way to have flexibility in your life (nine months on, three months of vacation!) or to experience a company sans commitment. Many contractors who perform well in their jobs do make the transition to full-time employee. To do so, you need to perform well, build connections, discover open positions, and, yes, interview just like anyone else off the street.

Get Creative

While most candidates wouldn't get much crazier than colored paper to print their resumes, some candidates go a bit further. One candidate applied to Google by affixing his resume to a giant bouncy ball. Another candidate applied to Twitter by printing his resume on a cake. It won't help them get the offer, but you can bet someone reviewed their resumes.

These nonconventional applications not only show a bit of creativity, but they also show passion. And in some cases, they can show that you get (or don't get) the company or its culture.

As a recruiter for the document-sharing application Scribd, Kwok saw two applicants who used Scribd itself to submit their resumes. Both were interviewed, and one became the company's first engineering hire.

Still want that Google recruiter to notice your resume? What if you imported your resume to Google Docs and shared it with her (along with a nice cover letter in the share invitation)? It might not work—but it just might! What have you got to lose?

But be warned: these quirky resume submissions may turn off the wrong company or recruiter. A company with a more formal culture may not be so amused by these antics.

Official Groups

In an attempt to reach out to new candidates, many of the biggest firms have created groups on Facebook, LinkedIn, and other websites. Getting involved in the pages—by both stating your interest as well as helping out other candidates—is a great way to show your interest, as well as your communication skills and personality.

Networking

Networking is not about collecting as many business cards (or LinkedIn connections) as you can. It's not about being fake or exploiting anyone. It's about establishing professional relationships, just like you would your social relationships. In fact, your social connections could well be a very valuable part of your professional network.

Attributes of a Good Network

A great network is broad but deep, while also focused but diverse. If these sound like contradictions, they are—sort of. It's about *balance* between these attributes.

Broad but Deep

A broad network is a large one with many connections, none of which are very close. A deep network is the opposite: you don't know that many people, but those you know really like you. You want *both*.

A broad network offers you a lot of people you can reach out to. When you need to talk at a particular company, you're more likely to know someone if you have a broad network.

However, if they don't really know you well, they're less likely to help you—especially if that means connecting you with *their* connections.

Focused but Diverse

Whatever your career goals are, there's a particular role that is most relevant for you to network with. Typically this is people in your own role: a software engineer benefits most from networking with fellow software engineers. They will be able to tell you who's hiring, who's growing, and which companies have the best cultures.

On the other hand, you might need help from all kinds of people. What happens when you want to shift careers? Or you need advice because you don't understand things well outside of your specialty? You'll value this more diverse network then.

How to Build a Great Network

Good networkers understand that quality matters much more than quantity, and that they must cultivate deep relationships by forgetting about the fact that they're just networking.

Always Network

Networking is not a thing you do when you need it. If you need to connect with a new job, you don't just flip a switch and say, "Okay, it's time to network!" By the time you need to build a network, it's usually too late—at least to fulfill that one need.

Networking is an all-day, all-year sort of thing. You build new connections by being open and interested in other people, and you deepen your connections by focusing on the value that you add to other people's lives. Networking is about what you do when you don't need a network.

Be Giving

Cameron, a former Microsoft program manager, wants more than anything to be a successful entrepreneur. He values building a strong network because he knows how important it is, but he's constantly stretched for time and money. When someone asked him for help reaching out to a former teammate of his at Microsoft, he delayed responding for a week and then said that he wasn't sure he had the time to do that. Later, someone else asked him for help with some technology decisions over coffee. He was very busy that day and said he would get back to her; he never did. While there's no anger or hostility toward Cameron, these people don't feel especially inclined to go out of their way for him. Unfortunately, neither does anyone else.

People quickly learn when working with Cameron that it's all about his needs and his desires. It's not that he's trying to be selfish; he's just shortsighted and incredibly focused. People like Cameron never build a network that is of any use to them.

Those who focus on giving—without worrying when they'll get repaid—wind up with hordes of people in their gratitude.

Be the Connector

Mehdi is everything that Cameron isn't. He's not only a giver; he's a connector. Sure, he'll be happy to chat with you about an idea or make some phone calls for you. But he'll also be happy to share his network with you.

Need to reach out to someone at Company X? Want to talk to someone who does Y? Mehdi knows just the guy—or at least knows how to track him down.

Not only do people feel like they owe him, but they want to help him. And how do you help Mehdi? You introduce him to people. And everyone wants to know Mehdi, because he knows everyone.

People with friends attract friends. That's how the game is played.

Where to Network

Your network is an outgrowth of your friend circle, your professional circle, and also your online identity. To expand your network, you should be actively cultivating those relationships. Get to know people. Talk to them about what they do and what they're interested in. And find ways that you can add value to their lives.

There are countless places you can network—alumni clubs, sports teams, even bars! But here are some of the most productive.

Immerse Yourself in Start-Ups

In many cities, the start-up community is one of the most active and engaging and—lucky for you—often centers around technology. And because many of these people are or wish to be entrepreneurs, they want to build a relationship with you.

Immerse Yourself in This Community

Go to happy hours, meet-ups, and lunches. Listen to tech talks by local start-ups. If you're an engineer, a designer, or in a related profession, attend hackathons. Simply by showing your face regularly and talking to people about their jobs, you'll start to build an identity in the community—and a network.

And remember, Kwok says, "If you're working so much that you can't network, you better make sure that your work is really good." You'll need it to push your way ahead of all the candidates who can network their way into a job.

Social Networking

Though many people lump Twitter, Facebook, and LinkedIn into the same general category of networking tools, they serve substantially different functions.

Facebook and LinkedIn help you maintain existing relationships. Generally speaking, you don't start conversations with strangers on Facebook—and if you do, you probably don't expect such connections to develop into professional contacts.

Twitter, however, can help you communicate with existing friends, but it's also extremely effective as a tool to expand your network.

Here's how to make the most of these connections.

LinkedIn

LinkedIn can be used to connect with both friends and professional contacts. One venture capitalist encourages his entrepreneurs to "add everyone they meet with—and add them immediately." To get additional value out of LinkedIn, encourage your connections to write recommendations for you by writing recommendations for them.

Finally, you should search out groups that are relevant to your interests and get involved in the discussions. Recruiters sure do love to hang out in them!

Facebook

Because Facebook is so good at truly *social* networking, many people overlook its professional value. In reality, Facebook's value to professional networking is expressly because it's a social service.

Your friends can serve a powerful role in connecting you with jobs, and Facebook provides a wonderful way of reaching out in mass. Not only that, but Facebook makes it extremely easy to loop in friends-of-friends. A single post could be the trick to connect you with your next job.

Twitter

If you're willing to put in the effort, Twitter can be an extremely effective tool to connect with people or join in on conversations. Most people fail to use Twitter successfully because they can't expend the sustained, daily effort.

If you think you can do this, set up a Twitter account and start tweeting relevant thoughts and interesting articles. If you don't have an engineering background, tweeting about technology news (and your reaction to it) can be a great way to demonstrate your interest, as well as to learn more.

If you can maintain a steady flow of posts, then it's time to start building up your following. Follow interesting and relevant people—they may follow you back. Put a link to your Twitter profile on your e-mail signature, on Facebook, and on LinkedIn. And start connecting with the people you most want to meet by responding to their tweets with your own opinions.

Build an Online Portfolio

Portfolios are for everyone, not just designers. You might be showcasing your prior projects and work, when relevant. If you don't have projects, you can still build a website or online profile.

The goal is to go beyond the basic social networking tools and become an online contributor:

- Create a website, with at least basic information about you. Include your resume, a picture of yourself, and a list of projects.
- Start a blog about technology, or whatever you're interested in.

- Write guest blog posts. Many bloggers are happy to let people write a guest post—less work for them! Guest blog posts are still written under your name and will allow you to link back to your own website.
- Answer questions. When you come across questions on forums (especially field-specific ones) that you know the answer to, respond! Recruiters actually look through people's profiles.
- Get involved with GitHub, if you're an engineer. Download interesting software and tools, and see if you can improve them or customize them. If you find bugs, report them back to the original developer.

Taking these actions will allow you to demonstrate your skills even before a recruiter talks to you. Many recruiters source candidates based on their online profiles. This is a great way to make a recruiter chase you.

Questions and Answers

Applying from Afar

I currently live in Chicago, but I will be relocating in two months to San Jose when my wife finishes up her residency. The problem I'm facing is that the smaller start-ups I'm applying to won't even consider me since I don't live in the area. They don't like to pay for relocation, interview travel expenses, and so on. How do I explain to them that I'm relocating?

I wouldn't necessarily tell them that you're relocating—I would just act like you're already in San Jose. You should never lie, of course, but you can just tell them on a need-to-know basis. As long as you're willing to pay for all travel and relocation expenses, this should not present an issue.

Rather than listing your full address on your resume, list just "San Jose, CA." Employers don't really need your address for anything anyway until they send out offer paperwork. It's becoming

(*continued*)

(continued)
increasingly common to not list your address, and most people probably won't even notice the absence.

When they call you to schedule an interview, that's when you should tell them the truth: that you're actually not moving to San Jose for another two months at most, but you'll be making a trip there in two weeks. Will there be a time then that can work? You'll make your life much easier if you can batch your interviewers into the same week.

Because you're applying to start-ups, there's a good chance that they can't wait two months. They needed you, well, yesterday. You may need to be a bit more flexible with your move, and spend a few lonely weeks away from your wife.

Distant Relations

My mother recently mentioned that her friend Eliza had a friend Eric who worked at Facebook. I know it's not exactly a close connection, but I've been trying to get an interview there for months. What's the best way to make this introduction?

There are actually two problems with this introduction.

First, it's not a close connection. The connection goes: you -> your mother -> Eliza -> Eric -> whoever he needs to forward your resume to.

Second, all of the connections are *personal* connections. No one has the trusted "I worked with you" relationship.

Your approach should try to tackle both of these challenges as much as possible.

Address the closeness by reaching out to Eliza directly—or even Eric, if you've ever met him. That at least shortens the chain a little bit. If you can't do either of these, try to get looped in on the e-mail rather than getting your e-mail directly forwarded on.

To tackle the credibility aspect, you'll need to give them a reason to trust you. Make sure your e-mail comes off very professional, and drop in little tidbits about why you're a good fit. And absolutely attach your resume from the beginning. If someone has to go through the extra effort to ask for your resume, he might just ignore it entirely.

Keep the maternal connections out of the e-mail if you can. Your e-mail might just be forwarded on directly, and "my/your mom connected us" is even less a sign of credibility than it coming from a friend. That is, if a stranger reads your e-mail, it's better if it appears to be a connection through friends than through parents. You choose your friends, not your parents.

You could also consider arranging to meet Eric in person. If you make it easy for him—offer to come to his office for lunch—he'll likely be happy to take the meeting. This immediately shortens the connection chain because now you're a (semi-)direct referral.

Note that the policy around referrals varies across companies. While some companies want referrals to be meaningful—that is, only refer people you can actually vouch for—others encourage you to refer anyone. The thinking behind the latter philosophy is that even a distant referral means *something* and more candidates is a good thing.

Just Following Instructions

I just attended a career fair at my school and had what I thought was a good chat with a recruiter there. But at the end of the conversation, she told me to apply online. What gives? Did I misinterpret the tone? What should I do now?

I was, however, able to snag her business card from the stack on the table.

It's unlikely that your recruiter was blowing you off. If she told you to apply online, she probably told everyone that.

What's probably going on internally is that paper resumes are difficult to deal with. People are spread out, and sheets of paper are just not an effective way to manage content. So, HR is now pushing all the recruiting online. It's a bit disconcerting, but—if handled properly—it doesn't have to hurt you at all.

Do as your recruiter said and submit your resume online, and then follow up with her. Thank her for the wonderful conversation and throw in a few unique details to remind her of your conversation. You are writing, essentially, a cover letter, and you should handle it as such. Tell the recruiter why you're a good fit ("As we discussed earlier today, I've built . . .").

Finally, explain to her that you applied online as she instructed, but you also wanted to attach your resume here for her reference. If she could give you an update as to your status and/or keep an eye out for your application, that would be fantastic. You are confident that you would be a great match for the company, and you look forward to hearing from her soon.

4 Resumes

Most resumes are broken—even from exceptional candidates. They have fantastic accomplishments, but you only learn this is if you spend a long time studying the resume. Or, perhaps their accomplishments aren't clearly stated and you can't really make out *why* the accomplishment is so impressive.

A good resume clearly highlights a candidate's relevant skills. It must present the candidate in the best possible light because, after all, it is one's first chance to persuade the reader that she is the best candidate for the job.

How Resumes Are Read

Part of the problem with people's resumes is that they don't understand—*truly* understand—how resumes are read.

The reality is that resumes aren't read so much as they are glanced at. A recruiter (or another resume screener) picks up your resume, skims it, and then makes a snap judgment: yes/no. You often get no more than 10 seconds to impress the reader.

The next time your resume will be read is by an interviewer. Even then, many interviewers don't read your whole resume, word for word. They skim it to get a sense for your background.

Either way, your resume must be designed to highlight your best accomplishments with only a brief skim.

Nine Hallmarks of a Powerful Resume

A powerful resume should leap off the page saying, "Me! I'm the one you want to hire!" Each and every line should contribute to that goal. Why, then, does a candidate list his vague, totally unprovable, and generic love for running? One has precious few lines on a resume, so unless you're applying to work in a health club, skip the fluff.

Before submitting your resume, go through each line on it and ask yourself why it would help convince an employer to interview you. If you can't give a reason, there's a good chance it shouldn't be there.

The nine hallmarks of a powerful resume is a checklist that your resume should pass with flying colors. Does yours?

1. Short and Sweet

Many candidates make lengthy resumes, thinking that they need this space to sell their experience. It's quite the opposite. In fact, many of the longest resumes are by candidates with less experience.

Generally, the rule of thumb is to keep your resume to one page if you have less than 10 years of experience. If you have more than that and multiple jobs, then you *might* be able to justify more than one page.

However, longer resumes often make you look worse. Imagine a candidate creates a one-page resume and a two-page resume. Typically, the stuff on the two-pager that isn't the one-pager is the worst content. Thus, if a recruiter just glances through each resume, the average item he reads from the two-pager will be less interesting than the items on the one page. You've added more content, but it's *worse* content. It brings down the average.

Additionally, if something really cool—like a great project—is on the second page, the reader won't see it as first. There goes your first impression.

You should also avoid large blocks of text on your resume; people hate reading, and will generally skip right over paragraphs. Your resume should be a collection of bullets of around one to two lines.

Keep your resume short and sweet.

2. Accomplishment Oriented

If your resume reads too much like a job description, then there's a good chance you're doing it wrong. Resumes should highlight what you did, not what you were supposed to do.

Example:

- Responsibility oriented: "Analyzed new markets and explored potential entrance strategies for China division."
- Accomplishment oriented: "Led entrance strategy for Foobar product in China, and successfully persuaded CEO to refocus division on the enterprise market, resulting in a 7 percent increase in profits."

The accomplishment-oriented resume packs a much stronger punch. Everyone wants an employee who gets things done.

Watch out for words like *contributed to*, *participated in*, or *helped out with*. These are good signs that you have focused more on responsibilities than accomplishments. After all, someone at Microsoft could say that they "contributed to the implementation of Microsoft Office." But what does that really say?

3. Quantifiable Results

Ever seen an advertising campaign that says, "A portion of our profits is donated to charity"? The convenient thing about that statement is that the portion could be 0.0001 percent, and it's still technically true.

This is what a resume reader thinks when she sees a resume that says "reduced server latency" or "increased customer satisfaction." If you really did this (and it had a remotely meaningful impact), why can't you say how much?

Quantifying your results makes them meaningful by showing employers the impact that you had. If you've implemented a change that reduced company costs or increased profits, employers want to hire you.

For business roles, quantifying results with dollars may make the strongest impact. However, if this isn't possible, you can instead quantify the results with change in employee turnover, reduction in customer support calls, or whatever metric is the most relevant. You may want to consider offering the percentage change in addition to (or sometimes instead of) the absolute change.

For technical positions, it may be more impactful to quantify some results in more technical terms: seconds of latency, number of bugs, or even an algorithmic improvement in big-O time. However, be careful to strike a balance here: while your accomplishments may be impressive to a fellow engineer, a less technical HR individual might be the one reviewing your resume. You want to make sure that your resume impresses everyone.

Example:

- Original: "Implemented crash reporter and used results to fix three biggest causes of crashes."
- Newly quantified: "Implemented crash reporter and used results to fix three biggest causes of crashes, leading to a 45 percent reduction in customer support calls."

Before, you communicated that you did something reasonably important, but the reader didn't understand how important. The quantified revision, though, leaves the reader with a "wow!"

4. Well Targeted

Back in the days of typewriters, a generalized resume could be forgiven. Editing a resume was a laborious process, and candidates frequently made 200 photocopies and sent off the same resume to every company. A well-targeted resume undoubtedly performed better, but it wasn't as strictly required.

Now, with resumes being easy to tweak and rarely even printed, tailoring your resume to the position can give you the edge.

Your resume should be tailored to the position, and potentially the company as well. What does the company value? Does it want developers to wear many hats? Talk about the different roles you played. Are they very data focused? Talk about how your analyzed website metrics to drive decisions.

Observe that the targeting is in potentially three ways:

1. **Targeted to the company's product.** If the company makes maps, you could talk about your map-related experience.
2. **Targeted to the job description.** If the job description wanted people with particular skills or experience, tweak your bullets to bring out these aspects.
3. **Targeted to the company's values.** If you know the company puts the user first, discuss how you went above and beyond for the user.

This is especially important for job switchers. For example, if you're applying for a technical lead position after years of being a software engineer, you'll want to mention the time that you led the design of a new feature. Or, if you're applying to a start-up that you know is facing customer support issues, you'll want to emphasize your prior experience in handling upset clients.

Luckily, figuring out how to target your resume isn't especially hard. Discovering information about the company or position is usually quite straightforward; you merely need to check the website and/or the job description. Ask yourself, what are the company's biggest issues? How would my role impact those? Even if you haven't solved the exact problems the company faces, you hopefully have skills one would need to solve them.

5. Universally Meaningful

Some resumes are so littered in position-specific jargon that it's hard to discern meaning from them. Position-specific jargon could be fancy sales terms, marketing terminology, or even internal expressions.

This can be an especially big problem for candidates from big companies. Some language that was commonplace within their company isn't well understood elsewhere.

Your resume should be meaningful to recruiters as well as to your future managers and teammates. Avoid acronyms, and translate highly technical terminology to plain English. Explaining the impact or goals, particularly in a quantifiable way, can help laypeople understand your value. You still can't please everyone, and that's okay; just make sure that everyone will get the gist of your resume.

That said, some terms are more understandable than one might think. Google recruiters in Seattle certainly knew what it meant for a Microsoft employee to have been promoted from a Level 60 to a Level 63 during her career.

6. Professional

Many recruiters will toss your resume away for a single typo. They figure that they have so many resumes to go through, why waste time on someone with poor communication skills?

Tech companies tend to be a bit more forgiving, due to their less formal atmosphere and their large international workforce. However, that's no excuse for sloppiness, particularly in communication-heavy roles.

Make sure to check your resume thoroughly for the following potential issues:

- **Spelling and grammar.** You can use Microsoft Word's grammar checker, but don't rely exclusively on this. If you are not a native English speaker, make sure to have a native English speaker—one who is strong in grammar and spelling—review your resume.
- **Consistency.** You can use either commas or semicolons to separate items in a list, but be consistent. End every bullet either with a period or with none. Make sure that your formatting is consistent in terms of bold, underline, italics, and the like. Your formatting decisions are often not as important as being consistent with them.
- **No first person.** Although it can be tough, avoid using *I*, *me*, or *myself*. Use the third person throughout your resume, with the exception of the objective statement, where first person is more expected.
- **No personal details.** A resume within the United States should never list personal details like marital status, age, or gender. This is obvious for most people born and raised in the United States, but international applicants are sometimes unaware.

The goal here is to present your resume, and therefore you, as professional. You want to show that you are a good business writer. After all, if you can't write a resume correctly—given ample time and motivation—you might not be able to write good e-mails and work documents.

7. *Well Formatted*

When a recruiter picks up your resume, her eye jumps to certain things. She wants to know your education (school, degree, major, and graduation year) and your professional experience (companies, titles, length of employment). For software engineering jobs, she may also look for a set of technical skills.

Remember that the path of least resistance for the recruiter is always to toss the resume. If she can't find the information she's looking for, there's a good chance she'll just toss your resume so she can move on to the next candidate.

Consider the following items in your format:

- **Columns.** You want to have distinct columns for your job title, companies, and dates. Putting these in their own columns make it faster and easier to find them.

- **Text formatting.** Then, think through how to format this text. Small formatting changes can matter. Consider the following (very abbreviated) resumes for the same candidate:

Bob Jones (Resume 1)	**Bob Jones (Resume 2)**
Program Manager (2008–Present)	**Microsoft Corporation (2008–Present)**
Microsoft Corporation	Program Manager
. . .	. . .
Product Manager (2006–2008)	**Intel (2006–2008)**
Intel (Santa Clara, CA)	Product Manager
. . .	. . .
Software Developer (2000–2006)	**Cisco (2000–2006)**
Cisco	Software Developer
. . .	. . .

While these resumes convey the exact same information, resume 1 emphasizes that Bob held product management roles. That's very relevant, of course, but it's hardly a highlight of the resume. Resume 2, however, emphasizes the fantastic company names: Microsoft, Intel, and Cisco. Which one do you think will pack a strong punch?

- **Margins.** Extremely small margins look, frankly, ridiculous. Margins should generally be .75 inches or greater, but certainly no less than 0.5 inches.
- **White space.** Using ample white space will make your resume easy to read. Recruiters have to deal with enough in their day; don't add to strain with a crowded resume.

When you are writing your resume, ask yourself, what will differentiate me the most from other applicants? Figure out your three selling points and make sure those stand out.

8. List Your Projects and Extracurriculars

Whenever I help someone with their resume, there's one question I always ask: What did you *not* include?

About half of the time, the applicant mentions something that is, arguably, the selling point of his resume—or it would be, if it were on his resume.

These might be things like

- (From a nontechnical product manager) I volunteer for the Star Wars museum and built them an e-commerce website.
- I teach stand-up comedy on the weekends.
- I organized a 10,000-person music festival for my city.
- On the side, I built a first-person-shooter game by hiring a number of designers and developers.

Invariably, the candidate describes that she didn't list it because she thought it either wasn't relevant or wasn't appropriate (because, for example, the game never launched).

Think again. The Star Wars website shows technical skills. Stand-up comedy shows communication skills. The music festival and the game show leadership skills. And *all* show initiative and just make you special.

Don't be too quick to ignore stuff that isn't relevant. Fluff doesn't belong on your resume, but the things that show a different side of you just might.

9. Be Different (If You Want)

What makes a good tech resume is much like what makes a good resume in general, except for one big difference: it's okay to be a little unique. And the further you get away from the stuffy business roles, the truer this is.

All these rules are really just rules of thumb. It's okay to break them, if you know what you're doing.

Your goal ultimately is to show that you would be a great employee. This usually means you want to stay within the rules of what a great resume should be. The rules were created because they're generally effective.

However, the rules were also created for the typical candidate. Breaking the rules can be, on rare occasions, valuable. For example, one candidate provided a picture of each app he built next to the project's listing on his resume. Another candidate wrote entirely in the first person—and wrote blocks of text rather than bullets—but it was so beautifully written and effused such passion that people read it.

Quirky is accepted, and even celebrated, at tech companies.

The Structure

Although we usually see resumes structured chronologically, there is an alternative structure: the functional structure. Under the functional structure, your resume is grouped into categories such as Leadership, Engineering, and Sales. Each category lists your relevant accomplishments, often without dates or positions clearly labeled. Many resume writers have recommended functional resumes for those whose job titles don't match their true accomplishments, or for those with significant job gaps. Functional resumes tend to mask those issues.

However, recruiters tend to be wise to this strategy and will spend their time trying to figure out what you want to hide—or, more likely, just toss your resume since it's not worth the trouble. Functional resumes may be powerful in theory, but with so many people having such a strong distaste for this structure, it's probably not worth the risk. If you must separate your accomplishments by skill set, I would recommend a cover letter instead.

We'll focus on standard resume format: the (reverse) chronological structure. Chronological resumes tend to almost always have at least an Employment (or Work Experience) section and an Education section, but may also include an Objective, Summary, Technical Skills, or Projects section. Which sections you choose to include depends on your skills, background, and desired position.

The Objective

Objectives are usually generic blobs of text that do little more than describe what role you are looking for.

When they are noteworthy, it's rarely a good thing. For example:

> To dive at such depths into my subjects and work that I am no longer a prisoner to the confines of my mind and I am instead engaged in the rapture of understanding.

This was a real objective. It was trying to communicate that she loved learning, but it really communicated that she's not that good at communicating. No one was impressed.

While this objective might be unusually philosophical, most objectives do little other than waste precious space. Objectives are not necessary and should be used only if they add important information.

For example, if you were previously in product management but would like to focus your job search on marketing roles, an objective could be valuable to point recruiters in the right direction. If, however, you're applying for a sales role and your prior position was also in sales, you probably don't need to specify this. Most software engineers do not need objectives, as their experience is clearly indicative of such a role.

An effective objective statement will not only direct your resume toward the right roles, but will also tell the reader why he should hire you:

> Project management and marketing professional with 10 years of experience growing new business unit from $10 million to $100 million seeking a position as a marketing lead in consumer software.

If you don't need to redirect your resume to a new role, you should probably stick to just a summary or a list of key accomplishments.

Unless you really screw up, an objective probably won't hurt you. It might shut off opportunities outside of the stated objective, though, and take up precious space.

Summary (or Key Accomplishments)

While summaries can wow the reader, they're usually so vague that they have no impact at all. Roy, an ex-Microsoft and current Google developer, says, "I would never look at a resume and say, 'Well, this person says he's a go-getter. Let's hire him.' It's like putting 'Loves to Laugh' on a Match.com dating profile. No one's buying it."

Your summary should read much more like key accomplishments—so much so, in fact, that these sections are often called Summary and Key Accomplishments.

The following objectives will demonstrate your value-add to the prospective company:

- "Software engineer lead with several years' experience implementing large back-end systems in Java and C11, including three as a lead/team manager; led re-architecture of critical system that serves 50 million requests per month, reducing request latency by 20 percent; designed new API for financial product used by 5 of the 10 biggest banks, which accounted for an additional $10 million in revenue; awarded the prestigious 'Green Sticker' award, given to the top 5 percent of engineers based on total impact to firm."

- "Program manager with five years of experience leading feature design of enterprise-oriented products; proposed solution and built team to solve number one cause of customer complaints, and completed project three months ahead of schedule; reduced development costs by 35 percent by creating plan to merge related products into one, more generalized product; oversaw integration of acquired technology by leading 17 developers and 9 testers from two companies, resulting in an additional $50 million of sales."

Don't just summarize the number of years of experience (this should be pretty obvious from your resume). If you choose to include it (which most candidates don't), use this section to highlight your biggest accomplishments.

Work Experience

For most candidates, the Work Experience section is the most important section of their resume. Your work experience should, at the minimum, list your job title, company name, firm location, and dates of employment. If you are working for a large firm with many products, such as Microsoft or Amazon, you may also want to list your team.

Your most recent job should have around four or five bullets of one to two lines each. Each bullet should focus on your accomplishments, not your responsibilities, and should be backed up with numbers whenever possible.

If you have trouble creating this section, start with listing your biggest accomplishments on a sheet of paper. Remember, though, that what was the most impressive to you or your team, who understand the full complexities of the problem, may not be as impressive when described out of context and in a mere 25 words.

How Far Back Should It Go?

Without showing any gaps, you should list only as far as the positions are relevant—and usually no more than three to five jobs. This means that if your career started as an information technology (IT) technician, but you then moved to testing, and then later had a few programming positions, you can probably cut the IT technician. A resume does not need to be a complete employment history.

Projects and Leadership Experience

If you have projects, you should list them. This section is a must for software engineers. For recent graduates or current students, this is a great way to diversify your resume and show some additional accomplishments.

> **Desktop Calendar** (Fall 2010, Individual Project): Implemented web-based calendar supporting online storage and syncing, meeting invites, and conflict resolution. Python, JavaScript, AJAX. 20,000 lines of code. Awarded Honorable Mention in Senior Design Projects.

If you are not applying for a software engineering position but have other substantial work, you can rename this section with a more appropriate title. For example, if you founded a club that accomplished some concrete goals and led your school's shift to electronic course review, you might make this a Leadership Experience section.

Education

Even if you have a 4.0 GPA from MIT, your experience usually matters more than education. Education is a checkbox, but an important one nonetheless.

In addition to the standard items (university name, dates attended, location), your education section should list the following:

- **Major, minor, and degree.** If your major has a nonstandard name, you should explain the curriculum on your resume—and you can do so in a way that shapes the reader's perception. For example, the University of Pennsylvania offers a major called digital media design (DMD), which is a fusion of computer science, communication, and fine arts (think: future Pixar engineers). A DMD student who is applying for a software engineering role at Amazon might describe it as "a computer science–based major with additional courses in design and communications."
- **GPA.** Generally, recent graduates should list their GPA on their resume if it's at least a 3.0 out of 4.0. If your school lists GPA in a nonstandard way (such as on a 10.0 scale), you should consider translating your GPA to a more understood system, such as class rank.
- **Activities.** Recent graduates should list their most serious (that is, most impressive/relevant) activities on their resume. Don't list everything you did, though—everyone can have a lot of half-hearted activities, so an extensive list won't impress anyone. More experienced candidates usually will not include activities.

- **Related course work.** Current students and some recent graduates may want to list relevant courses. Make sure the courses are truly relevant, though. If the course names aren't clearly understandable to someone not familiar with your university, you may want to give them more user-friendly names. You do not need to list this section though. If you have better uses for the space, do it.
- **Awards.** If you received any awards in college, you could list them here. However, be aware that this sometimes makes the awards blend in too much. If your awards are particularly impressive, you might want to have an awards section on your resume.

While you must always include education on your resume, this section should get shorter with more work experience. Many candidates with even two or three years of experience list just their major and degree.

What about High School?

High school almost never belongs on a resume. There are probably only three exceptions to this—and two of them occur only very rarely:

1. **Freshmen and sophomores.** Freshmen and sophomores might consider listing their high school on their resume, but only if they really have nothing better to list. It's unlikely to impress anyone.
2. **Building a connection.** In rare cases, you might know that you're sending your resume to a fellow alum or someone else strongly connected to your high school. One candidate, Mark, included his small private high school on his resume and wound up interviewing with someone whose daughter attended the same high school. He says it helped them build a connection.
3. **A very impressive accomplishment.** If you have some very impressive accomplishments from high school and the only way to include them is to list your high school, this might be acceptable. However, it's more likely that these accomplishments should go elsewhere, such as under an Awards section.

If you're not sure, ask yourself, what would I use this space for if I removed my high school experience?

Which Comes First?

The rule of thumb is that education should be listed before work experience for current students (or graduates with no postcollege work experience). For everyone else, work experience is listed first.

However, tech companies aren't really sticklers for rules. If your education is much stronger or more relevant than your work experience, or vice versa, you could deviate from custom. It is unusual, but the benefits might outweigh the costs.

One candidate, Arun, had an electrical engineering degree and had been employed for several years as a software tester. While working full time, he had enrolled as a part-time student at Stanford, where he had recently completed four computer science courses. In this case, he was helped by listing his education first. His work experience would usually eliminate him from software engineer; his only saving grace was that he was taking computer science courses at Stanford.

Skills

This is a must for technical positions. For nontechnical positions, it can be useful to add anyway *if* you have truly deep technical skills (e.g., coding).

This section should list any software, programming languages, foreign languages, or other specific skills you know. To avoid a lengthy, disorganized list, it is useful to divide up this list into appropriate categories.

However, just as a native English speaker would never list "English" as a skill, you should not list obvious skills such as Microsoft Office. It's assumed. Likewise, familiarity with Windows and Mac can be left out unless you are also listing something less obvious, such as Linux.

Anything on your resume is fair game, including all of your programming or foreign languages. Once, a candidate at a start-up tried to claim he was fluent in Romanian, Portuguese, Greek, and Italian. He mostly did very well, and would have surely received an offer—except that the small company just so happened to have Romanian, Portuguese, Greek, and Italian employees, and they just so happened to be available for an interview that day. The company didn't care about the languages, but they did care about the honesty.

Similar things have happened when candidates attempt to list unique skills like riding a unicycle. Surely, the company won't have unicycles lying around! Perhaps not, but they might talk to you about this passion of yours. If you can't back it up, it's going to be a major red flag for the company.

Don't hesitate to list legitimate passions or skills, but don't feel obligated to include anything. If you leave this section out, no one will notice or care.

Awards and Honors

If you have awards or honors, you can choose to list those either with your work experience/education or in their own Awards section. The best decision largely depends on how much space you have and how much you want to emphasize your awards. Are your awards a key differentiating factor between you and other candidates?

Either way, you should list the dates and why you received the awards. When your recruiter sees an award like the Vincent R. Jacobs Award, she has no idea what that means. Your awards should instead be listed as something like "Recipient of Vincent R. Jacobs Award, given annually to the top woman by GPA out of the 3,000-person senior class." If you can quantify your award to suggest the selectivity, that's even better.

How Do I Shorten My Resume?

As discussed earlier, shorter resumes often do a better job of highlighting your bigger accomplishments.

For many candidates, shortening their resume is easier said than done. They know they should shorten it, but it's difficult to figure out how.

If this sounds like you, try the following tips:

- **Start from scratch.** If you're trying to go from a three-page resume to a one-pager, cutting out individual lines will be tedious and will often lead to a weird, stilted resume. If you're going to majorly cut down your resume, it might be best to just start from scratch and build up.
- **Cut your college experience.** Things like course work and activities can often take up more space than they are worth. Remove these, unless they truly add a new perspective or accomplishment.
- **Reduce time on older jobs.** The older the job, the less relevant it usually is. Often, a job from years ago will only have one or two bullets under it.
- **Look for dangling words.** You should never have a line with just a few words on it. It's a waste of a perfectly good line. Find a way to shrink the bullet so that it fits on just one line.
- **Reduce paragraphs.** Paragraphs (blocks of three or more lines of text) are typically bad, but especially so if you're trying to save space. Find ways to reduce paragraphs to just one or two lines. Rewriting from scratch might be best.

- **Think about what matters.** Review each job you had. What matters? A resume does not need to be a comprehensive description of what you did, particularly if your responsibilities are fairly clear from your job title. Instead, think about why this particular job matters on your resume. What does it show that your other jobs don't? Is the company a strong brand name? Did you get promoted quickly? Spend extra time thinking about your older jobs. If you worked in a similar function as your current role, then the attributes demonstrated might be duplicates. If you worked in a very different function, then they might not be relevant.
- **Cut your objective/summary.** Your objective probably doesn't add much. And, if you can get your resume to one page, then it's already a summary. You don't need to spend a couple of lines resummarizing it.
- **Evaluate a new format.** A different format can create as much as 25 percent more space. Try experimenting with the format (especially the columns), but don't shrink the font size down too much or remove all the white space. It's there for a reason.

Everyone has trouble shortening their resume. You get attached to your accomplishments, and you just hate to see them wiped off. Try giving your resume to a friend and ask him to cut items, line by line. What do you not need?

Resume Action Words

Sometimes, it's all in the way you say it. Using strong action words can give your resume a bit more oomph!

Accomplishing
accomplished
achieved
attained
completed
obtained
realized
Analyzing
analyzed
compared
critiqued
detected
distinguished
evaluated
reviewed
Assisting
aided
assisted
helped
supported
Building
architected
assembled
built
coded
compiled
constructed
created
designed
developed
engineered
established
experimented

fabricated
formed
formulated
generated
improvised
prepared
produced
programmed

Calculating

budgeted
calculated
computed
forecasted
measured
projected
tabulated

Changing

adapted
adjusted
augmented
broadened
edited
effected
maintained
manipulated
modified
molded
overhauled
reconstructed
redesigned
reformed
remodeled
repositioned
reshaped
revolutionized
supplemented

Communicating

articulated
assured
briefed
clarified
communicated
corresponded
demonstrated
distributed
explained
illustrated
informed
justified
presented
proposed
publicized
recommended
reported
responded

Connecting

acquainted
collaborated
consulted
interfaced
networked
partnered

Determining

approved
assessed
balanced
charted
classified
defined
identified
pinpointed
prioritized
specified
validated

Giving

contributed
delivered
extracted
fulfilled
gave
offered
provided
retrieved
served
supplied

Improving

advanced
eliminated
encouraged
enhanced
expedited
facilitated
fostered
furthered
gained
improved
revamped
revitalized
stimulated
strengthened
upgraded

Increasing/ Decreasing

amplified
boosted
conserved
cut
decreased
doubled
downsized
enlarged
expanded
increased
maximized

optimized
quadrupled
reduced
saved
trimmed
tripled

Influencing

convinced
dissuaded
empowered
enabled
influenced
inspired
lobbied
motivated
negotiated
nurtured
persuaded
pushed
shaped
sold
solicited

Initiating

conceived
conceptualized
devised
founded
initiated
introduced
invented
launched
originated
pioneered
started

Leading

chaired
delegated
directed
governed
guided
headed
hired
led
managed
oversaw
presided
recruited
represented
spearheaded
supervised

Ordering

administered
arranged
authorized
enforced
enlisted
operated
ordered

Organizing

allocated
centralized
collected
concentrated
consolidated
contracted
diversified
focused
formalized
gathered
integrated
organized
packaged
redirected
reorganized
streamlined
systematized
unified

Performing

acted
applied
attended
conducted
coordinated
enacted
executed
implemented
installed
instilled
instituted
monitored
performed
planned
scheduled
secured
utilized

Researching

catalogued
discovered
examined
explored
inspected
investigated
processed
researched
searched
surveyed
unearthed

Solving

addressed
answered
committed
determined
diagnosed
ensured

fixed
forced
rectified
repaired
resolved
restored
solved
treated
Teaching
advised
coached
counseled
educated
instructed
lectured
mentored
reeducated
taught
trained
tutored
Winning
awarded
earned
exceeded
excelled
mastered
promoted
won
Writing
authored
composed
documented
drafted
published
summarized
translated
wrote

Questions and Answers

It's a Family Matter

The only school activity I've done is the waterskiing team—and that was just my freshman year of college. I was hoping to get more involved with college activities, but then my father got sick.

I didn't have to take time off school, but I did have to help him out a bit at work. He runs a local chain of jewelry stores, so I've had to do everything from hiring and training salespeople for a new store to reorganizing our accounting system. Being family and all, I didn't get paid a dime(!).

I'm a junior now and about to apply for internships. Is there a way to tactfully explain my family situation on my resume? It looks rather sparse as is, and it doesn't look like this situation is going to change anytime soon.

While you can absolutely briefly explain your situation if an interviewer inquires, personal details like this do not belong on

(*continued*)

(continued)
a resume. Your resume is about what you actually did, not your excuses (even if reasonable) for not doing more.

However, you can—and should—list your experience with your father's business on your resume. No one has to know that it's your father's business and, frankly, it doesn't matter anyway. The good thing, as you said, is that you've done a wide variety of things.

Think through your past couple of years on the "job," and make a list of your most tangible accomplishments. These will become your resume bullets. Tailor your selections to the positions you're applying for. That is, if you're applying for product manager jobs, your work building a new team for a new store is very relevant, as well as anything else that shows leadership. Then, come up with an appropriate job title. You can be called anything you want (within reason), as long as you clear it with your boss/father.

In the future, ask your father if you can focus your activities on particular aspects of the business that are most relevant to your career. This could be a win-win for you and your father—and even for your future employer.

On the Up and Up

I had a low GPA freshman year—very low. It was 1.93. I've worked really hard and pulled mostly As, but still my GPA is only a 2.98. That places it just below that 3.0 cutoff that many companies have.

Should I just not list my GPA?

Conventional wisdom is that you don't list your GPA when it's below a 3.0, but I do feel that yours is somewhat of a special case. Your grades now are, in fact, quite good. I worry that by leaving off your GPA, the assumption will be that it's lower than a 3.0.

My advice is that if you have academic awards, like the Dean's List, list those without your GPA. That will remove the employers' assumption when they didn't see a GPA.

If you don't have such awards, you should list your GPA—but only your GPA after freshman year. Something like this will do the trick:

GPA: 3.6 (Junior Year), 3.4 (Sophomore Year)

It'll be plainly obvious what you're doing, but that's not really an issue. The important thing is that your grades are good now, and they have been for a while.

When your interviewer asks what happened freshman year, don't beat around the bush. Tell him the truth. You were a bit overwhelmed, both academically and socially, with college. You realized at the end of the year that you really needed to straighten up and focus, and you've done just that.

Personally, if I heard an answer like that, I'd be pretty impressed. You've shown honesty in your answer and maturity in your reaction. Way to go!

But Seriously

I have about two years' work experience in two different roles. I also have three internships from college, plus a double major and a few extracurriculars. I'm having trouble fitting it on two pages, let alone one.

If I need it, I can use more than one page, right?

I would strongly discourage you from expanding to multiple pages.

Not all recruiters are strict on the one-page rule, but some are. Do you really want your recruiter's first thought to be frustration?

(continued)

(continued)

Even if a recruiter gives a vague "Oh, any length is fine" statement, it doesn't mean longer is better. Focus on the best, most relevant accomplishments. You can fit them all on one page, I assure you. Diluting them with weaker items will only make you look worse.

5 Deconstructing the Resume

In the previous chapter, I told you what makes a good resume, and it was things like conciseness, structure, accomplishments, and so on. But seeing a bunch of A+ resumes does you only so much good.

In this chapter, I'll walk you through some sample resume excerpts and show what could be improved about them.

When you are reading these, first study the original resume and see if you can diagnose the issues.

Resume #1

This candidate applied for a position as an account manager.

Sample Resume

Account Manager, Cisco. (2009–Present)

- Cultivate client relationships for suppliers in home and beauty industry and help them achieve short- and long-term goals.
- Create marketing and sales plans for cross-functional teams of 10+ people.
- Analyze and determine customers with best ROI.
- Prepare detailed monthly and quarterly reports for each business and present findings to senior management.

Assessment

This candidate has described her job responsibilities, which isn't all that useful. Responsibilities only tell us what she was instructed to do. It doesn't tell us if she was actually successful in them. Additionally, responsibilities are often fairly obvious from the job title, so describing them really doesn't offer much value.

Additionally, if you look at what she said, it's a bit fluffy and ambiguous. Cultivated client relationships? What exactly does she mean by that?

Improved Resume

It would be better if she said something like this:

Account Manager, Cisco. (2009–Present)

- Managed 30 accounts annually, representing over $10 million in sales. Awarded company's two largest accounts.
- Achieved a 90% retention rate by focusing on frequent communication and customer happiness. Retention rate was the highest of the 15-person department.
- Designed and proposed new sales plan to scale to Asian markets, which grew to be company's second largest territory.

These bullets demonstrate her responsibilities as well, but do so via clear, measurable accomplishments. She also shows how her accomplishments compared to other people. This sort of comparison makes her success more tangible, since we might not otherwise know if managing 30 accounts is a good or bad thing. When you're outperforming your team, it's clear that you're doing very well.

Resume #2

This candidate applied for a position as a software developer.

Sample Resume

Quality Assurance Manager, Omnicom (2013–Present)

- Designed test plans for automated and manual testing of website and responsive mobile web page.

- Hired and managed remote team of 15 testers in India and the Philippines.
- Organized and taught monthly workshops on test-driven development to 30-person software development team, resulting in 10% reduction in priority 1 bugs.
- Implemented scripts to test website features.

Assessment

This resume is fine—except that it's not a *software development* resume. This candidate talks only about his testing experience. There is one bullet about software development, but there aren't even many details there.

For software development, recruiters care primarily about your coding experience. Much of this candidate's actual job will be in testing, but he doesn't need to provide a comprehensive list of his work experience. He only needs to describe the *relevant* parts.

Improved Resume

It would be better if his resume looked something like this:

Quality Assurance Manager, Omnicom (2013–Present)

- Designed and built internal dashboard that monitored website activity and alerted developers via text and e-mail when high-priority issues arose. (Python, Perl).
- Implemented tool to import error logs and display simulation of user's path through website, enabling developers to more quickly locate source of error.
- Hired and managed remote team of 15 testers in India and the Philippines.
- Organized and taught monthly workshops on test-driven development to 30-person software development team, resulting in 10% reduction in priority 1 bugs.

Some of the bits of the old resume are still there, but the focus has been shifted toward coding. Bullets that show leadership, such as managing a team and teaching a course (especially a coding-related course), can also remain.

Resume #3

This candidate applied for a position as a project manager.

Sample Resume

Project Manager, MusicNow (2012–Present)

- As leader of customer happiness team, organized and directed the roll out of new cloud infrastructure, which resulted in stronger relationships across development, product management, customer support, and marketing teams. Analyzed costs of alternatives, created slide deck of projections, and successfully pitched new project to senior management.
- Facilitated improved relationships with most successful independent artists on platform by prioritizing their needs and ensuring regular contact. This resulted in greater retention and was the building block to a new approach to client management, which has since been rolled out to the full team.
- Pulled together four-person cross-functional task force to rethink how company handles payments. Narrowed down options to three proposals and selected one that best matches company's long-term objectives. Designed launch of new strategy before turning responsibilities over to coworker to complete implementation.

Assessment

This candidate might have some good experience, but the resume reader probably won't know it. People may not spend more than about 5 or 10 seconds on a resume. These large blocks of text are too long to grasp in that time, so they likely won't be read at all. (Did *you* even fully read those paragraphs?)

Your resume should be designed such that someone can grasp the gist with a quick skim. Keep your bullets short—just one or two lines. This also has the benefit of making the details easier to comprehend since you're focusing on the most important stuff.

Improved Resume

Here is a fixed-up resume.

Project Manager, MusicNow (2012–Present)

- Directed roll out of new cloud infrastructure in order to improve inter-team collaboration after analyzing ROI on alternatives and successfully pitching to senior management.

- Conceived of and implemented new approach to client management that improved retention rate of most successful independent artists by 10%.
- Led four-person team to design new payment strategy that better aligns with company objectives and led initial launch and implementation.

By making the bullets shorter, a reader is more likely to read them and more likely to be able to understand them. Your bullets do not need to tell a complete story; they only need enough to show an impact.

Resume #4

This candidate applied for a senior business analyst role.

Sample Resume

Business Analyst, Yahoo! (2011–Present)

- Designed and built metadata management tool.
- Worked with team of developers and UX designers to redesign new customer experience.
- Analyzed data to determine root cause of major customer conversion issue.
- Updated database to new schema and wrote SQL to transform entries.
- Automated process to distribute monthly logs to users.
- Managed close of $3 million acquisition deal.
- Prepared weekly and monthly reports for division-wide meetings.
- Led training of remote team in India.
- Won Initiate Award at end of first year.

Assessment

This candidate did indeed focus on accomplishments, but there's just too much stuff here. When you list this many bullets, your reader doesn't know where to focus. Most likely, she'll read one or two bullets here before going on to the rest of the resume. Don't you want those one or two bullets to be the strongest ones? Unfortunately she's basically watered down the resume with weaker content.

Additionally, the individual items lack power and impact. In some cases, I don't understand why the item is important. In other cases, I don't understand what exactly this person did. I have no idea what it means if someone "worked with" a team to do something. That could mean anything.

Improved Resume

Here the candidate decides to limit each item and focus on just the most important things, thus strengthening the overall content.

Business Analyst, Yahoo (2011—Present)

- Achieved 10% improvement in customer acquisition rates after analyzing web traffic data and identifying two major issues.
- Designed and built tool to facilitate editing and managing metadata (SQL, Slimpy).
- Acted as project manager for successful close of $3 million acquisition deal: managed time line, led cross-team collaboration, and gathered and analyzed necessary data.
- Led training of seven-person analyst team in India.
- Won Initiate Award at end of first year, awarded to the business analyst who, out of 50 total cross-company, shows the greatest initiative in identifying and resolving issues.

These bullets offer a bit more context, while also keeping some (like the training one) fairly short. Varying the length of the bullets can present an easier reading experience.

6 Cover Letters

Back in the days of typewriters and snail mail, cover letters were nearly as widespread as resumes. Candidates dutifully banged out a custom note, affixed their resume, and sent them off in a stamped and sealed envelope.

With virtually all resumes submitted electronically nowadays, cover letters are often optional. In fact, many job seekers say that they haven't ever had to write one.

That's probably not entirely true, though. Your first e-mail reaching out to a recruiter or potential referrer is essentially a cover letter. Your cover letter is a key marketing document; a strong cover letter will make someone open up your resume to learn more.

Why a Cover Letter?

Many job seekers don't understand why companies value cover letters. After all, your resume already describes your background. Why require another document that just repeats this information?

A good cover letter, though, can serve a number of purposes. First, it builds a case for yourself about why you are a good match for the position, rather than making the recruiter evaluate your background with respect to the job position. Second, it offers context and color to the drab, factual list of accomplishments on your resume—explaining the *why* not just the *what*. Third, it lets you explain why you want the job—something that a resume just can't do. Fourth, it provides a writing sample, and writing is valuable for almost all professions.

Understanding these goals can help you perfect your cover letter.

The Three Types of Cover Letter

Whether your cover letter is solicited, unsolicited, or broadcasted, it will follow a similar format and will have similar goals. Your goal is still to excite the reader enough that he puts down your cover letter and picks up your resume—and, hopefully, the phone. The difference lies in the degree to which the cover letter can be targeted.

Solicited Cover Letter

Most cover letters are solicited; that is, the cover letter is responding to a specific job opening advertised online, on your campus, or anywhere else. The job opening likely lists specific skills or backgrounds desired, and you need to appeal to those specific attributes. Your cover letter should explain exactly how you match those qualities, and should provide evidence using your prior experience.

"If you don't exactly match every requirement, don't let that stop you," says Matt, a former Apple recruiter. "Sometimes ads are written by recruiters or managers who don't understand that the combination of skills they want is impossible or very unlikely. Or sometimes you have other skills that may compensate for your weaknesses."

Unsolicited Cover Letter/Cold Call Letter

An unsolicited cover letter taps the hidden job market by contacting recruiters about positions that may not be advertised. Obviously, getting a job through these means is more challenging, but not at all impossible. Sometimes positions are created only when a sufficiently good candidate comes along, as is often the case with start-ups. Or other times, a friend inside the company might be able to tip you off to a new opening that has only been advertised internally.

Either way, your approach is the same: you need to identify what you think the company would want and match that. You can often extrapolate the company's needs from looking at the company's other job ads, or from looking at ads for the equivalent job at other companies.

If you think this approach seems hard, you're right. But the good news is that you will have substantially less competition if you pursue it.

Broadcast Letter

While all cover letters should be tailored, sometimes you have no choice but to create a generic cover letter. This is often the case when using online job boards. The job board might encourage you to post a cover letter along with your resume.

What to do? You should be as specific as possible, while not excluding yourself from any desired positions. If you're looking for a sales or customer support role, emphasize the skills that those positions have in common (communication, etc.).

Recruiters won't expect your cover letter to be very specific but will look at it for a quick list of your accomplishments and skill set, so make sure to really emphasize what you've achieved in your career.

The Structure

The vast majority of cover letters are fairly mediocre. They basically get the job done and they don't hurt your chances, but they don't help you either. They follow a set pattern or structure.

Part 1: Introduction

The first paragraph introduces why you are interested in the company. Perhaps you heard a keynote by the CEO. Maybe you are really fascinated by the revolution in online payments. Or perhaps you have a personal connection to using the product.

> As a long time coupon-cutter and dog lover, I get a little thrill every week when I open my discount e-mail from DealsForFido. It's not just the savings that catch my eye; the quirky touches on the e-mails build a connection to me, the customer. Naturally, I was thrilled when I saw an opening for a customer service position.

Part 2: Who You Are

In this paragraph, you explain what your background is, making sure to touch on the key points of your background. If all you do is restate your resume in written format, that will put you in the solidly mediocre bucket. It's what most applicants do.

When you write this paragraph, select two or three key skills, attributes, or accomplishments that you want to make sure the reader knows. Is it that you are great with design? Is it your surprisingly deep technical skills? It might even be a company or school you are associated with, if it's an elite company/school.

An exceptional cover letter does all of these things, but it does them in a way that turns you into a person. It adds color to the accomplishments on your background.

> As a sales representative at Nordstrom four years ago, I learned the value of not just appeasing customers, but delighting them. I spent my first few weeks learning how to do this from my fellow sales reps and, by the end of my first year, became the store's top sales person.
>
> I took this focus on customer happiness into my current role as a support representative for Chicago's largest social media management company. I quickly moved into managing a team of 10 contractors, where my focus on people has resulted in the lowest turnover that this department has ever seen.
>
> Seeing the power of technology, I spent the last year learning JavaScript and CSS. I used these new skills to design and build a tool for the local dog rescue charity, resulting in a 20% increase in successful adoptions.

This candidate has demonstrated an excellent understanding of people, passion for the position, and technical skills. She's also demonstrated initiative and leadership.

Part 3: Why You Want the Position

Finally, you connect yourself with the position. Why do you want it? Why specifically are you a good fit?

> This position with DealsForFido is a perfect blend for my customer service skills, technical skills, and passion for animals. Moreover, I love the cute touches that represent the company's culture, and I look forward to bringing that same flair to customer service.
>
> Thank you,
> Bethany

Bethany spent less time on justifying her passion for the company since this was already partially done in the first paragraph. If your first paragraph is more generic, then you might want to spend more time here.

Part of the value of explaining why you want the position is that it shows that your letter isn't totally generic.

Five Traits of a Strong Cover Letter

A cover letter is not a chance to tell your life story, nor is it a chance for you to list every accomplishment you've ever had. A cover letter should introduce you, demonstrate how your background matches the job description, and state your interest in the position.

When writing yours, keep these five suggestions in mind.

1. Tailored

Recruiters are busy and, frankly, often just looking for an excuse to toss your application in the trash. One down, a few hundred to go.

Of course, they want to hire, too—their job depends on it. Their job description will tell you what they're looking for; it's up to you to show that you match it as closely as possible. If they say they want a highly quantitative marketer, then you must address that in your response.

Be wary of simply modifying an existing cover letter for a new position. This can save you time, but it can also result in a worse cover letter. You might be attached to what you wrote and thus leave in lines that are not as relevant to this specific position. Or, you might change what you wrote so piecemeal that your final letter doesn't flow well.

Ideally, you should write a fresh cover letter for each application. If you won't do that, though, be sure to keep one finger on the Delete key. Be prepared to completely scrap what you've written.

What If There Is No Job Description?

In cases where there is no job description to be found, then you'll need to guess at the preferred skill set. If it's a software engineering job, try to find out what languages or technologies the team uses. For a job that's heavy on communication, call attention to your public speaking skills.

You can also track down other job ads, both from similar positions with the same company and from the same position at other companies. Look for similarities. If you find that the company always looks for someone with a particular background or that one skill is highly in demand for your position at other companies, then you can safely assume that this position will desire it, too.

2. Supported with Evidence

Anyone can say that they are hardworking or have strong communication skills; not everyone can prove it. Use your education, work experience, and accomplishments to show the recruiter that you have the skills he needs.

> I have strong public speaking skills, a skill which was honed through four years of college Speech and Debate Team. In my final year on the team, I placed second in the statewide Impromptu Speaking category.

Unlike a resume, which must be strictly facts, a cover letter offers more freedom to make subjective statements about your strengths in a particular area. However, those statements are much more powerful when backed up with evidence.

3. Structured and Concise

If you want to have any shot of your cover letter being read, you need to keep it short. Long cover letters won't be read.

Additionally, an overly long cover letter reflects poorly on you. Structure and brevity is valued at work, so you should be able to clearly and succinctly communicate your interest in the position. Keep your cover letter under about 250 words (about half a page).

4. Simple, Direct Writing

Some people who are considered great fiction writers are lousy business writers. Subtle, hidden meanings and descriptive writing is great in fiction, but direct, simple writing is better for business. You should write to communicate, not to impress. Use short, familiar words, and get to the point. If people have to reread what you're saying, it's not good writing.

5. Professional

As a cover letter is often the best and only writing example a company has, being professional and using correct spelling and grammar is extremely important. You should proofread your own letter multiple times, and give it to a trusted friend to review as well.

Additionally, you should address the letter to the individual, if you know his or her name. If you do not know the recipient's name, never assume a gender. Who would do this? Lots of people, it turns out.

One start-up founder discovered this firsthand when she posted a job opening for her new company. The ad lacked her name, but mentioned that her background included a PhD in electrical engineering. Over 70 percent of applicants chose to address the recipient of the cover letter as "Dear Sir" instead of a more gender-neutral opener.

The Daring A+ Cover Letter

Want to move away from the boilerplate cover letter? Check out this A+ cover letter:

> Let's get the bad things out of the way first: I went to a mediocre university, had a 2.7 GPA, and skipped many classes. There's good stuff, too, though. I took all three of the university's most difficult classes, aced two of them, and am now a teaching assistant for one of them.
>
> You see, I love learning, but formal education takes a carrot-and-stick approach. When a class meshes with my learning style—when it inspires and motivates—it's a wonderful experience. This is why the position of instructor coordinator is such a perfect fit for me.
>
> After my so-so college experience, I spent two years freelancing where I filled in whatever gaps a start-up had. I did marketing, social media management, support, and technical writing, and my scrappiness earned me projects with big name start-ups like Dropbox, Twitter, and Snapchat.
>
> While freelancing with Impy.io, I was offered and accepted a full-time role as a project manager, where I've been for the last three years. I've overseen the launch of three features and a major redesign, which required international and multi-team collaboration. I continue to wear many hats, though: I designed a training program for our clients and co-led a new recruiting initiative.
>
> I want to contribute to something greater, though, and your company is just what I'm looking for. I am excited by your approach to "inspired learning," and I excel in fast-paced, flexible environments.

(*continued*)

> *(continued)*
> If you want someone who will do what it takes, whether in or out of their job description, that's me.
>
> I can't wait to be part of this.

This cover letter is daring. It breaks from a very standard structure and, rather than just boasting about successes, it admits major failings.

In doing those things, it is an excellent cover letter *for the right company*. The candidate writes with passion and energy. He clearly wants this job—this isn't a form cover letter. He's also done a great job of selling his prior accomplishments. The context behind his work experience makes accomplishments that might not look that exceptional shine.

The Traditional A+ Cover Letter

If being adventurous isn't your style—or isn't the style of the company—that's okay. You can be enthusiastic while sticking to a more traditional style.

> I was excited to see an opening for a software developer within the Swords team, as this is one of what I consider to be the most addictive games. I've nearly uninstalled it from my phone but, well, I just couldn't. While the game play is fantastic as a whole, I've been particularly impressed with how the game leverages the iPhone features to implement realistic collisions.
>
> When I picked up the job description, I knew that not only was the position a perfect match for my interests, but I was perfect match for its requirements. I have over three years of experience with writing mobile games and pride myself on having an artistic eye despite being "just" a developer. I would love the opportunity to utilize both the artistic and the technical aspects of my brain. My games have been shipped to three mobile platforms, with over 100,000 downloads on the iPhone itself.
>
> Additionally, I place high value on the long-term maintainability of a code base, and have implemented systems at my previous company to improve code quality. Most notably, I restructured our coding cycle to match industry best standards. Gone were the days of bang-it-out; developers needed to write design documents for any external APIs and have them peer reviewed by at least two people. All source must be code reviewed before being checked in. Bugs at the critical level dropped 19 percent with the implementation of this new system.

> I think that Swords and I could have a wonderful working relationship; we're compatible down to the last little detail.
>
> I look forward to talking with you more about this opportunity.

While more standard than the last example, this cover letter still effuses passion. It shows character while also demonstrating one's relevant skills (that were presumably mentioned in the job description). The discussion of skills is backed up with evidence, and the candidate has obviously done her research.

The So-So Cover Letter

Unfortunately, most candidates struggle to write a great cover letter that shows their fit for the position. If a letter like the preceding examples is very difficult for you, try something like this:

> Dear [Recruiter or Hiring Manager's Name]:
>
> I am interested in the [job title] advertised on [website or other source]. With a strong background in [list of tangible skills], and [number of] years of experience in [area], I am confident that I can [general problem you can solve].
>
> My qualifications include the following:
>
> - [Desired Qualification #1]: [Proof that you have qualification #1]
> - [Desired Qualification #2]: [Proof that you have qualification #2]
> - [Desired Qualification #3]: [Proof that you have qualification #3]
> - [Desired Qualification #4]: [Proof that you have qualification #4]
>
> I would love to discuss this opportunity further. I will follow up within a [time frame] to confirm that my application was received and to schedule a time to talk further.
>
> Sincerely,
> [Your Name]

While this letter certainly won't win any awards for prose or creativity, it's short, concise, and gets the point across: that you match the employer's needs and that you can perform the job effectively.

Many candidates shy away from using bullets in business writing—don't! In cover letters, as in business, you don't have to be—and shouldn't be—William Shakespeare; you just need to communicate clearly and effectively.

Questions and Answers

New Form, Same Great Content

I've tried to write a cover letter multiple times, but each time I feel like I'm just turning my resume into prose. Is this normal? And is it okay?

Normal? Yes. Okay? Maybe.

Many people hit the same issue, so if you do, it's not the end of the world. A good part of the reason for a cover letter is to check that you can write. Employers can check your spelling, grammar, and structure just about as well in this boring, regurgitated form.

However, it may be a missed opportunity to give your employer more information than they can read on your resume. Your goal here is to prove that you have the desired skills. You can do that using accomplishments (which will likely be repeated on your resume) or by using slightly softer evidence. For example, you can call out that you're detail-oriented using something like this:

> I was the go-to person on any design doc, not only because I understood the company's technology at a broad level, but also because I had a knack for picking up on issues that were otherwise overlooked.

This is the sort of context that's otherwise difficult to explain on a resume.

With all that said, the vast majority of cover letters are just mediocre. They don't help you, they don't hurt you, and they might not even be read at all. Don't overly focus on your cover letter at the expense of your resume.

Optional

Many companies I'm applying to say that providing a cover letter is optional. Is it truly optional? I feel like it will look like I don't care if I don't submit a cover letter.

Generally, optional means optional. They're not trying to trick.

Companies make cover letters optional because they know that some people have something useful to add in there, and they're trying to gather all possible information about you. Sometimes, candidates put valuable information in their cover letter that they wouldn't have put in a resume.

Why not just require them then? Because *most* companies don't. A company doesn't want to make you go through unnecessary work. They also don't want to go through unnecessary work themselves!

If your cover letter won't add anything new to your application, and the company specifies that it's optional, feel free to skip this. You'll save yourself *and* the company some time.

That said, you should consider if you could make a cover letter actually valuable. An amazing cover letter can help you.

Additional Resources

Please visit crackingthetechcareer.com for sample cover letters and other resources.

7 References

"One time I called a candidate's reference and she said that the candidate had been fired for theft—a fact the candidate had not revealed to me," recounted Matthew, a serial tech entrepreneur. "Another time I called and discovered that the reference himself had been fired months earlier. And then there was the time that the reference paused, took a deep breath, and explained to me that he's found that giving bad references comes back to haunt him. He prefers to avoid that situation now, and he hoped I would understand. The pause before the last word was suggestive, to say the least. Oh, and I can't forget my favorite: I once called a reference only to notice that her voice sounded remarkably similar to the candidate's. I called back later for some additional clarification, only to get redirected to the candidate's own voice mail."

These are not mistakes that you want to make. Bad references are *really* bad; you will lose an offer for them. But even if your references are just okay (not terrible), managing them can turn those okay references into great ones.

How References Are Used

References serve potentially three purposes.

1. **Assessing.** A reference can be used to *assess* you. Were you a good employee? What were your strengths? What were your weaknesses? How did your teammates feel about you?
2. **Sanity checking.** A reference can be used as a sanity check. Is there anything really worrisome that an employer should know about you?

3. **Verifying information.** A reference can be used to verify past employment. What was your title? How long did you work there? Did you quit or were you fired?

In many cases, a company *hopes* the reference can be used to assess or at least sanity check you, but can actually only verify information. Some companies, especially large employers, prohibit for legal reasons revealing anything other than basic employment facts.

Whom You Should Select as a Reference

The perfect reference—assuming it's a strong one—is your most recent manager. This manager will typically have the best information about your performance. It will also be a more realistic and fair reference. Nearly everyone can find one person out of one's whole team who will speak fondly of them; not everyone has a manager who does.

However, there are many occasions when you can't use your most recent manager. Perhaps she doesn't know that you are leaving, or perhaps you're on bad terms with her.

When you need to find someone else, or need multiple references, look for people with the following attributes:

- **Knowledge of your work.** A strong reference will be one who has worked directly with you for at least six months, if not several years, and who can speak in-depth about your skills and accomplishments. And, of course, this should be someone who liked you.
- **Articulate.** You've worked with your references long enough to know if they communicate well. If they sound ditzy or speak with terrible grammar, they may not inspire confidence when they speak about your intelligence. You want someone who can elaborate just the right amount and can cite concrete examples.
- **Positive communicator.** Not everyone who likes you will be able to speak well of you. Some people are just too negative, while others may not be able to communicate clearly. John, a Microsoft employee looking to switch careers, opted not to have his manager as a reference, turning instead to his manager's manager: "My direct manager liked me, but he was a poor communicator—one of those guys who almost never seemed pleased, even when he was. His manager, on the other hand, knew my work very well, and was generally more prone to positive reassurance. The choice was a no-brainer."

- **Understands the desired position.** A reference who understands the position will be able to more effectively communicate your ability to fulfill the responsibilities.
- **Available and eager.** When a reference can't spare the time to talk to a prospective employer, it can seem as though the reference isn't sure about your skills. Make sure that your references are happy to do this favor for you, and don't burden them any more than necessary.

When you select your references, think about what skills are most important to a new position. Your references may come from a number of sources, including peers, mentors, vendors, or even customers.

Be aware that in some cases your future employer will explore beyond the references you provided.

Make a Good Reference Great

An unprepared reference tends to say the first thing that pops out of her mouth—or, even worse, she says little. When a reference doesn't elaborate on her answers, it can give the impression that she is saying little because she doesn't want to harm you.

A prepared reference, on the other hand, can speak clearly about your strengths (and sometimes weaknesses). Managing this process in the following seven ways will help you get the best reference possible.

1. **Ask permission.** The first time you give a reference's contact information, you should ask his permission. This is not just proper etiquette; it also helps ensure that you have the appropriate contact information. Some references might prefer to be contacted on their personal e-mail and cell phone, while others prefer their work e-mail and office number. After you've given out the reference several times and the reference is clearly comfortable, simply notifying the reference might be sufficient.
2. **Describe the position.** Tell your reference about the position. Why do you want it? What are your career goals? Why do you think you would be a great match?
3. **Refresh their memory.** Your reference might have forgotten about some of your greatest accomplishments. Remind her of what your responsibilities were, what your accomplishments were, how you accomplished them, and what your greatest challenges were. At a minimum, if your reference would be expected to know about some of your accomplishments listed on your resume, make sure to discuss

the details of these with her. References will typically appreciate your doing some of the legwork for them.

4. **Update them.** If you've taken any additional courses or had any significant experiences, describe these to your reference. These may come in handy.
5. **Suggest areas to emphasize (or deemphasize).** While you can never ask your reference to lie, offering suggestions on areas to stress is acceptable and even helpful. If you want to make sure that the caller knows that you're a strong negotiator, you can mention this to your contact. Likewise, if you want to deemphasize some aspect of your application, you can mention this to your reference.
6. **Discuss the bad stuff.** Your reference may be asked about your weaknesses or failures. This is a bit more awkward to discuss directly, but it's feasible depending on your relationship with your reference. You can mention a few different topics, and let him decide what to discuss. If you don't feel comfortable addressing this issue directly with your reference, you can send an e-mail encouraging him to be prepared for this:

   I did some research on what sorts of questions references are typically asked. It seems that it's common to inquire about strengths and weaknesses, and to ask for some examples. If you want some guidance on this, I'm happy to help out. I really want to make this process as easy on you as possible!
7. **Follow up.** Thank your reference for his assistance, and make sure to follow up with him about what happens.

Don't forget to maintain a positive relationship with your references, as you might need to use them multiple times.

When Things Go Wrong

Your hiring process seemed to be proceeding just fine—until the employer called your reference. Shortly thereafter, you were told that you won't be receiving an offer. What happened?

This pattern is fairly common, and it's very easy for candidates to conclude that they got a bad reference. After all, they were going to get an offer up until the reference was checked, and then—*bam!*—no offer!

The vast majority of the time, it's not the reference. Something else happened, and these reasons can be basically benign:

- The recruiter accidentally misled you into thinking you did better in your interview than you did. The company was checking references to see if that could salvage you, and it couldn't.

- You and another candidate were both being considered for the position. Both of your references checked out fine. However, on the grounds of interview performance, your competitor got the offer.
- The company learned in the course of reference checking that you didn't have sufficient experience in a particular area. They were already concerned about this and your references confirmed it.
- The company's hiring process is being frozen due to financial problems.

It's usually not a bad reference, since people will typically decline giving a reference for you rather than give a bad reference.

Sometimes, though, it *is* the reference. If this appears to be a trend, it's worth your time to understand what might be happening. Ask your references to run through what they've been asked, and what their responses have been. Encourage them to be open about the negative things as well, because, after all, a 100 percent positive review is never credible.

If you still can't figure it out, ask yourself these questions:

- Do your references have any major black marks themselves? If they've been fired or significantly demoted, they may not offer a ton of credibility.
- Are your references effective communicators? When you challenged their positions on a matter, were you able to understand their reasoning?
- Do your references communicate in a positive way? Think back to your reviews. Did they focus on the positive or the negative?
- Are they knowledgeable about your prior projects? They may just need a refresher course on what you accomplished under them, or they may need to be yanked completely.
- Are they familiar with what you're doing now? If you've lost touch with your references, invite them to grab coffee with you. Discuss what they're working on—and what you're doing.

Bad references can be caused by many things. If you suspect a contact is offering a negative review, you may want to play it safe and remove him or her entirely.

What If Your Bad Reference Is Your Former Boss?

If you have personal differences with your current boss, this will likely not present an issue. A prospective company should never call your current company without your permission.

But what if you've left your old company and your potential future company insists on speaking to your former boss? You have many options, and none of them involve asking someone to lie. (Never, ever ask a reference to lie. Do you really want someone to think of you as dishonest right before they talk about your weaknesses?)

First, you should call your old manager and discuss your concerns upfront. Explain what you think your strengths were, and be blunt about your weaknesses. Without making excuses for yourself, tell her why you faced these issues and how you've been working on them. What sort of progress have you made? This will deemphasize the weakness, and you may even be able to suggest less harmful vocabulary (such as "is very passionate about opinions" instead of "has a quick temper").

Second, if the review is particularly bad (such as being fired for exposing company secrets), you need to be upfront about this with the new HR department. It's better that they hear it from you, rather than being caught off guard by your ex-manager.

Finally, you may be able to offer additional references in certain cases to compensate for a poor reference. Audrey, a technical sales representative, quit her job after being assigned a manager who frequently yelled at his employees for even small mistakes. She had no chance of improving this review. Instead, she explained the situation to her prospective employer and offered contact information for three former teammates. They would not only corroborate her story, but they would also offer a strong reference for her. She got the job.

Questions and Answers

Full Disclosure

Should I tell my manager that I'm looking for a new job? I'm coming to the end of a rotation program, so my leaving shouldn't be a complete surprise, but it's still not exactly encouraged.

I'm worried that prospective employers will contact my manager for a reference, and I wouldn't want him to find out the wrong way.

There's no need to tell your manager. Your prospective companies should not contact any references without your explicit permission. Just to make extra sure, though, you should let the prospective company know the situation. It's quite normal—in fact, the norm—for people not to tell their manager until they've accepted the new offer.

However, perhaps you have some reason to believe your manager stands a very good chance of finding out. If, for example, you know that your manager has a close friend at the companies or teams to which you're applying, I wouldn't count on this friend's discretion. In this case, given that your leaving is not totally unexpected, discussing the situation with your manager might be wise.

What's the worst he can do—fire you?

After college, I founded my own business. We did okay for a little while and I hired a few people, but things took a turn for the worse.

Anyway, here I am, looking for work. Employers want to check references, but I've never had a boss. Whom should I give?

Former employees, clients, investors, and partners all make great references, and they all have their pros and cons.

Investors make great references. They may not know you quite as well as a manager would in most jobs, but they're the closest thing you have to a boss.

Your employees will know you extremely well, but with the power dynamic (even if it shouldn't be an issue), employers may not trust that they're being fully honest.

Clients and partners can also be useful. They'll know certain aspects of you quite well, and won't have much reason to be misleading like your employees might.

The best thing to do, really, is to explain the situation to the employer. Ask your recruiter which type would be the most valuable, and then track down the relevant references. There's no reason you shouldn't check with your recruiter about logistical questions like this.

Remember, though, that just because you didn't list a particular client doesn't mean your recruiter won't track that client down. Some reference checkers will do more than just check off a preapproved list.

8 Interview Prep and Overview

Rumors fly wild about the crazy interview questions at tech companies, most notably Google. Bloggers and journalists write articles about the intense, mind-stumping questions. Every six months or so, a new series of articles circulates about how so-and-so company has revolutionized its interview process.

But, more often than not, those articles contain mostly false or misleading information. A single offhanded remark by someone not that knowledgeable of the situation gets twisted into a much bigger story, and no one cares to fact check the piece. After all, it's the crazy stories that get the clicks.

The interview process is mostly consistent across the major tech companies. They're all looking for people who are the classic "smart and get things done" person. The specific way that is assessed varies across positions, of course.

Interview Questions

Most interview questions fit into one of the following four categories:

1. **"Define yourself" questions.** These include the standard interview questions like "Tell me about yourself," "What are your strengths and weaknesses?," and "Why are you interested in this position?"

2. **Behavioral questions.** Behavioral questions are sometimes asked as hypotheticals, but are typically asked in a form like "Tell me about a time when . . ."
3. **Intelligence/problem-solving questions.** Rightly or wrongly, tech companies place a high value on intelligence. Candidates (although rarely software developers) are sometimes asked brainteasers, but more often they're asked other sorts of problem-solving questions, like estimation questions.
4. **Job-specific questions.** Job-specific questions include coding/algorithm problems for solver developers, such as "How would you market ___ to ___?" for a marketing position, product design questions for product managers, sales-related questions for a salesperson, and so on.

Note that problem-solving questions do overlap with job-specific questions; some questions fall into both categories.

We will cover these types of questions in later chapters.

The Tech Interview Culture

Passion. Creativity. Initiative. Intelligence. And a "getting things done" attitude.

Tech companies operate a bit differently from the rest of corporate America. The employees don't wear suits. Few arrive much before 10 a.m., due in part to horrendous traffic in tech hubs like Seattle and Silicon Valley. Post-lunch (or midmorning, or midafternoon) foosball and Ping-Pong games are standard.

They pride themselves on their funky and innovative culture, and they want people who will fit into this. "You have to prove why you are there, and that you know you fit within their community, that you enjoy the lifestyle," says Andre, a (successful) Apple candidate. "The moment my interviewer said, 'We are very informal' I took off my tie."

- **Passion for technology.** Passion for technology can be shown through your course work, but it doesn't end there. Do you read tech news sources? Do you use technology in your day-to-day life (beyond just e-mail and basic web browsing)? Are you interested in finding new ways to leverage or improve technology?
- **Passion for the company.** Do you know the company's products? Do you use them? Why or why not? What would you improve?
- **Creativity.** When asked to design something from scratch, can you brainstorm lots of features you'd want? When you're asking to solve a

problem, do you think outside the box and push back on assumptions or constraints?

- **Initiative.** How have you gone above and beyond? Have you started a blog? A business? Organized a charity auction? Remember that initiative might be something as nontraditional as putting on a photography show.
- **Getting things done.** Regardless of where the idea came from, do you have a demonstrated ability to accomplish great things? Think beyond just your academic or professional work: what have you done outside of work?
- **Intelligence.** Your GPA can be one show of intelligence, but people with GPAs well below a 3.0 out of 4.0 can and do get hired at the best tech companies. Intelligence can be tested through problem-solving questions, or hinted at through your resume.

At the end of the day, it comes down to this: can you communicate how you can help the company? Passion, creativity, initiative, intelligence, and a "getting things done" attitude are all signals of that.

Do Your Homework

Recruiting is expensive, and companies want to know that you're excited about the job. The more excited you are about the job, the more likely you are to accept it, the more likely you are to work hard, and the more likely you are to stay at the company for a while. Companies look for enthusiasm, and researching the company, position, and people is one way to prove that.

Additionally, by doing this research, you'll be able to forge stronger connections with your interviewers, learn more in the process, and sometimes even predict interview questions.

"Before my Amazon interview, I bought a Kindle," Dave, a (now) Amazon employee, says. "It was expensive, but I needed that job badly. I also explored S3, EC2, and basically every Amazon product I could get my hands on. I was interviewing with a back-end team, but people move around—I knew that my interviewers had likely worked on other teams in the past. And I was right. Several of my interviewers had worked on Kindle and other products, and I was able to ask informed questions about their teams. Needless to say, they were impressed."

Company

Company research starts with the basics: what does it make, how does it make it, and how does it make money? These answers sometimes appear more straightforward than they really are. Amazon, for instance, makes money by selling or reselling products at a small profit. The interesting question is how: how is the company able to sell so many things? By having some of the best distribution systems and infrastructure out there!

- **News.** Stay on top of the latest news about a company, especially if you're interviewing for a nontechnical role. The more important current events are to your role, the more important it is for you to know about this for your interview. Twitter can be a great source for unfiltered company news if you search what other users are saying. The corporate blog can also be valuable, but keep in mind that those blogs are usually more of a PR machine than anything else.
- **Competitors.** Not only are competitors likely to have similar problems, but a competitor's success is the company's problem. Research who the competitors are, as well as why: in what ways is one company doing better than another? Why is it doing better?
- **Current and former employees.** Use Twitter, Facebook, or your friends network to reach out to current and former employees. They may be able to share with you some insights about the company, and, if you're lucky, offer some interview tips.
- **Culture.** Companies with a particularly strong culture are likely to select for culture fit, and are likely to openly discuss their culture. Zappos.com, for instance, is known for having a very fun and quirky culture. Don't be surprised if the interviewer asks you for a time when you broke the rules or invented a new type of pizza topping. The interview questions reflect the company's weirdness, and Zappos.com will look to see if you're weird enough to fit in.

In particular, think about these questions in relation to *your* job. Think about things like:

- **If you're a marketer:** How would you market this product? What are the challenges you might face? What has the current marketing done well or poorly?
- **If you're in sales:** How would you sell this product? Who would you sell it to?
- **If you're a developer:** How would you design this system from scratch? What did the current team do well or poorly?

Oftentimes, candidates will be asked questions directly based on these points. Doing this sort of research and analyzing the company's decisions will help you be well prepared.

Interviewer Research

You won't always know your interviewer's name in advance, and it's not necessarily a must to research your interviewer. However, it can be useful to do so.

Knowing your interviewer's background can offer hints as to what she is likely to focus on. For example, a product manager interviewer who used to be a designer is more likely to focus on design-related questions.

Additionally, the companies that the interviewer used to work for can also point you in the right direction. People's interview styles are influenced by where they work, and they often bring these influences into their next job.

Finally, your interviewer's background can give you some hints of interesting questions to ask. For example, if your interviewer has worked on several teams at that company, it can be useful to ask your interviewer about how the culture varies across teams.

Prepare Questions

At either the beginning or end of each interview, your interviewer will give you a chance to ask questions. The quality of your questions will be a factor, whether subconsciously or consciously, in his decision. Ask open-ended questions in order to create a more natural conversation.

Consider questions from the following three categories:

1. **Genuine questions.** These are the questions you actually want to know the answers to. These questions might be:
    - "How much of your day do you spend in meetings?
    - "How many people are on the team? What is the breakdown of different positions?"
    - "What are the biggest issues facing the team?"
    - "How does the decision process work? Who makes the final call? Who drives the decisions?"

2. **Insightful questions.** These questions show that you've thought deeply about the issues facing the team or company. Research you do in advance will come in handy here. For example:
   - "Office has been aggressively pursuing an online strategy. Is this a play at the consumer market to protect Microsoft from Google? Or is there a role in the business market as well, since that's where Microsoft makes most of its money?"
   - "Why did Google opt to use an open protocol for this product? Is it mainly a PR move, or are there actually technology advantages? What sort of limitations is Google usually concerned with when leveraging open source?"
3. **Passion questions.** Passion questions are designed to show you as someone who is excited about technology, about the company, or about learning. These questions include:
   - "Though I don't have a coding background, I love learning how software is implemented. As an employee, what sorts of resources are there to do this?"
   - "I'm not familiar with the technology you mentioned earlier. Could you tell me a bit about it?"
   - "Thinking back to people who have had this job in the past, what separates the successful person from the unsuccessful?"

While some questions may come to you during the interview (which is great), you can—and should—prepare about 10 questions in advance. This will ensure that you have at least a few unique questions to ask every interviewer.

Avoid asking questions that you can easily look up, as this will reflect poorly on you. Companies expect that you have done research prior to your interview.

Additionally, remember that you will likely interview with HR, a manager, and teammates as well. What perspective can they each offer about the company?

Working with Your Recruiter

Your recruiter serves as your advocate during the recruiting process. He wants you to do well—after all, his performance evaluation is largely determined by the quantity and quality of candidates he brings in. He's unlikely to be making the final hire/no hire decision, but he can be a voice that fights for you.

No one knows this better than Ravi. Ravi was applying for a position at Microsoft—his dream job. Ravi breezed through the on-campus interviews at his college and was flown out to Redmond, Washington, for five interviews with two different teams. He met with his recruiter at the end of the day, who thanked him very much for his time and scooted him out the door. He left the rainy city with no offer in hand. A week later, he started sweating—why hadn't she called? Finally, two weeks after his interview, he learned the bad news: though he had done well, she said, neither team would be moving forward at this time. Ah, the generic words every candidate hates to hear!

Normally, that would be that. However, instead of shutting the door on him (and his dream job), she invited him to return to Seattle for another set of interviews. He flew out again, completed another five interviews, and again, days passed with no word. Finally, she called Ravi: "Neither team will be moving forward at this time, but we have a different team that would like to speak with you." Two phone interviews later, and—*bam!*—he got the offer and went on to have an amazing summer internship experience.

Why was Ravi special? He and his recruiter clicked, and she believed in him. She recognized that interviews are a bit random and take some practice. She was willing to give him a second—and then a third—chance.

Your goal, during a recruiting process, is to build a connection with your recruiter like Ravi did. Though they may not have the hire/no hire decision, they can and do fight for you to get an offer—or not.

Getting the Recruiter on Your Side

Simply by respecting the recruiter's role, you're off to a great start. Far too many candidates see recruiters as just a minion in the recruiting process—someone who is just there to do their bidding.

- **Be polite.** Always show your recruiter politeness and courtesy. Follow up with him, but don't pester him. Respect that he's busy and works with many candidates. When he doesn't get back to you as quickly as you'd like, give him the benefit of the doubt.
- **Use good grammar and spelling.** Using correct grammar and spelling when e-mailing your recruiter will show professionalism. Minor grammatical mistakes will probably be forgiven, especially for international candidates, but text messaging style abbreviations are not acceptable.

- **Ask questions.** Ask the recruiter questions about the company, the position, and so on. Make sure that these questions don't have easily discoverable answers online. By asking insightful questions, you show that you're passionate about the company—and about learning.
- **Seek their advice.** Though the recruiter may not be an expert in finance, engineering, marketing, or whatever position you're applying for, she's probably seen a lot more interviews than you have. Seek the recruiter's advice about what skill sets are more important, how to prepare for the interview, and the like. Even if she can't answer your questions, she'll appreciate that you respect her opinion enough to ask.

Your recruiter's first allegiance is of course to the company, but this is not totally misaligned with your interests. On the contrary, your recruiter wants you to do well.

Communication and Behavior

Your personal interaction with your interviewer not only can be a direct factor in deciding whether you have an offer, but it can also bias your interviewer. If an interviewer likes you, she is more likely to perceive you as talented. She *wants* to hire you, and that will cause her to perceive your answers in the best possible light.

What Your Interviewer's Attitude Really Means

"How do you know when an interview is going well or poorly?" someone asks online. Responses are varied:

- "When the conversation with your interviewer seems strained, or if you have to constantly look for ways to make conversation, that's a bad sign."
- "Look for signs of positivity in the interviewer's reaction. If an interviewer is happy, it'll be obvious. Interviewers will tell you—directly or indirectly—that they liked your answer."
- "Constantly firing off questions is never a good sign."
- "If you don't get an interview with the hiring manager, that's a bad sign."
- "Struggling on interview questions is obviously bad."
- "If they seem to be selling you on the company, that probably means you're getting an offer."

It turns out that none of these are particularly indicative of performance.

A good interviewer will do his best to leave you with a positive impression, regardless of your performance. He should smile, offer positive reassurance, and give you his full attention. Even if he has effectively written you off as a "no hire," you have friends and colleagues who may interact with the company down the road. Recruiting is too important to a company's future to just disregard anyone's perceptions.

Of course, there are still unfriendly interviewers. There are interviewers who push back on your responses with a condescending tone, and there are interviewers who are distracted and don't give you their full attention. This is much more about their personality than about your performance. In fact, for *them*, their attitude toward you might actually be quite friendly.

Controlling the Interview

Your interviewer might walk into the meeting with a set list of favorite questions, but the interview is not totally predetermined. By dropping little nuggets along the way, you can encourage your interviewer to ask you certain questions. That then gives you the opportunity to highlight your best stories (and avoid the interviewer focusing on the worst ones).

For example, consider this interaction:

Interviewer: What did you work on at Google?

Candidate: I joined just after Google acquired YouTube, and I was responsible for figuring out a plan for merging YouTube's technology with Google's. The two companies were working with some of the same basic technologies, but I needed to figure out how much to merge them—if at all. I quickly discovered that YouTube could be made much more cost-effective by leveraging the Google Video libraries. I spent most of my time working on the video compression library, where I encountered some of the most interesting challenges.

What do you think will be the next question the interviewer will ask? If she's at all interested, she'll probably ask you to elaborate on the challenges you faced. If she's not interested, then aren't you glad you didn't ramble?

By leading your interviewer like this, you'll be able to drive the conversation in a way that's positive for both you and your interviewer, rather than drown her in details.

Alternatively, you can be more direct and say: "I can elaborate on that if you'd like." This is a good way of skipping over details in a story that an interviewer may or may not want to hear.

It's actually quite helpful when a candidate does this. Your interviewer wants to hear about your best accomplishments, but doesn't know where to dig. Offering this information helps guide interviewers toward the information they want to here.

Six Ways to Keep the Interviewer's Attention

Newly minted interviewers are often quite eager to speak with you. They open your resume well in advance, research your projects, and maybe even check out the website that you conveniently listed on your application.

But, as interviewers become more experienced, their enthusiasm tends to wane. The walk over to the interview room becomes the ideal slice of time for resume preparation. While you're diving into the nitty-gritty details of how you saved your current employer from impending doom, your interviewers are picturing the ever-growing mountain of work waiting for them. They know the importance of the interview both to you and to the company, but at the same time, they just want to be done already!

You can't really blame your interviewer (too much), but you can be proactive in detecting when they're losing focus and in bringing them back to you.

To keep your interviewer more engaged, try these six tips:

1. **Be aware of talking too much.** If you find that your interviewer rarely has follow-up questions, that's often a sign that you talked too much. Be more brief and cut out details, with a mention that you can go into more detail if the interviewer would like.
2. **Be aware of talking too little.** If your interviewer asks a bunch of follow-up questions, particularly if those follow-up questions are ones that you could have covered initially, that might indicate you didn't elaborate enough. For example, a question like "So what did you do to

resolve this?" is something that you possibly should have covered initially.

3. **Talk from the heart.** Bringing emotion into your story can be a powerful way to connect with your interviewer. Lines like "It was really difficult for me to see my coworker struggle, because I remembered being in his shoes" engage your interview.
4. **Vary your speech.** Try varying the volume or tone of your speech. Speaking a bit louder or a bit quieter may be the kick needed to grab your interviewer's attention. Or, if you can show some additional passion or enthusiasm in your voice, your interviewer might absorb some of this emotion.
5. **Tell a story.** Minor changes in word choice can flip your response from a bland description of what happened to a memorable story. Consider the difference between "The servers were experiencing significant downtimes during peak ordering times, which made us lose money" and "I answered the phone to hear a customer raging at us because our website was down. As we looked into it, we discovered this was a widespread issue that caused our department to lose about $10,000 each month." Adding action to the story will grab the listener's attention, while quantifying the impact will ground what you're saying in fact. Be careful not to go overboard, though—you don't want to drown the interviewer in details, either.
6. **Structure your responses.** Have you ever listened to someone speak and ask yourself, "Where is this story going?" Sometimes this is because the person is talking too much, but sometimes it's just due to a lack of structure. Picture your response as a set of bullet points and sub-bullets—and use them while speaking! For example: "We had two major issues with this design: one, our customers are very cost-sensitive, and two, it would take too long to implement. As far as the first point is concerned, we believed that . . ." Hand gestures can help make the division between your points even clearer.

If your interviewer's attention drifts, she's probably just like that in general. Don't lose hope or get discouraged, but do act on it.

Projecting Confidence

Confidence is a delicate balancing game: too much confidence and you appear arrogant; too little confidence and you appear insecure. You need to find the sweet spot—the point where you are assertive with your own opinions and are bold enough to take some risks, but you also listen and respect others.

Whether you have lots of confidence or little, keep in mind this advice:

- **Eye contact.** Making eye contact with your interviewer shows confidence, and—short of starting a staring contest—you probably can't go overboard with this. If you are the type to stare at the desk or up in the air while trying to construct an answer, then make sure to maintain steady eye contact.
- **Match your volume.** Roughly matching your voice to your interviewer's will ensure that you speak at an appropriate volume that doesn't get read as too aggressive or too passive. Of course, don't go overboard on this—if your interviewer is barely audible, you should just soften your voice only as much as is easily comfortable for you.
- **Don't argue (too much).** Occasionally, your interviewer might say something you disagree with—and you might even be correct. Speak up, but gently. Use wording like "Interesting—I thought that Apple had stated they wouldn't enter this market," and then if your interviewer stands firm, "Oh, all right, I must be thinking of something else." No matter how sure you are, always remember that your interviewer thinks you're wrong. And it's your interviewer's opinion that matters.
- **Watch out for nervous habits.** Fidgeting with your watch. Chewing on pencils. Twirling your hair between your fingers. Do any of these sound familiar? Nervous habits like these not only suggest that you lack confidence, but they can also be distracting or even offensive to your interviewers.

If people have told you that you're arrogant, then you'll want to be aware of this. Try softening your voice, really trying to listen, being reassuring toward your interviewer's opinions, and exposing a bit of your feelings.

Special Interview Types

While most interview advice is broadly applicable, there is some advice that is most applicable to specific types of interviews.

The Phone Interview

Do not assume that phone interviewers are simple weeding interviews that filter out the very worst. The standard for phone interviews is often just as high as for in-person interviews, and they are conducted in much the same way.

What to Bring

You'll usually be doing your phone interviews from your own home or office, so make sure to have the following out in front of you:

- **Calculator.** For many roles, you may have to do basic calculations. It's useful to have a calculator of some sort in front of you. This doesn't have to be a physical calculator. In fact, Google.com works quite well as a calculator since it allows you to enter longer equations—as long as you don't get distracted by being online.
- **Pencil and paper.** Use these to jot down notes or potential questions to ask the interviewer.
- **Your resume.** Your interviewer will be using your resume to ask you questions, so it's helpful to be able to look at the exact document to know what he's reading from.
- **Computer.** Have it out in front of you in case your interviewer needs you to open up a document, reference a website, or do a calculation for which you'll need Google.com. But keep it closed until then. If you try to look up answers on your computer, it'll only distract you and it's unlikely to fool your interviewer.
- **Your interview preparation grid** (covered in Chapter 10, "Behavioral Questions"). A phone interview is a perfect time to have it out in front of you.
- **Questions.** You've prepared a list of questions in advance (one hopes), so have this out in front of you. You can also jot down any new questions that come up during the interview.

These materials can be useful, but don't let them distract you. Your first priority should be to focus on the conversation with your interviewer.

The Human Resources Screening Interview

The HR screener probably won't deeply evaluate your job-specific skills, but that's no reason to blow off this interview. This is the company's first impression of you and, like all first impressions, it matters. Even strong candidates sometimes get rejected at this stage.

What Is It?

The HR screening interview serves as an efficient way to determine if a candidate meets the basic requirements. The screener is essentially trying to match you against the backgrounds of those who have done well. Are you a match?

Matching this skill set is often simply a matter of educational background and work experience, but may at times delve into extracurricular discussions. One interviewer mentioned how she loved to hire soccer players. This seems silly (and it probably is), but she said the strongest two interns from the year before were both varsity soccer players. Soccer players possess the determination and teamwork that she was looking for.

The HR screen is often skipped when a candidate's background is clearly and directly relevant (for example, a Microsoft developer applying for a developer position at Google). Therefore, do not assume that the first interview is automatically an HR screening interview—even if it's called a "phone screen." If you are unsure, ask your interview coordinator what position your interviewer has.

What Happens?

The HR screener will likely ask questions to evaluate your character, background, and basic intelligence. Any skill-specific questions should be at a cursory level. Questions may also be designed to probe any potential red flags, such as frequent job-hopping.

These interviews are usually conducted over the phone, but may also employ video chat or computer tests.

How to Do Well

In addition to the usual guidance for interviews, consider this advice:

- **Look for red flags.** A core goal of the HR screening interview is to evaluate any potential red flags on your resume. Do you have several jobs of less than two years? Did you switch from a seemingly more prestigious company or position to a less prestigious one? Give your resume to a friend and ask him what the weakest point on it is. What would be his biggest concern if he were a recruiter?
- **Be prepared for salary questions.** Like it or not, HR screeners will often ask you for your salary requirements. They need to know if you're too expensive. Before your interview, use the Internet and your friends network to get a feel for salary ranges. If you are asked for

your salary requirements, you should try to avoid giving a specific answer so as not to set your sights too low or too high. However, the interviewer may continue to press you on this question, in which case you will be prepared to give an answer.

- **Practice discussing your background in layperson's terms.** Your screener interview likely understands a bit of your field, but is not an expert. Learn how to use simpler terminology to describe your accomplishments. It's often useful to relate your accomplishments to understandable metrics, like dollars or time saved.

Follow-Up Interviews

In some cases, you might be scheduled for a follow-up interview after completing a full set of on-site interviews.

There are three main reasons this happens:

1. Your interviewers neglected to assess some aspect of your background sufficiently. This is their fault, not yours.
2. A red flag came up. For example, one interviewer thought you lacked depth in a particular skill and they want to double-check this.
3. They want you to meet with a specific person, like the hiring manager, who wasn't available on your interview day.

If this happens to you, try asking your recruiter if there's any particular focus for this interview or if it's standard procedure. He might not tell you, but it doesn't hurt to ask.

If you aren't given any specific direction for this interview, you should reflect on your last set of interviews: what do you think you did more poorly on, or were there gaps in what they asked you? This may offer one focus area, but remember that you might not be correct in your assessment. You should therefore do general prep, with just a slight focus on certain areas.

Finally, you should be prepared with two to three new questions that show additional thought or research. What you learned in your prior interviews is a great source of inspiration for your questions.

After the Interview

That unmistakable relief that you're done with your interview is soon replaced by an unmistakable anxiety about how it went. You replay the entire interview in your head: Did you do okay? Did you make any mistakes? What did the recruiter mean when he said, "We'll get in touch with you soon"?

Here's what you should be doing after your interview.

The "Thank You" Note

Although postinterview thank you notes are essentially required in many interviews, they're fairly unusual in tech companies. Howard Wu, a T-Mobile and former Amazon interviewer, estimated that he received thank you notes from fewer than 10 percent of his candidates. For engineering candidates, this number is probably closer to 1 percent.

Eric, a former Amazon interviewer, joked, "For tech companies, a thank you note is like wearing a suit to the interview. It's out of place, and it looks like you're trying to compensate for something." While other people may be less negative, it's generally agreed that a thank you note won't help you much. After all, feedback is usually submitted so quickly after your interview that you couldn't impact the decision.

However, a short note to your recruiter thanking her for coordinating your interview can certainly be nice. If you decide to send a thank you note, either to your recruiter or to an interviewer, these notes usually follow a format similar to this one:

> Dear Leslie,
>
> I wanted to thank you for your time today. I was particularly interested in the discussion we had about the upcoming scalability and power constraints that the company is expected to soon face. I've been interested in big system design for some time now, and I am eager to learn more about it.
>
> During my time in college, I enrolled in several courses on distributed systems. My current position has offered me an excellent foundation in designing reliable software, and I've continued to pursue my interest in large system design through implementing various web automation projects during my free time.
>
> I feel confident that I can leverage my academic, professional, and extracurricular experience with software development to make an impact on Google. I look forward to the opportunity to continue discussions with the company.

This sample thank you note does several things that you should look to replicate in your own letter:

- **Specificity.** The references to a specific discussion make it impossible for it to be completely cut-and-paste. This shows passion for the position.
- **Highlighting of skills.** This letter reminds the recipient of how the candidate's background matches the desired skill set.
- **Enthusiasm.** The candidate has reiterated interest in the position. No lengthy explanation—a brief mention will do.
- **Brevity.** Time is precious, and people are less likely to read longer e-mails. Additionally, conciseness is valuable in employees, so showing this skill here is useful.

If you're sending multiple thank you notes to the same company, you should vary the format and word choice a bit. People talk.

Following Up with Your Recruiter

Although recruiters should be proactive in updating you about your status, they deal with many candidates, and sometimes people fall through the cracks. If you haven't heard from your recruiter (and haven't been given a time line), feel free to e-mail your recruiter after about one week to check in. A simple note like this will suffice:

> Hi Jamie,
>
> I wanted to thank you for helping coordinate my interview last week, and I also wanted to check in about my interview status. Do you know when I could expect an update?
>
> Thank you!

If there's no response, you can e-mail them after another three working days with a short note like:

> Hi Jamie,
>
> I just wanted to check in again. I understand you're probably busy with other work, so I'll most likely just give you a call tomorrow or the next day if I haven't heard back from you before then.
>
> Thanks!

Of course, if at any time your recruiter updates you with a time line, that time line completely supersedes this schedule. That is, if your recruiter says you'll hear back in two weeks, you must wait those two weeks, as painful as it is.

Virtually all companies have a policy of informing candidates when they're rejected. If your recruiter doesn't respond, there can be many reasons for it—but being rejected is not one of them.

Dealing with Rejection

For each offer a company gives out, a company rejects an average of five to ten candidates. This means that, as a candidate, you can expect to get rejected—a lot. It may mean that the position was a poor match, it may mean that you didn't prepare adequately, or it may mean that you just had bad luck.

In the unfortunate case that a company does not extend an offer, focus on not burning bridges. Companies will usually let you reapply within six months to a year, and a positive relationship with your recruiter is critical for doing this. Try to offer a polite response like the following:

> Okay, well, I'm sorry to hear that, but thank you very much for the opportunity. I really enjoyed the experience, and I hope to be able to revisit it down the road.
>
> How long will it be until I can reinterview? Are there any particular weaknesses in my application that would be good to focus on in the meantime?

You can also try asking for feedback directly on your interviews. A larger company usually won't tell you why you're being rejected, but a smaller one might.

Questions and Answers

Run for the Hills

I've been shy and nervous talking to new people my entire life. As a result, I've never liked interviewing, but I'm especially dreading this upcoming interview.

HR has informed me that at the end of the day, I'll be expected to give a short, five-minute talk about a prior project I've done. All the interviewers from that day will be attending, and will have a chance to talk afterward.

I'm terrified. Any tips?

Don't get nervous! (That's probably easier said than done.)

First, pick a recent project. You'll feel more comfortable with the topic and will get less nervous. You can even dumb down some of the details—they won't know the difference.

Second, tell a story. Introduce the issue you were faced with, and walk them through how you solved it. You might not have access to a slide deck, so use hand gestures to show when you transition from one point to the next.

Third, get the slides—if any—right. Many people put too much content on their slides, especially people who are nervous. The slides should be helping you prove your point; they shouldn't tell the whole story themselves. Consider not even using slides if you don't really need them. In some cases, you can be more effective speaking without slides.

Fourth, brainstorm the questions the interviewers are likely to ask, and prepare your answers. They could take the questions two directions: (1) interview-y questions (hardest challenges, etc.) or (2) real-world questions (impact, issues, etc.).

Fifth, practice! Do this in front of a mirror, your friends, or just the family pet.

Sixth and finally, admit to your interviewers that you're nervous. They'll probably smile and do what they can to calm you down, and you'll get away from this uber-serious-professional tone. Getting out this bit of vulnerability can actually help you.

On a more serious level, though, if you really dread public speaking, you may want to reconsider this position. Public speaking is obviously an important enough part of the job that they're putting it into the interview process. Are you prepared to take on a job if it is an integral part?

Too Much Information or Just Enough?

I have Tourette's syndrome. While I don't curse or do anything inappropriate, I do twitch, especially when nervous. Should I give my recruiters a heads-up about this? I'm worried that this may make them uncomfortable or, even worse, open me up to discrimination.

You'll hear advice both ways on this, but I think it really depends on how severe the condition is. Will it distract significantly from your interview? Would you feel more comfortable if your interviewer knew why you twitch? If the condition is relatively subtle (i.e., noticeable but not distracting), you may not need to say anything. Here's why:

- There are no accommodations to be made for you. You don't need to ask your interviewer to speak lower, talk louder, write larger, and so on. In short, there's no action they should take, so the information would likely not even leave the ears of your recruiter.
- It's obviously medical. If you had, say, a black eye due to recent surgery, you might want to inform your interviewers of this, lest they think you decided to rough someone up on your way to the office. In this case, though, there's no other way they can interpret a tic. It's clearly a medical issue; who cares if it's Tourette's or something else?

As far as I can see, specifying the condition in advance can only hurt you. Some people might assume that you shout out obscene words at random and (unfairly) be concerned about the impact of your condition.

However, if either of these points were wrong—if you do need accommodation or there might be an alternate, worse explanation for your condition—then I would suggest telling your recruiter well in advance.

Playing Hard to Get

I interviewed with a company two weeks ago, and they haven't notified me of a decision. I even tried e-mailing the recruiter—no response. Does this mean I'm rejected?

In one word: no. After you interview with a company, they will always tell you if you're rejected.

Delays can happen for many reasons—good, bad, and neutral:

- They are going to give you an offer, but would like to have all their paperwork together.
- They prefer another candidate, but are waiting for her to make a decision. You are their second choice.
- The team is being "reorg'd" and the current head count is unclear.
- Your recruiter went on vacation.
- The recruiting team is being "reorg'd."
- You have a bad/lazy recruiter.
- One of the many people you interviewed with is slow about entering feedback.

You should continue to check in with your recruiter regularly for updates, but no more than once every few days.

Additional Resources

Visit www.crackingthetechcareer.com for additional preparation resources, and the preparation grid template.

9 Define Yourself

Of all interview questions, these are perhaps the most despised by candidates. Some people think they're trick questions. Some think they're just demanding crafted answers rather than honest ones. And some are just sick of how overdone and cheesy the questions are.

All this may or may not be true, but an interview is probably not the right time to take up this battle. Roll with it—unless you're willing to sacrifice the job for this.

Prepare for these questions by knowing what you'll say in advance. Think about what are the bright spots and blemishes of your background. Know what you want and why.

If you get nailed with a question you weren't expecting, just speak honestly. These questions, even the annoying, overdone ones ("What is your biggest weakness?"), are usually best answered with genuineness.

Your interviewer is not expecting perfection. In fact, many of these questions are aimed at trying to understand exactly how you're not perfect. The worst thing you can do is to pretend that you are.

The Pitch

Many of your interviews will begin with an open-ended question like "Tell me about yourself" or "Walk me through your resume."

This question is so common that there's no reason not to be entirely prepared for it.

Your response should typically take about two minutes. The following structure usually works well.

Part 1: Introduction

Start off with a one- or two-sentence introduction about yourself. Keep it short; you'll go into more detail later.

> "I'm a sales manager for Orthogonal Ads, where I lead a team of six salespeople. I have worked there for two years and manage sales for our mobile integration components."

All you really need to mention here is your job title, company, how long you have worked there, and maybe one detail about your responsibility.

Part 2: Chronological Resume Walk-Through

Walk through your resume, usually starting from your college experience. The more recent the experience, the more time you'll spend on it.

This should be a fluid, natural story. Your goal is not to expand on your key stories, but you do want blend in:

- Your key accomplishments
- What you learned
- What drives you

As you jump from one job to the next, try to connect the dots. Why did you switch? How did you make that transition?

> "To back up, I did my undergraduate degree at the University of Pittsburgh, where I was the president of my fraternity. I found that I really enjoyed the recruiting side—trying to identify and recruit the right members. It required me to quickly assess people, filter who is and isn't a good match, build quick relationships with people, and sell them on our strengths. This was what drew me into sales.
>
> "When I graduated, I ended up actually taking a job in customer support for a health care start-up. I joined when the company was only about 15 people and worked very closely with the sales team. When the company needed to ramp up its sales efforts, I transitioned completely over to sales. I met my sales quota every year, and eventually got poached by an ex-manager who was starting a new company."

Note how this candidate has worked in his skills, interests, and key accomplishments. The mention of getting poached is intentional; it clearly shows that he has been successful.

Part 3: What You're Doing Now

You've already mentioned what you're doing, but here's the chance to go into it in more detail.

> "This was when I got brought into Orthagonal. The company had customers very early on, but little idea on how to manage a sales time line. I launched the sales org at the company and have grown the company from under $10,000 in annual revenue to over $5 million. I've recruited my own team, developed a sales training program for them, and worked closely with developers to shape the product based on customer feedback.
>
> "One of my major initiatives at the company has been ensuring strong connections across all parts of the company. Sales, marketing, engineering, and support really need to be tightly linked. I've rolled out several tools to ensure better transparency, and created a cross-company rotation program."

This is a good place to dangle little tidbits, to prompt your interviewer to probe more. You can shape the direction of the interview.

Part 4: Extracurriculars

What do you do outside of work? If there's something interesting—and "interesting" can be very broad—mention it.

> "Outside of work, I've been learning how to do home remodeling. I love learning new things and getting my hands dirty—literally, in this case. I've so far remodeled my bathroom and I'm halfway through my kitchen."

This offers something interesting about you, which is usually valuable. Although home remodeling doesn't sound particularly relevant to sales, not being afraid to do things that aren't usually up your alley is attractive to employers.

Why Should We Hire You?

Erin, a recruiting coordinator from Microsoft, reminds us, "Whatever you're asked, you're always answering the question 'Why should we hire you?' It is the thesis of your interview." This question is explicitly asking for the thesis.

Although this question sounds aggressive to some candidates, it's usually not intended to be. The interviewer isn't trying to say that you shouldn't be hired. Rather, he's giving you the opportunity to sell yourself. Take it.

Focus on a few core (related) skills or attributes that you think you offer. Three is a good target; fewer than three seems weak, and more than three loses the interviewer's focus. Back up each with a short amount of evidence or an explanation.

Where possible, try to hit a diversity of aspects. For example, you could select one personal attribute (persistence, etc.), one skill (sales experience), and one culture/position match.

> "There are a few things I offer.
>
> "First, I have a deep background in statistics. This will allow me not only to perform complex analysis, but also to drive changes by teaching the rest of the team how to do this.
>
> "Second, I am not afraid of trying something new and failing. I don't stick to just what's easy; I push my limits. This has made me a leader in tackling top challenges at my prior positions and will do the same for you.
>
> "Third, I'm passionate about the quantification of body metrics. I will enter the company excited, and I will stay excited. I am always reading up on the latest trends."

Thinking in advance about your strengths and weaknesses will help you prepare for this question.

Why Shouldn't We Hire You?

Resist the urge to say something snarky. There's a small chance you'll come up with something genuinely funny, but it's more likely that you'll turn off the interviewer.

This question is very similar to asking about your weaknesses, but allows for a bit broader range of responses.

Here's one that would work:

> "Obviously, I am really excited about this opportunity. But to be honest, I can't say that I am absolutely, definitely the perfect fit for this job. I don't think it's realistic to claim such insight.
>
> I guess I'll tell you what could be reasons why I might not be a good fit.
>
> "I do best in environments where people's roles aren't narrowly confined. The shiny-happy/put-a-good-interview-spin-on-it way of saying this is that I enjoy wearing many hats and getting my hands dirty. The more blunt, realistic, negative way of putting this is that I get bored and lose focus if I'm doing just one thing all day.
>
> "Please don't misunderstand. I love doing this work. I wouldn't be in this profession if I didn't. But I also want to work closely with other job functions and maybe even take on little aspects of their responsibilities from time to time.
>
> "If you're looking for someone who will be happy doing only their core duties, it's not me, unfortunately. I wouldn't be happy, so, from a strictly selfish perspective, don't hire me.
>
> "Less selfishly, I should also advise you that there are some things I'm not good at. Specifically, I just don't have a good attention to detail. Again, the positive side of this is that I execute quickly and get things done—but it comes with a trade-off of making little mistakes.
>
> "Ever heard of Quora? I swear it is impossible for me to write a Quora answer without dropping a word or making a typo. I'm one of the most active writers on the site, but any lengthy answer will generally have a mistake or two. I would never, ever go into, say, air traffic control or become a surgeon. The costs of mistakes are too high.
>
> "I am getting better at this. I know to check my work carefully, and I have a good sense for where I'm likely to make mistakes. But still, being detail oriented does not come naturally to me. If little mistakes are critical (or seen as critical), then I probably wouldn't be your best hire. Does that make sense?"

As with the weaknesses question, you want to select an issue that is a genuinely bad thing, but not a deal breaker. A software tester probably would not want to admit to a poor attention to detail, because that's critical. A manager might be able to get away with this, though.

Why Do You Want to Work Here?

The key to this question is answering it in a way that boosts your chances. It's all about your motivations and skills. Think about the skill sets for the job or the area you'll be working in. What excites you? Do you love working with people? Are you fascinated by tough algorithm problems? Do you want to make an impact?

Try to keep your answers as specific as possible to the company or even the team. You might even consider mixing in some comments about your background and how the company is a great match for that.

This is also a great time to flex all the research you've done about the company.

Here's a great response for an engineering position at Google:

> "There are two major reasons.
>
> "First, I'm really interested in the design of large systems. I've taken a lot of courses on distributed systems and explored this for my senior project. I feel Google is the best place to deepen my knowledge in this area.
>
> "But, second, and perhaps more important, I really believe that the most important thing for any job is to make sure that you're learning a lot. Whereas at many companies you really learn only about your own team, at Google employees seem to be encouraged to transfer between teams, to share knowledge across teams, to do tech talks about their team's architecture, and so forth. I can't think of any place where I'd learn more than at Google."

In providing this response, the candidate has shown himself to be excited about learning, to have done research on the company, and to be knowledgeable about a core skill set.

Why Are You Leaving Your Job?

When a friend asks you this question, you'll likely respond with something like "I'm just so bored, plus I have a bad manager."

You want to be honest in your interview, but not *that* honest. Stay positive. Negativity reflects poorly on you as a candidate because people don't like negative people. Additionally, most of the negative remarks you could make indicate some blemish in your background.

- **"I'm bored."** You haven't been working on interesting challenges, so you haven't learned as much in your current job as one might hope.
- **"There's little room for promotion."** Is that your company's fault or your fault?
- **"My coworkers aren't very good."** If your coworkers aren't skilled, then you're probably not being challenged.

These assumptions might not be true in every case, but they're true in enough cases. Companies take a risk-averse approach to hiring—it's better to reject a good candidate than hire a bad one—so these sorts of red flags can be deal breakers.

No matter how bad your situation is, stay positive. Focus on the good things about the new position rather than the bad things about the old one.

> "My current position has been great in certain ways. It has taught me a lot about communication, negotiations, and how to manage many clients at once. However, I've found that I excel most in building longer-lasting relationships with clients, and I'm looking for an opportunity where this is a primary focus."

Assuming that the new position matches this requirement, this would be an excellent response. It focuses on your strengths.

Where Do You See Yourself in Five Years?

Before answering this question for your interviewer, answer it for yourself. Where *do* you see yourself in five years?

Many candidates assume that their five-year goal must be at the same company. That's not really the case.

Unlike some other industries, the tech community is pretty understanding of switching jobs frequently. A lifelong commitment isn't expected (or even admired); technology moves too fast for that.

It's okay not to be certain about where you'll be. Your interviewer just wants to get a feel for your goals and to know that you are ambitious and you care about your career.

This is one answer you could give.

> "I'd like to move into a marketing role eventually. I'm good at thinking about product positioning—it's one of the things that makes me a good fit for this role—but I know I need more formal business experience before doing that. I hope to develop some of those skills

> here. I'm also taking classes online on statistics to develop my quantitative side.
>
> "I've also considered starting a company one day, but I don't know if that will be within the next five years or not. I love working in close-knit teams, moving fast, and pushing the envelope of what's realistic."

Note that it's okay to admit that you might not be at the company in five years. In this case, the candidate says that she might leave by then, but she does so in a way that shows valuable attributes: risk taking, teamwork, and tackling big challenges.

It's also okay to be uncertain. Openness is good, but total lack of goals suggests that you're not ambitious.

What Are Your Strengths?

You're probably great at many things, but you want to pick a set of three attributes that are most relevant to the job and provable, while also being unique. Intelligence, for example, is probably very applicable as well as provable, but it's also so common that it's bland.

A better set of strengths are things like communication skills, energy, creativity, working well under stress, motivating others, and so on. When you state each one of these, try to cite a specific example. For instance:

> "I think there are three core strengths.
>
> "First, I have strong communication skills that have been refined through five years of prior teaching experience.
>
> "Second, I'm a very creative person. Whether it's writing new song lyrics for my band or designing a novel interface, I'm able to find unique solutions to problems.
>
> "Third, I am passionate about learning. I recently finished up a certificate in psychology at the local university, and I'm starting a new program now in art history. I may never directly apply this education, but I love learning new things."

Note that there is a difference between your knowledge and your skills. It's okay for one of your skills to be knowledge-based (e.g., "I am good with statistics"), but most should be personal attributes (persistence, risk taking, etc.). Personal attributes will stay with you throughout your life; knowledge-based skills are acquirable by anyone.

What Are Your Weaknesses?

Many years ago, someone started a vicious rumor that your weaknesses should be strengths in disguise: "I think one of my biggest weaknesses is that I work too hard. I struggle with creating a healthy work/life balance."

Candidates who do this come off as arrogant, dishonest, and out of touch. In the vast majority of cases, it's far more damning than the honest answer.

Weaknesses should be genuine weaknesses. When delivering your weaknesses, it's common to do either of the following:

- Discuss how you're mitigating the issue.
- Mention the silver lining of the issue.

See how one job seeker has done this:

> "I think I have three main weaknesses.
>
> "First, I sometimes lack attention to detail. While this is somewhat good in that it enables me to execute quickly, it also means that I can make careless mistakes. I have learned that I need to double- or triple-check important work before submitting it.
>
> "Second, I am a very quantitative person, and sometimes I can lose sight of the personal aspects of a decision—who is impacted and why. I've learned the hard way that I need to consider who all the stakeholders are in a decision, and how they'll react.
>
> "Third, I am too critical of ideas—both my own and sometimes those of others. I've largely masked this by focusing on offering positive feedback, but I know I have some room to improve my internal reactions."

These weaknesses certainly aren't good things, but they aren't deal breakers (for most positions).

If you're worried about delivering a weakness that's a huge red flag, relax. This is actually relatively unusual. Most candidates—even those who are worried that their weakness is too big—actually give a weaknesses that's too little.

Be genuine. You are not expected to be perfect.

Layoffs, Firing, and Unemployment

Sometimes, the toughest questions are the ones we already know about and don't want to answer. Maybe it's a layoff, maybe it's a pattern of job-hopping, or maybe it's a sudden career switch. No matter how much we don't want to be asked these questions, we must be prepared for them. Practice your story for this, both to yourself out loud and to your friends. Does it appear honest and credible? Are you prepared for any follow-up questions that your interviewer might ask?

The biggest mistake you can make in this question is brushing it off. Your interviewer may not press you for your answer, but she won't be impressed.

Whatever you're trying to hide, be honest and don't assign away too much blame. Admit your mistake, and focus on what you've learned and how you've grown since then. This sort of answer will show maturity and honesty, while leaving your response on an honest note.

Layoffs

If you were let go during a round of layoffs, you're in a better position than many. However, even these routine layoffs might raise a red flag: some people are usually kept—why weren't you?

The important thing is to stress evidence that you were performing well.

- "The recession hit my company really hard. I was able to survive three rounds of layoffs, but the fourth one included me, too. Frankly, I can't really blame my company: my role was about client service, and there weren't many clients left."
- "My firm laid off about 25 percent of its workforce, and it hit the mobile division the hardest. My manager fought hard for me, but given the new direction of the company, it just didn't make sense."

Try, if you can, to give some indication of good performance. Don't be defensive, though; that will be obvious and will come off as dishonest.

Being Fired

You don't need to volunteer that you were fired. But if you are explicitly asked, you can't lie.

Interviewers know that there are two sides of the story. If you claim it's not your fault that you got fired, they'll just dig elsewhere and discover the truth eventually. It's better if it comes from you.

Accept the blame, and show what you've learned from it:

- "My company had expectations of my working upwards of 70 hours per week. I had a new baby at home, and I couldn't do more than 40 or 50 hours. I held on longer than I should have, but it taught me a valuable lesson about setting mutual expectations up front."
- "Honestly, it just wasn't the right fit for me. I was hired primarily off of a strong reference from a prior employer, and it ended up that they needed a very different skill set than I had. Neither I nor the company did the mutual research we should have done to see if there was a good fit. They needed someone who could do deep quantitative analysis, and this is a big weakness of mine. I kept trying to learn this, but there was too much of a gap there."

Offer a crisp and concise answer. Don't play the blame game. Don't bad-mouth your former employer. And don't lie.

Everyone fails sometimes; it's important that you understand how you failed and that you learned from it.

Unemployment

If you've been unemployed for an extended period of time, interviewers may want to know what you have done during your time off. "Looking for a job" is probably not a complete answer. How many hours a day could you have really spent doing that?

The best answer involves accomplishing something or brushing up on new skills.

One job seeker discussed a seven-year gap in his career. He explained that he had taken time off to raise his two young children. Once they started preschool, he spent his days learning to program. This candidate spun what was initially a red flag—an extended career gap—into a big plus. Coding wasn't a necessary skill for the position, but being willing to learn something new is valuable.

If you're currently unemployed, find something to do that's productive. Can you help out your friend's start-up? Can you take some classes online? Unemployment is an excellent time to beef up your resume.

Questions and Answers

Barrier to Entry

I've lived most of my life in India, before relocating to the United States, and still have a very thick accent. This isn't as much of an issue for technical questions, but I have trouble maintaining a conversation during the more conversational parts.

If my interviewer is from a country other than India or the United States, this issue is exacerbated. Is there any way to request specific nationalities of interviewers?

You can't ask for specific nationalities and, even if you could, what would that say about you? No one wants to hire someone who can work only with specific nationalities.

Instead, I'd work on how you communicate. Speaking more slowly and using simpler words can help with comprehension.

I'm not sure that this issue is as big as you're making it out to be, though. Interviewers are fairly accustomed to dealing with candidates with different accents and typically try not to judge them for this. Many candidates exaggerate the impact of this obstacle.

If you're finding communication to be a real challenge for you, though, you might want to think about speech classes. Many people have reported a lot of success with improving their pronunciation. This would help not only your job search, but also your career.

Just Joking

I know it's important to show yourself to have strong interpersonal skills, and part of that is a sense of humor. I was thinking about preparing a joke to ask my interviewer. What do you think?

This is a risky maneuver. I would proceed with caution here.

A sense of humor isn't the same thing as a joke. A sense of humor helps you roll with things better and smooth over interactions on the team. It keeps people in good spirits. It's about how you *respond* to events. A joke is about being proactive to make people laugh.

Additionally, a forced joke can be really awkward, and it sounds like that's what you're trying to do here. It's very difficult to have a preplanned joke fit into the conversation naturally. Instead, it will likely come off as awkward: "Hey, want to hear a joke?"

If you do proceed down this path, though, think carefully about what joke you're going to tell. A lot of funny jokes are offensive to someone. You probably wouldn't tell a joke that's overly racist or sexist, but you might tell one that comes off elitist or ignorant in some way.

Do try to show a sense of humor, though. Keep a smiling, upbeat attitude. If you can say something moderately funny, go for it. But don't try to plan or force a joke. It's unlikely to help you and might very well hurt you.

10 Behavioral Questions

Gone (mostly) are the days of hypothetical questions; instead, interviewers prefer to know how you have actually handled specific situations:

- "Tell me about a time when you overcame an obstacle at work."
- "Tell me about a time when you've had to build a team."
- "Tell me about something you're proud of."

For many candidates, behavioral questions will form the bulk of their interview. It's important that you're well prepared for these questions. Preparation—in both the content and the communication—makes an enormous difference.

Evaluation

When an interviewer asks behavioral questions, she's trying to learn about what sorts of situations you've faced in the past and how you handled them. She might enter with a predetermined list of areas to probe (risk taking, initiative, customer focus, etc.), or she might just be seeing what she can learn about you.

In either case, you want to think about both the content and the communication of your answer. Both are important, and they influence each other. Stronger communication makes it easier for someone to understand the content. Better content simplifies your communication.

Mastering the Content

Blindsided by an unexpected question, many candidates just try to give any answer that matches the question. When possible, try instead to think about what the *best* answer to a question is.

What Interviewers Look For

There are three big things interviewers will be looking for:

1. **Did you really do that thing on your resume?** It's easy to carefully wordsmith your resume such that it's not technically lying, but it certainly magnifies your accomplishments. This sort of exaggeration is more challenging when unexpected questions are lobbed at you and you must come up with examples from your experience.
2. **Have you accomplished big things?** The best predictor of future performance is past performance, so interviewers want to understand the issues you have faced. In this case, the specific issues you're asked about will likely relate to the position. For a management or team lead position, you'll likely be asked about leadership or about working with struggling employees.
3. **How did you accomplish those things?** Your responses to behavioral questions reveal something about your personality. They show whether you're the type of person who takes charge through analysis or through building relationships, and whether you're outspoken or soft-spoken. No specific personality trait is inherently better than another, but some might be a better fit for the company culture.

Prepare for the questions with these aspects in mind.

Review Your Resume

From past projects to your foreign or programming languages, anything on your resume is fair game. If you claim that you're fluent in German, be prepared for a company to verify this. Tech companies are extremely international, and it's not hard to find someone who speaks a language.

The day before your interview, pick up your resume and explain each bullet point out loud, just as you would if your interviewer asks, "What did you mean by this line?" Make sure you can explain the what, how, and why.

Preparation Grid

Imagine that your interviewer throws you the following question: "Tell me about a time when you had a difficult situation with a coworker." Could you answer it? Possibly.

Now imagine he asks you to pick a time from a specific project that you worked on three years ago. You know you've experienced difficult times, so why is it so hard to think of one? Because that's just not the way our brains work.

That's why it's so important to create a preparation grid. The preparation grid allows you to construct answers in advance to each major type of question for each project or role you've had. The columns represent each project, and the rows represent the most common behavioral questions. If you are applying for an engineering role, the rows should instead be the common technical questions, such as the hardest bug or biggest algorithm challenge.

	Support Job @ Acme	**Sales Job @ Mobile Device Company**	**Independent Project**
Leadership/ influence			
Teamwork			
Successes			
Challenges			
Mistakes/ failures			
Learnings			

Fill each cell with a story that would respond to the question. When you fill in your grid, limit each story to just a few key words—this will make it easier to recall. If you do a phone interview, consider having the preparation grid in front of you.

For your most recent or current job, you might want to have multiple stories for some categories. Most of your responses will be about this job.

You can download a fresh copy of the preparation grid from www.crackingthetechcareer.com.

Five Key Stories

Once your preparation grid is complete, you now need to select about five stories to really master. These will be your go-to stories, but you might still need others, too.

Fill in the next grid, making sure to have coverage of each category of question.

- **Category.** The category should probably be one of the earlier-mentioned ones (leadership, teamwork, etc.), but if there's something else, that's fine too. It's also okay—even good—if some of your stories fall into multiple categories.
- **Nugget/thesis.** Give a few words describing the title of the story.
- **Situation.** Describe what the situation was that motivated the issue or action.
- **Action.** Tell what you did to solve the problem. Try to expand on this. If you had to do multiple things, that's ideal. List them separately so that your response can be structured when you discuss this with your interviewer.
- **Result.** Describe the final result. One hopes (depending on the question) that the situation was resolved well. Try to provide some sort of metric or proof for this.
- **What it says.** Consider what your action says about the way you solve problems.

We'll describe the nugget, as well as the situation/action/result more later.

	Category	Nugget/ Thesis	Situation	Action	Result	What It Says
Mobile App Pivot	Leadership	Motivated team to pivot	Team attached to failing product	• "Sold" influencers first • Analyzed data • Emotional appeal	Reduced time to market by 50% Top app in store for 3 weeks	Data driven Challenges assumptions Empathy

(*continued*)

(continued)

	Category	Nugget/ Thesis	Situation	Action	Result	What It Says
Story 2						
Story 3						
Story 4						
Story 5						

As you fill out this grid, look for diversity in all aspects. You want stories from multiple aspects and/or jobs (although most will usually come from your current job, depending on how long you've been there). You also want to have shown different aspects of yourself. If you keep proving that you are data driven, it will stop being interesting and might even be worrisome. Plus, you will have missed out on the opportunity to show other things about yourself.

With each of your stories, also think about what you'd do differently, if you could do it all over again. That's a common followup question from interviewers.

Mastering the Communication

Communication is really half the battle. This is a good thing, though. Even if you can't deliver an awesome answer in terms of content, you can at least deliver an answer that is well structured and clear.

There are two structures that work well: (1) nugget first and (2) situation, action, result (SAR). These two structures are not necessarily independent. In fact, they're often quite powerful when used in conjunction with each other.

Don't forget about your personality, though. Be real and genuine. Talk with passion about things that you are or should be excited about. Be willing to be humble. Be willing to show vulnerability; it's okay to have failed before.

- **Communication.** Can you respond off the cuff in a clear and concise way? Is your communication structured, and do you refrain from rambling? Do you speak in an interesting and engaging manner?
- **Personality.** Do you come across as being real and not arrogant? A certain amount of emotional openness, particularly when talking about a big failure, can be effective in connecting with your interviewer.

When possible (and it often isn't), try to quantify your accomplishments or offer some sort of concrete proof. This can even be something like "And my mentee ended up being the first person to be promoted." Your proof doesn't have to be numbers, but that is often nice.

Nugget First

Nugget first means that the first thing out of your mouth should be the thesis, or the answer to the question.

Interviewer: Tell me about a time when you influenced a team.
Candidate: Sure, let me tell you about the time that I motivated the team to switch directions. So, what happened was . . .

This simple action holds tremendous value.

In interviews, job seekers will often give extraneous details—sometimes they're not really sure where they're going with their story. Giving this one-sentence opener will help you focus on the point of the story.

Additionally, it will also focus your interviewer on the point of the story. The interviewer will be able to understand and remember the little details more easily if he knows that this is about motivating a team to change their minds (not, say, dealing with a mistake).

Almost any response should start off with the nugget. If you can't do this, beware of diving into your answer, as you will likely ramble.

Situation, Action, Result

Behavioral questions are not just about whether you can come up with an example of, say, your leadership, but about what the example says about you. Do you subtly influence people, gaining their support in advance of a decision? Do you try to motivate the people around you? Are you a person who finds it easy to diffuse tense or stressful situations?

Your response to behavioral questions will suggest not only what you've accomplished but how you've accomplished it.

Situation, action, result (SAR) is an effective way to structure responses to behavioral and other questions in a way that clearly explains what the problem was, what you did, and why it matters.

Question: *"Tell me about a challenging interaction with a teammate."*

- **The situation** should include a brief description of the problem. Provide enough details so that the interviewer can understand what the problem was, but don't offer much more.

  On my last project, I was asked to oversee the work of a man who was much older than me. He was working too independently from the rest of my team and not keeping us informed, and this ended up introducing a lot of conflicting work. When I went to discuss the issues with him, he blew up at me—practically shouting that he had been working since before I was even born.

- **The action** describes what you did. It's generally the most important part of the story.

  I did three things to resolve the situation.

  First, I sought the advice of a teammate who had worked with him for much longer, to see if she could help me understand what happened. What she told me was that he was really insecure and tended to lash out.

  Second, I went back to him and took the responsibility on myself, saying that I screwed up in not keeping him informed of my work. I told him that I was new to this and didn't really know what I was doing, and asked him to advise me on how to manage it. This helped him feel better about himself, and also allowed us to work together to find a solution.

  Third, I pushed these changes out to the team since, really, it was a broader problem of how to keep two semi-independent projects in sync. I set up a process for weekly check-ins and goals, empowering individual people to ensure their completion.

- **The result** explains what happened, and sometimes what you learned from it.

  This solution ended up largely resolving the situation. He and I worked together very well from then on, since he no longer saw me as a threat. He even started seeking out my advice, and he had never done that with anyone before. The new teamwide process was also very successful and reduced a lot of the friction in project management.

Note how the candidate skipped over a lot of details. He never explained what the project was or what the conflicting work was. It's not relevant to this story.

The candidate does, however, clearly call out what he did. He broke down his story into different steps and suggests some of his personal attributes: being willing to ask for help, being willing to take responsibility, not backing down from conflict, thinking broadly about scaling a solution, being empathetic to others, and so on.

Most of the discussion should be about the action. The situation is not that important, and the result doesn't need many details.

Common Mistakes

In addition to a lack of structure and poor preparation, the mistakes that follow are common with applicants. While rehearsing your stories, pay close attention to these issues. Most people make at least one of these mistakes, and many people make all three.

Too Much "We," Not Enough "I"

Many people have been trained by business leaders to focus on the team, not themselves. The *team* completed the milestone. The *team* accomplished an important pivot. The *team* increased page views.

That's great advice—just not as much for interviews.

In an interview, it's really about yourself. Merely being a part of a team's success doesn't say much about you. The interviewer wants to know what *you* did. Instead of talking about the team, you should discuss the changes *you* made to *lead* the team.

The majority of people in leadership roles struggle with this one. Listen to your stories and pay close attention.

Simple Actions

The action part of many people's stories lacks depth. They see the story as compelling because it was a challenge at the time. But when it comes to delivery, there's little substance.

For example, one candidate discussed an issue where her supplier was late in delivering a product. She then went on to discuss the implications for the buyers and how they were reacting—threatening to cancel their orders and so on. "Finally," she says, "I wrote a detailed e-mail explaining what was happening and giving them an update. A few canceled their orders, but most stayed on."

An interviewer listening to her story gets a clear impression that it was a stressful situation, but it doesn't really sound like she did much. Ultimately, all she did—as far as we know—was write an e-mail.

Instead, she should delve deeper into her actions. If possible, she can break them into multiple steps so that she can describe doing two or three actions rather than just one thing.

Where's the "Why"?

Your interviewers are asking these questions because they want to learn about how you act in certain situations. Make it easy for them by calling out semiexplicitly why you did something.

Of course, you don't want to say, "I did this because I'm empathetic"; that sounds fake and the interviewer won't trust you. But you can *nearly* say that:

I understood that my customers were most upset about the unexpected change and that they were losing trust in us. There were too many customers for me to talk to all of them, but I could talk to the biggest ones. I knew that they would value that personal touch; it helps build trust. Just having them hear my voice and know that I'm a real person helped them feel that we cared.

This candidate doesn't actually use the word *empathy*, but the answer was all about that.

Reflect on the "what it says" column of the five stories grid. These are the things that you can call out for your interviewer.

Five Example Questions

There may be no one right answer to behavioral interview questions, but there certainly are a lot of wrong answers. In this section, we'll give example responses (or discussions) for five common behavioral questions and highlight what makes these strong responses.

1. Tell Me About a Time When You Gave a Presentation to a Group of People Who Disagreed with You

Sample answer:

Sure, let me tell you about when I convinced our team to launch a new product.

In my last team, I became concerned with a decision the team was making on how to extend our small-business accounting software to personal users. My team thought that we should just create a slightly tweaked version, and I disagreed. I thought we should build a brand-new tool, and I wanted to present this proposal to the team.

I took a three-step process here.

First, before the presentation, I tried to understand the perspective from the team leaders. I spoke with each of the key decision holders—namely, my manager, the tech lead, and a VP—prior to the meeting. I talked with them about why they felt we should do one thing versus another, and then gathered additional data based on their responses.

Second, I delivered an initial presentation about the data I'd gathered. Rather than presenting it as a pitch (which would be met with immediate resistance), I focused on understanding what would need to happen for us to make a different decision. We had a very fruitful discussion as a team, rather than anyone feeling like we were fighting. We were able to set guidelines to guide our decisions.

Third, I met privately with key influencers, showed them what I had learned, and got them on board. This was important because negative energy can build on a group in a room, so it's not the most productive way to present a controversial decision. I asked them to help me develop a plan for rolling this out.

When we met the following week, much of the team was on board. The remaining members were given compelling data and a clear plan, plus they saw many people they respected supporting this new plan.

I was able to show that we could hit the targets they needed, and that we should reverse our decision. The decision was taken to senior management, who ended up agreeing with the new proposal. We saved our company about $16 million.

This candidate has shown herself to be analytical, data driven, empathetic, and collaborative. She made a point of showing how she sought feedback from her team, while still effectively asserting her opinions. She has shown herself to be a good teammate and leader.

While this story has a happy ending, this is not strictly necessary for an effective response. A candidate could, instead, give a humble answer about how she made a mistake in the presentation, and what she learned from it. In fact, the next response is about just this.

2. Tell Me About the Biggest Mistake You Made on a Past Project

Sample answer:

The biggest mistake I made was when I underestimated the time line of a project.

I was filling in for our tech lead. She had just left for maternity leave, and I was responsible for developing a new schedule to get us to the next milestone.

I really wanted to do a good job (I knew this was essentially a trial for a full-time tech lead position), so I solicited input from everyone on the team about the schedule. Each person gave me an estimate, and I essentially averaged them.

Then I showed the schedule to everyone; they all thought it made sense—or at least they said so. Management was impressed by the short time line and signed off on it.

We weren't super late on the deadline, but we had to cut several very important features.

I did a few things wrong here that I corrected when I created the Milestone 4 schedule.

First, I shouldn't have relied so much on the pure numbers. Yes, data's fun, but it's important to understand why someone is providing a certain bit of information. That person who tells you that the feature will take a year might know something I don't. I should have probed deeper.

Second, I forgot to take into account human ego. I didn't realize that just as I'm trying to impress people as a new (even if temporary) tech lead, everyone else is also trying to impress me. They wanted to show me that they were A+ employees who could surely get this done quickly.

Third, I forgot about groupthink. I asked people as a group, "Does this look okay?" People have a tendency to just confirm that sort of thing. Instead, I should have asked more open-ended questions like "What are the biggest challenges?" or talked to people privately.

I corrected these things for the next milestone and added in some comfortable padding, and we ended up coming in just ahead of schedule.

In this response, the candidate has been open and honest and has admitted a genuine mistake. Many candidates give responses here about how they "took on too much at once" or "didn't ask for help early enough." While these may indeed be large mistakes, they're also very stereotypical and don't reveal that you can admit your faults.

The candidate has also clearly explained how he fixed the situation for future issues.

Remember that this response is as much about learning from your mistakes as it is about understanding whether you can be honest.

3. Tell Me About a Time When You Had to Deal with a Teammate Who Was Underperforming

Sample answer:

Hmm, okay. One example that comes to mind is when I had to deal with a new coworker who was accomplishing very little.

In this case, I was actually assigned to mentor the teammate. Vivek had transferred to our team from another division where, to the best of our knowledge, he was doing pretty well. The work was fairly similar, so we expected he would fit in well.

By his fourth week, we realized something was wrong and I was asked to mentor him. Most candidates have submitted at least a bit of code by then, but he hadn't submitted a thing. Every time I asked him about his progress, he said he was doing fine and was "almost done." I suspect that he was struggling in multiple areas and didn't want to expose himself by asking too many questions.

Partially based on his prior (rumored) performance, and partially because I just wanted to give him a second chance, I tried a different approach.

I pulled him off his current task (which should have taken him only a few days anyway) and put him on a new and pretty different project—one that he and I would be working side by side on. This allowed him to start fresh, and not have to feel stupid asking questions. It also allowed me to walk him through the project (outlining steps, etc.) without his feeling like I was micromanaging him.

He was able to get through the project with some help from me, but more important, I was able to understand exactly what he was struggling with. It turned out that, while he was smart and generally capable, he had some pretty substantial gaps in his knowledge that we needed to deal with.

For some topics, I ordered some additional books for him and taught him some of these areas myself. For others, which I felt the team could use a refresher course on, I had the whole team go through them.

He improved dramatically, and all without having to hurt his ego too much. Within three months, he was performing at expectations, and after another year, he was actually mentoring new hires himself.

The candidate has shown an awareness of other people and has demonstrated that she's a positive person who believes in others. She has proven that she is willing to get her hands dirty; she sat down and worked with Vivek side by side, and then taught him much of what he needed to know. She cares about her teammates, and that's the sort of person you want on your team.

4. Tell Me About a Time When You had to Make a Controversial Decision

Sample answer:

Sure. Let me tell you about responding to a poorly launched redesign.

We'd spent a few weeks working on a major redesign that, when we launched it, resulted in a 10 percent drop in our active user rates. Many people wanted to just instantly revert the changes, but my gut told me this wouldn't be the right thing to do.

I thought about the problem from three aspects: what was the right thing for the users, what was the best thing for company morale, and what would set the company on the right move for the long term.

For the users: At first glance, the metrics pointed to reverting the changes. In my opinion, though, numbers don't lie, but they sure can be misleading. That's why it's so important to understand why something is happening. As I pored through the data, I saw that engagement of the active users was up. So there was a silver lining. Some users were turned off, but some were turned on.

For the company morale: This was tricky because people don't want to be on a sinking ship, but they also don't want to have their hard work cut. I felt that sticking with the redesign—if I pitched this in a motivational I-believe-in-us way—would show that we had a vision.

Finally, for the long term, I really believed the right thing to do was to have a vision. Data is very important (don't get me wrong), but I've seen companies get so fixated on numbers that they are scared to make any big changes. Any changes that are made are just incremental fixes, and you'll never go far that way. I'd rather take big risks and be prepared to fail.

I pitched it to the team by telling them that it's their choice if they want to revert the redesign, but that I think we should move forward with the existing work. We should focus on the future—if this was the right thing for our vision, then we should fix the issues rather than scrapping everything. We needed to be able to look forward, and reverting it would be the opposite of that.

The team walked into the meeting assuming that we would revert the redesign, but walked out inspired for the future. We decided, as a team, that this would be the new baseline. We would try to keep engagement high while bringing active user rates back up.

Within two months, our active user rates had returned to where they were and engagement was an all-time high. More important, though, it outlined an expectation that taking risks and failing were part of the adventure.

What have you learned about this candidate? You've learned that he's value-driven and motivational. He's comfortable with data and metrics, but he understands their limits. He's also logical, as he broke down his thought process for the interviewer.

Observe how he takes a slightly different structure for this answer. Rather than saying, "I did X, and afterward I did Y," he elaborated on his thought process. The implementation of the decision was almost an afterthought.

It's okay to approach this answer from either direction. You can dive into what guided your thought process, or you could dive into the implementation and execution. You could even do both, as long as your answer doesn't get too complex.

5. Tell Me About a Time When You had to Use Emotional Intelligence to Lead

Sample answer:

Sure. One time that comes to mind is encouraging my old company to give junior employees more responsibility.

When I joined, I was struck by the division between junior and senior people. The company was large and had rather rigid hierarchies. The older (tenurewise, not agewise) people got to pick what they wanted to do, while the newer employees got stuck with menial tasks. This resulted in high turnover as well as a lack of diversity on projects.

I wanted to do away with this system, and I knew that I'd meet a lot of friction along the way. People are reluctant to give up their privileges, even if they know it's what's best for the company. Plus, I too was junior. I didn't really have the power or influence to roll out such a major change.

The first thing I did was just observe. For the first project, I did it their way. This gave me a chance to see the good and bad things, and get to know the people. As much I objected to their system, I didn't want to mess around with something I didn't understand. It was also important that people saw that I'd given it a fair chance.

The second thing I did was understand what the younger employees wanted to do. Some valued learning, while some valued visibility. Without making any promises to them about the future—I didn't want to get myself into trouble—I asked them to envision what things they would want to do one day when they had this ability.

Then, third, I went and talked to the senior people, expressing the junior employees' desire to have additional learning and visibility opportunities. I asked the senior folk to do me a "huge favor"—stressing that it was totally up to them—and let the younger people try out some bigger tasks while being mentored by more senior people. This allowed everyone to have a stake in the important projects. Because I was seeking their help and therefore respecting their seniority, they were fairly happy to help out.

After this project was done, people were reasonably receptive to switching to this system full-time. I realized that most of this issue was really about the ego, and as long as I respected people's seniorities (hence the mentorships), they were pretty happy to work on some less important projects. So far at least, turnover has seemed to drop.

This candidate has demonstrated with this response an ability to understand people. She accurately saw the problems, understood the real driver (ego), and created a plan. She acted carefully and methodically, always making sure she really saw the full picture. She's the kind of manager people want.

Questions and Answers

Misleading Information

I have a full-time job, but I also volunteer at a nonprofit most weekends. How much is it okay to talk about my volunteer work? What about my past jobs?

Assuming you've been at your company for at least two years, it's probably a good idea to have 60 to 70 percent of your answers discuss your current job. Less than that and an interviewer might question if you've really been successful at your job.

Talking about the volunteer work, though, is great. You should definitely bring that into your pitch, especially if you're doing something "business-y" or something that truly shows another side to your profile.

Your past work is also very relevant. If you have strong stories from your prior jobs, you should bring those in.

If you feel you might be talking about your old jobs too much, you might be able to leave it ambiguous whether the stories describe your current job or your old ones. It's often unclear (and, frankly, not very important), especially if you've held similar roles.

Overly Specific

How important is it to answer a question exactly as worded? Sometimes I have a story that would be great, but it doesn't exactly fit the question. For example, I was asked about a time that I influenced my manager. I didn't have a great answer for that question, but I did have a potential story about influencing some senior executives. Would this have been okay?

Typically, interviewers really aren't sticklers for the exact phrasing of the question.

When your interviewer asked about influencing a manager, what she was probably trying to understand was how you exert influence when you don't have power. She happened to say "manager," but your story would have worked well for what she *really* wanted to know. (In fact, in some cases, the interviewer might not even be looking for anything specific. She might just have wanted to know about situations you've been in at work and how you handled them.)

Feel free to tweak the question, just do so casually yet directly.

- *Casually* means that it should sound natural. You don't want to make it sound like you *can't* give a good story for the exact question. Rather, it's just that you happen to have a good story for this slight tweak of it and you're presuming that it's okay.
- *Directly* means that you want it to be clear that you're tweaking the question. If you start off your story without making that clear, it can be confusing.

Here's an example:

Interviewer: Tell me about a time when you influenced your manager.
Candidate: Sure. This wasn't actually my direct manager, but rather a senior executive—close enough, though. I successfully convinced the executive to pivot our product. What happened was . . .

(*continued*)

(continued)

Think of this like handing someone four quarters when they ask to borrow a dollar. You want to pretend like the new question you're answering is more or less interchangeable with the original one.

Be careful about doing this too much, though. It's okay to make one or two minor tweaks in the interview. If you do this for most or all questions, it suggests that you are overly rehearsed, refusing to play by the rules of the interviewer, not necessarily giving genuine answers, and only have a small number of stories to speak about.

11 Problem Solving

"You know how I interview electrical contractors?" Colin Jaques of Canzam Electric told me. "I give them a pipe and I tell them to bend it." Suddenly I pictured a Hulk Hogan–type man heaving as he bends a pipe with his bare hands. He can't be serious?

"No, no. It's not about strength." Colin reassured me. "It's about how they answer. Do they ask where you want it bent and at what angle, or do they just bend it? You see, we can't have contractors running around bending things at random with no idea what you or the client wants."

He had a point. In fact, this attribute of *make sure you know what problem you're solving* is common to many types of interview questions.

It had another thing in common with typical tech interviews, too: it's not what it seems. Too many candidates stress getting the right answer, as though there's always one single correct answer. Not so.

Rather, interview questions are about the process you take. Do you check your assumptions? Do you think through all possible cases? How do you break down the problem? Are you sure you're even solving the right problem?

You could debate at length the value of asking such questions, but these are things the interviewer is *trying* to ask.

Types of Problem-Solving Questions

Problem-solving questions can come in a variety of categories. Some of the most common are:

- **Estimation questions.** Also called Fermi problems, these questions are of the form, "How many nickels would it take to cover the

Golden Gate Bridge?" or "How many soccer balls are sold every year in the world?"

- **Case/business questions.** These questions could ask how you would launch a product in Germany or how you would market a pen to the elderly. Often these questions are focused closely on your profession.
- **Design questions.** You could be asked to design a real or fictional product, or to improve an existing one.
- **Brainteasers.** These aren't nearly as common as is sometimes rumored, but they do come up sometimes. These usually don't involve silly plays on words and are instead focused on solving a problem.

Estimation Questions

How many Ping-Pong balls would fit in a 747 jet aircraft? How many pizzas are consumed every year in the United States? Even if you knew, it wouldn't help you.

These seemingly bizarre questions are not about knowing the right answer, but rather about the process one takes to get there. The relevance of this to real life is debatable, but supporters of these questions argue that being able to ballpark and deduce numbers is valuable.

What They're Looking For

Estimation questions are designed to test your skills in a few areas:

- **Mathematics.** Can you do math in your head? If numbers are too big to easily estimate (3,124 × 8,923), can you make a reasonable approximation (3,000 × 9,000 = 27,000,000)?
- **Assumptions.** Can you make reasonable assumptions, such as the width of an aircraft? And if you can (such as the width of an aircraft seat), do you verbally call them out so that people can check them?
- **Deduction/intelligence.** Can you logically reason through an answer using the facts that you do know?
- **Carefulness.** Do you understand when not to generalize? For example, if computing the average amount of money spent on clothing the United States, do you treat adults and children differently?
- **Intuition.** Do you have a good gut feeling for when something doesn't sound right? For example, suppose logic leads you to conclude that one million pizzas are delivered each year in the United States. Do you understand that that sounds low (one pizza per 300 people per year)?

These questions are not looking for knowledge. If you just happen to know a lot about the pizza industry and you're asking how many pizzas are sold a year, this won't help you at all. Likewise, if you're asked question where you lack a background, this shouldn't hurt you.

For international applicants, this is of particular concern. Many questions involve some knowledge about the United States. For example, if you're asked how many schools there are in the United States, it's useful to have some knowledge about the U.S. educational system, right?

Yes and no. Yes, knowledge about the topic will help you arrive at a closer answer. No, it won't really help you do better.

It's the thought process that matters, not the accuracy of your answer. (Frankly, your interviewer likely doesn't know the correct answer.) Making incorrect assumptions because you're missing certain knowledge doesn't matter, especially if that knowledge is irrelevant to the job.

How to Approach Estimation Questions

These questions require logically deducing an answer from what you know, and there are often multiple paths to arrive at an answer. Four steps are helpful:

1. **Ask clarifying details.** You need to understand what the question is that you're trying to solve. For example, if you're asked how much money a company makes, you'll need to know if that's profit or revenue.
2. **Find a structure.** Break down the problem in separate chunks you can solve, almost like an equation.
3. **Compute each component.** For each component of this equation, make reasonable assumptions in order to estimate the answer.
4. **Sanity check.** Once you've come up with an answer, sanity check your value to see if it basically makes sense.

Let's see this with an example.

How Many Books Are Sold Every Year in the United States?

First of all, we'd need to ask our interviewer if he means physical books and/or electronic books. Let's assume the interviewer told us that he means both.

Here is one approach:

We could compute this by summing the following:

- Number of children's books (for pleasure)
- Number of schoolbooks (required reading and textbooks)
- Number of adult books (for pleasure)

Now let's solve for each of these.

Number of Children's Books for Pleasure

There are about 300 million people in the United States, so we can estimate about four million people of any given age (assuming a 75-year life span). We'll assume that children under age 8 are mostly reading (or being read to) only for pleasure. After age 8, kids are doing more homework and their parents don't read to them as much. This gives us 32 million children under age 8 reading or being read to for pleasure.

My friends with young children seem to buy about 20 books for each kid each year. But they're probably a bit more aggressive readers than most, so let's say this is 10 books on average per child.

With 32 million kids under age 8 reading 10 books per year each, that's about 320 million books, which we can round to 300 million books.

Number of Schoolbooks

If the average child takes six classes, then there's probably an average of about 10 schoolbooks per child per year. Some classes, like a writing class, will have multiple books.

But, schoolbooks are reused from year to year, so not all of those books are new. Assuming that schoolbooks have a two-year life span, this is about five books bought per kid per year.

Children are in school from age 6 to age 18, so this is about 48 million kids. At five books per year, we have 240 million schoolbooks.

This doesn't account for college books, but I don't think that's an enormous factor.

Number of Adult Books for Pleasure

I think I remember reading online that 25 percent of American adults haven't read a book in the past year, so this means that 75 percent have.

At 220 million adults, this means around 150 million people have read at least one book.

Let's say that a third of those people have read one to five books, a third have read five to 10 books, and a third have read 10 or more. This is probably gives us an average of seven or so books per person per year, of those who read.

This gives us a sum of about one billion books.

Total

We have 1 billion adult books, 240 million schoolbooks, and 300 million children's books. This is a total of about 1.5 billion books.

Sanity Check

A total of 1.5 billion books means about five books sold per person in the United States. This doesn't sound crazy to me.

The most popular books also seem to sell millions of books per year. So if we think the top couple of books sell 10 million combined, then this would mean that they account for about 1 percent of book sales. This seems like it's in the right ballpark.

Is this accurate? It doesn't really matter. What matters is our approach.

How Many Basketballs Would It Take to Fill a Basketball Gym?

We need to clarify with our interviewer that we're talking about filling the gym from floor to ceiling and not just covering the floor. Let's assume that we're talking about filling the gym from floor to ceiling.

We'll also need to make some assumptions about the size of the gym.

To be honest, I haven't played much basketball, so I'll have to do this based on what I've seen on TV.

A typical gym probably has about half the length of the floor taken up by the basketball court, and ditto for the width. This means that the total area is about four times the area of the court.

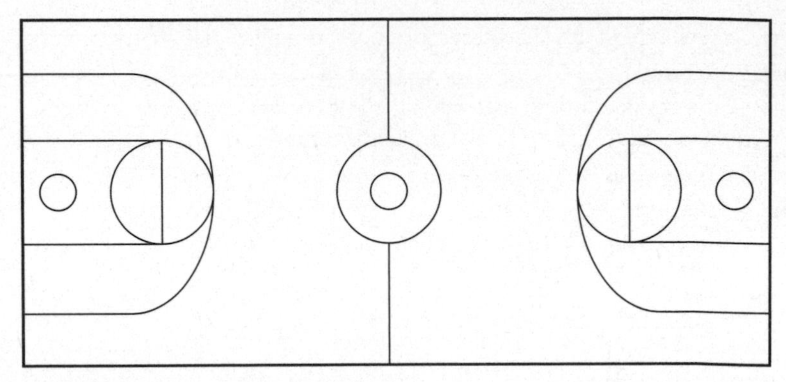

Figure 11.1 Basketball Court

Court Area versus Gym Area

There's a free throw line that is probably about a quarter of the way down the court. I've seen five people lined up between the hoop and the free throw line, and they're not too squashed together. If we assume 4 feet of space per person, this is about 20 feet. (See Figure 11.1.)

If the free throw line is a quarter of the way down the court, then the total court is about 80 feet long.

It's longer than it is wide, so let's say it's 50 feet wide.

Our gym as a whole is therefore 160 feet by 100 feet.

Height

How tall is the gym, though? I've tried to jump up to hit the basketball hoop, and I think I can brush the net but not hit the hoop. That sounds like about 8 feet to the net and 9 feet to the hoop.

The ceiling of the gym needs to be much, much higher, though—at least three times as high to not worry about having a basketball hit the ceiling.

Let's say the gym then is about 30 feet high.

Basketballs in the Gym

A basketball seems like it's not quite a foot in diameter, so let's say it's 9 inches, or 0.75 feet. So, on a floor with an area 160 feet by 100 feet, you

Figure 11.2 Stacked Basketballs

could fit about 200 basketballs lengthwise and about 125 widthwise. This is about 25,000 basketballs on the floor.

Now, stacking up the basketballs, you could fit about 40 basketballs. But you can actually fit a bit more than that because you can stack spheres more compactly by offsetting the spheres slightly. (See Figure 11.2.) Let's say that's more like 50 basketballs.

Therefore 25,000 basketballs × 50 basketballs = 1,250,000 basketballs that can fit in the gym.

Sanity Check

The total volume of the gym is 160 × 100 × 30 feet, or about 500,000 cubed feet. A ball is 0.75 feet wide, which gives it a volume (if you treat the ball as a cube) of around 0.5 cubed feet. Dividing these, you get about a million balls. This makes sense.

Does the height of the gym make sense? I think so. A typical ceiling is 8 to 10 feet, so a basketball court would be three times that.

The length seems right, too. A football field is 100 yards long, or 300 feet. This makes it about three or four times as long as a basketball court.

The width is derived from the length, so it should be about right, too.

If you don't know enough about U.S. sports to solve this, that's okay. Your interviewer wouldn't expect you to. It's about your approach, not your answer.

Example Questions

1. How many golf balls would fit in a school bus?

2. How many pizzas are delivered in New York City?
3. How many cell phones are sold each year in the United States?
4. How much would you charge to wash all the streets in New York City?
5. How many people work at fast-food restaurants in the entire world?

Design Questions

Design questions range from the normal ("How would you design a to-do list manager?") to the abnormal ("How would you design an alarm clock for the deaf?"), and are common for many positions, especially product managers. They often focus on specific markets: children, deaf people, blind people, and so on.

What They're Looking For

"We want to know if you are customer focused," Joon, a program manager (PM) at Microsoft, says. "So 50 percent of this question is being able to put yourself in the shoes of a customer—being able to understand who the target user is. Twenty-five percent is about creativity. Can you come up with a new, fresh perspective about how it might work? The remaining 25 percent is communication."

Many candidates focus too much on the creativity aspects—coming up with crazy new features and widgets. While that can be great, is that really what you would do in the real world? Remember that interviewing is supposed to mirror your real-world performance. In the real world, you'd figure out what the customers want and design for that.

As you answer these questions, remember that interviewers are trying to answer these four questions about you:

1. Are you creative? Can you think of an outside-of-the-box way to find a novel solution to a problem, rather than pumping out small tweaks on the same old stuff?
2. Are you customer focused? Do you think about what the customer's needs are, as well as the limitations? A 16-year-old girl has a lot in common with her parents, but she also has her own unique needs.
3. How do you deal with ambiguity? Do you recognize elements as being ambiguous, and clarify them? If you can't resolve ambiguity, how do you make a decision?

4. Can you communicate your ideas? On these questions, it's easy to wind up rambling about an endless set of features. Effective communicators will instead approach this in a structured way, wrapping up at the end with their conclusions.

How to Approach Design Questions

Let's walk through an approach with a sample request: "Design a key fob for a 16-year-old girl." (*Note:* A key fob is a key/remote for a car.)

Step 1: Resolve Ambiguity

Who is buying the car—the girl or the parents? Is this for a new car or an additional key fob for an existing car? Is it a regular car or an SUV?

The first question is important because it determines who the customer is: just the girl, or the girl and the parents. The second question is important because it determines what the first-time user setup is: will it just work, or will it take programming? The third question determines whether the key fob needs a button to pop the trunk.

Step 2: Understand the Customer

A big part of design problems is to understand the customer.

- Who is the customer?
- What are the customer's use cases?
- What does the customer value?

You can ask the interviewer some questions about this, but some of it you should be able to figure out. For example, it's reasonable for the interviewer to tell you that the user is a 16-year-old girl from a wealthy family. You should probably figure out on your own what the girl values (price, appearance, durability, etc.) and what her use cases are (throwing the keys in her purse, finding her car, etc.).

Think broadly about who the user is. The parents might also be users (or at least purchasers), so you would need to think about their use cases and values, too.

What do the parents need or care about? Price and safety are probably two of the biggest things.

Step 3: Compare to Existing Products

In some cases, it might also be useful to compare the existing product to these use cases. In what ways is a typical key fob not ideal for the girl or her parents?

Step 4: Design the Features

- **Appearance.** Offer the item in multiple colors with a glossy exterior, and have the key fold out from the key fob.
- **Durability.** We want a durable material, like a hard plastic, that doesn't scratch easily.
- **Safety.** Can we implement a 911 button on the key fob? What about a global positioning system (GPS) tracker—or is this too scary?

One other area to dig deeper into is the purchase process. Can someone upgrade to this type of key fob? To what extent should we optimize for this scenario?

Example Questions

1. Design a TV remote for six-year-olds.
2. Design an ATM for the blind.
3. You are given a million-dollar budget to redesign the bathroom of a famous tech executive. What would you do?
4. Most people dislike bank websites. Design a website for a new bank.
5. Design the heating/air-conditioning controls for a car. Assume that you're designing from scratch: no one has ever seen a car's air-conditioning/heating controls.

Brainteasers

Once standard at Microsoft and many other companies, brainteasers have dropped substantially in popularity. Interviewers are instead encouraged to ask behavioral or skill-specific interview questions. Unfortunately, they still pop up from time to time, either because no one can decide exactly what a brainteaser is or because some interviewers still feel that they are an effective way of measuring intelligence.

Luckily, software engineers need not fear these questions: the vast majority of candidates will not face a single brainteaser. Those engineers who do will likely find that the brainteaser has a quantitative or computer science basis.

What They're Looking For

Interviewers who ask brainteasers feel (arguably mistakenly) that these questions help measure intelligence. They want to know if you can tackle a hard problem and logically work toward the answer.

Fortunately, this means that the brainteaser is unlikely to be of the "word trick" variety and more likely to be one that can be approached through logic and deduction.

How to Approach Brainteasers

Brainteasers have a wide range, so it's difficult to offer a nice and simple path for tackling them. However, there are a few approaches that often work well. One or more of these might be useful in a brainteaser question.

In general, remember that these questions are about your approach. Talk out loud and show your interviewer how you're thinking about the problem. This lets him know that you're not stuck, while also letting him jump in when it would be useful to you.

Solve a Subproblem

If you find that there is a variation or a subproblem you can solve, you might very well be on the right track. Work with this for a bit and see where you can go.

- **Example:** You have two ropes that burn for exactly one hour each. The ropes are of uneven densities, so half the rope lengthwise might take more than 30 minutes. Use the ropes to time something that is exactly 15 minutes.
- **Subproblem:** You may realize that you can time 30 minutes by lighting a rope at both ends.
- **Solution:** Light rope 1 at both ends, and rope 2 at one end. When rope 1 burns up, 30 minutes will have passed and there will be 30 minutes remaining on rope 2. With rope 2 continuing to burn, light it on the other end as well and start your timer. Stop your timer when rope 2 has completely burned up.

Develop a Rule or Equation

When you get a problem, see if you can work through examples. Try to formulate any rules or equations that you discover along the way as specifically as possible.

- **Example:** You have 100 lockers. Someone starts off by opening every locker. Then they close every second locker. Then they open every third, and so on. At the end of 100 operations, which lockers will be open?
- **Rule 1:** The xth locker is toggled on the yth operation if x is divisible by y.
- **Rule 2:** The xth locker is open at the end of 100 operations if it has an odd number of factors.
- **Solution:** If you play with some examples, you'll find that almost all numbers have an even number of factors. This is because if a number n is divisible by x, it's also divisible by n/x (sort of like the complement). For example, since 12 is divisible by 3, it must also be divisible by 12/3 (or 4). Thus, the list of factors that a number has can almost always be paired off. Factors (12) = 6{1 and 12, 2 and 6, 3 and 4}. The only way that you could wind up with an odd number of factors is if a number is a perfect square: Factors (30) = 8{1 and 30, 2 and 15, 3 and 10, 5 and 6}. Therefore, the number of open lockers equals the number of perfect squares. There are 10 perfect squares for 100 or less: 1^1, $2^2, \ldots, 10^{10}$.

Simplify the Problem

Sometimes simplifying a problem or solving the problem for a specific case can help illustrate a general trend.

- **Example:** A group of people are on an island, and one night some are given magical hats. These hats are magical because the wearers can't see their own hats, but they can see everyone else's. To remove a hat, one must take a swim at exactly midnight (and there are severe penalties for taking a hatless swim). How long does it take the people to remove the hats? *Note:* They know that at least one person has a hat, but they don't know how many have a hat. They cannot signal or indicate to each other in any way if a person is wearing a hat. That is, a person must deduce whether or not he is wearing a hat purely by observation of other people.
- **Simplification:** What if only one person had a hat? In this case, the hat wearer would see no one else with a hat, and would know it must

be him. He would go for a midnight swim. What if two people (let's call them A and B) had hats? A and B know that there could be either one or two hats out there, but don't know which. They know, however, if there's only one hat, it'll be removed at midnight. When day 2 comes, they must conclude that there are two hats. They know they have the second one, and they both take a swim at midnight. What if three people have hats? A, B, and C recognize that there are two possibilities: two hats or three hats. When two nights pass and everyone still has a hat, they all know that there are three hats and they all go for a swim.

- **Solution:** Extending this out, we can see that if there are x hats, it takes x nights for them all to be removed. All hats are removed simultaneously. From the very first day, each person knows that there are only two possibilities: x hats and $(x - 1)$ hats. If there were $(x - 1)$ hats, they would be removed on the $(x - 1)$th night. The hats are not removed, so all the hat wearers conclude that there are x hats on the xth night.

Example Questions

You have 10 bottles of pills. Nine bottles are filled with pills of 1.0 grams, but one has faulty pills of 1.1 grams. With only one use of the scale, how would you figure out which bottle has the heavier pills? *Note:* The scale gives an exact measurement.

Let's simplify the problem. What if there were only two bottles of pills (with one faulty bottle)? In this case, we could take just one pill from bottle 1 and weigh it. If the pill weighs 1.0 gram, then we would know it was the lighter one.

What if there were three bottles of pills? If we took two pills, one from bottle 1 and one from bottle 2, and the scale read 2.0 grams, then we'd know that bottle 3 had the heavier pills. Unfortunately, if the scale read 2.1, then we wouldn't know whether the faulty pill was from bottle 1 or bottle 2.

We need a way of distinguishing between these, which suggests that we need to treat bottle 1 and bottle 2 *differently* in some way.

If we took one pill from bottle 1 and two pills from bottle 2, then we could identify the faulty one based on the weight.

- If scale = 3.0 grams (0 grams over expected), then bottle 3 is faulty.
- If scale = 3.1 grams (0.1 grams over expected), then bottle 1 is faulty.
- If scale = 3.2 grams (0.2 grams over expected), then bottle 2 is faulty.

We can scale up this solution for the 10-bottle case. Take one pill from bottle 1, two pills from bottle 2, three pills from bottle 3, and so on to bottle 9. The expected weight is 45 grams $(1 + 2 + 3 + \cdots + 9)$, so we just need to look at what the excess weight is.

If scale = 45.0 (excess = 0), then bottle 10 is faulty.
If scale = 45.1 (excess = 0.1), then bottle 1 is faulty.
If scale = 45.2 (excess = 0.2), then bottle 2 is faulty.
If scale = 45.9 (excess = 0.9), then bottle 9 is faulty.

You and I are playing a game. I give you two buckets: one with 100 white marbles and one with 100 black marbles. You can rearrange the marbles between the buckets however you'd like. Then, I'm going to pick a random marble from one of the two buckets. If it's white, you win a prize.

How can you maximize the odds of winning? The rules are: (1) all the marbles must be used; (2) neither of the buckets can be empty; (3) each bucket has an equal chance of being picked; and (4) given a bucket, every marble has an equal chance (you cannot, for example, put all the white marbles at the top).

If you just put the marbles randomly across the two buckets, then you would have a 50/50 chance of winning. This is a baseline. Every solution you come up with should be better than that.

Alternatively, you could put all the white marbles in one bucket and the black ones in the other. This is still 50/50.

Note, though, how the problem is stated—that's important. Each bucket has an equal chance of being picked.

Imagine you put only white marbles in bucket 1; then you have a 100 percent chance of winning if bucket 1 is picked. This is true regardless of how many white marbles are in bucket 1. If bucket 1 contains only white marbles, then you know that if I pull a marble from bucket 1 it will be white.

What you want to maximize, then, is the odds of picking a white marble from bucket 2. If you put only one white marble in bucket 1 and all the others—99 white marbles and 100 black marbles—in bucket 2, then you will have nearly a 75 percent chance of winning.

In our universe, everyone has their own unique lock that is opened with their fingerprint. I need to send you a precious stone without worrying about someone stealing it, so I get a box for it that takes locks. How can I send you the stone so that you can open

it but no one else can? It is illegal to send unlocked locks, so it's not feasible for you to send me your lock to use.

Let's make sure we understand the problem first.

- If I mailed you the box with my lock, then you couldn't open it.
- If you mailed me your unlocked lock, this would be illegal.
- If I mailed you the box unlocked, this would be dangerous.

Going through this thought process, we've actually narrowed down our possibilities substantially. I must mail it to you locked in a box. I can't access your lock, though; so I must mail it with my lock. But you can't open my lock!

There seems to be a contradiction here, but there's not.

A box can take multiple locks. Nothing in the problem forbids that.

1. I lock the box with my lock.
2. I mail the box to you.
3. You place your lock on it also.
4. You mail it back to me.
5. I unlock my lock.
6. I mail it back to you.
7. You unlock your lock.
8. You remove the item.

A lot of people get tripped up on this question because they make an incorrect assumption. Be very clear about what you do and don't know, and be careful to not make assumptions.

There is a building of 100 floors. If an egg drops from the *n*th floor or above it will break. If it's dropped from any floor below, it will not break. You're given two eggs. How would you find *n* while minimizing the total number of drops in the worst case?

Many people think that they'll first drop the egg from the 50th floor, then the 75th, then the 87th, and so on until it breaks. This is actually a bad scenario. What if the first egg breaks on floor 50? Then you'd have to drop the second egg at every floor from the first floor to (potentially) floor 49. This could be 50 drops total.

A second approach is to drop the first egg from floor 10, then 20, then 30, and so on. Then, if the first egg breaks at floor 30, you would drop the second egg at floor 21, 22, . . . floor 29. The worst-case scenario happens when the threshold floor is floor 99. Egg 1 is dropped 10 times and egg 2 is dropped nine times. This is 19 drops total.

Observe that it doesn't really matter if we improve the typical or best-case scenario. All we care about is reducing the worst case.

Also observe that egg 2 always has a range of nine floors, whether egg 1 broke at floor 20 (in which case egg 2 has a range of floors 11 to 19) or floor 90 (in which case egg 2 has a range of floors 81 to 89).

Can we cut down this worst case a bit? Yes. Suppose that we dropped egg 1 from floors 15, 30, 40, 50, 60, 70, 80, 90, then 100. This is shaving off one of the egg 1 drops at no cost to the worst case.

- If egg 1 breaks at floor 30 (after two drops), then egg 2 will have at most 14 drops (floor 16 to floor 29). This means a total of 14 drops.
- If egg 1 breaks at floor 100 (after nine drops), then egg 2 will have at most nine drops (floor 91 to floor 99). This is a worst case of 18 drops.

We've basically shifted work from egg 1 to egg 2.

Since we care only about the *sum* of their *worst-case* drops, we can set up a system where, when egg 1 has done less work (because it broke after only two drops), egg 2 does more. This points to a decreasing interval/spacing. For each additional drop that egg 1 has done, we want to ensure that egg 2 has done one fewer drop.

Let's play with these numbers a bit. We had a worst case before of 18 drops, so let's try to beat that with a 17-drop worst case:

- If egg 1 drops from floor 17 and breaks, then it'll take at most 16 more drops from egg 2 to find the right floor. This is a worst case of 17.
- Suppose it doesn't break. Now, let's move up 16 floors and drop it from floor 33. If it breaks, egg 2 has 15 drops to go. Note how with egg 1 doing *one more* drop, egg 2 has to do *one fewer.*
- We continue this pattern: move up 15 floors (to floor 48), then 14 floors (floor 62), then 13 floors (floor 75), then 12 floors (floor 87), then 11 floors (floor 98), then 2 floors (floor 100). This is a worst case of 17 drops.

This is good, but is it optimal? Not quite.

We can express the starting floor as floor x. The next floor will be up $x - 1$ floors, then up $x - 2$, then up $x - 3$, and so on. The goal is to wind up exactly at floor 100, or as close to that as possible.

We want to find an x such that $x + (x - 1) + (x - 2) + \cdots + 1$ is as close as possible to 100. If you know the equation for the sum of numbers between 1 and x, you can use that. Otherwise, you can do this by hand pretty easily:

- $1 + 2 + \cdots + 10 = (0 + 10) + (1 + 9) + (2 + 8) + (3 + 7) + (4 + 6) + 5 = 55$
- Add 11: 66

- Add 12: 78
- Add 13: 91
- Add 14: 105

The optimal starting floor therefore is 14. The sequence goes: floor 14, floor 27, floor 39, floor 50, floor 60, floor 69, floor 77, floor 84, floor 90, floor 95, floor 99, floor 100.

The worst case is also 14 drops.

You have a three-gallon jug and a five-gallon jug, as well as an unlimited supply of water. How do you use these to get exactly four gallons of water?

Let's start with something easier: how can we get *any* quantity other than three and five gallons? If I fill up the five-gallon jug and then use it to fill up the three-gallon jug, I will be left with two gallons.

We might as well then dump the water out of the three-gallon jug. We could always refill it from scratch afterward if we needed it.

Action	3-Gallon	5-Gallon
Fill 5-gallon jug		5
Fill 3-gallon jug with contents of 5-gallon jug	3	2
Dump 3-gallon jug	0	2

What can I do with those two gallons? They're not doing very much good sitting in the five-gallon jug, so let's pour them into the three-gallon jug. Let's also fill up the five-gallon jug again.

Action	3-Gallon	5-Gallon
Pour 2 gallons from 5-gallon jug into 3-gallon jug	2	0
Fill 5-gallon jug	2	5

Now let's try pouring more water from the five-gallon jug into the three-gallon jug.

Action	3-Gallon	5-Gallon
Pour 1 gallon from 5-gallon jug into 3-gallon jug	3	4

We're done! We now have exactly four gallons.

For the most part, this problem can be approached randomly—by just playing with the numbers. The only thing we were particularly careful to do was to notice that when a jug is completely full, holding on to this quantity doesn't offer much value. It's trivial to fill up a three-gallon jug with three gallons, but it's harder to fill a three-gallon jug with exactly two gallons.

There is an 8 × 8 chessboard in which two diagonally opposite corners have been cut off. You are given 31 dominoes, and a single domino can cover exactly two squares. Can you use the 31 dominos to cover the entire board?

We should probably first sanity check this. A total of 31 dominoes represents 62 squares. If the chessboard is 8 × 8 but two corners are cut off, then it also has 62 squares. It might be possible therefore to do this.

Let's picture a chessboard.

Imagine that the top left and bottom right (white) corners were cut off, and we are trying to cover the rest of the board with dominoes, starting from the top row. As our first attempt, we might try laying them horizontally along the edge. There are only seven squares remaining in this row, so one of our dominoes would have to poke into the next row. And, when we do this, the next cell is also left with an odd number of squares.

This is a good intuition that makes it *feel* impossible, but it's not a great proof.

Let's look at the board again. It has 62 squares. It did have 64, but the two white corners were cut off. That's interesting, actually: we have 30 white squares and 32 black squares.

Each domino, though, covers one white cell and one black cell, always. Therefore, 31 dominoes must take up 31 black squares and 31 white squares, meaning that it is impossible for the 31 dominoes to cover the 30 white squares and 32 black squares.

Questions and Answers

It's a Numbers Game

While I understand the basic approach of estimation questions, I always seem to make mathematical mistakes. I'm just not good at math in my head. Can I ask for a calculator, or is there anything else I can do?

You probably can't ask for a calculator, but there are ways that you can get better at these questions, especially since you say you have the approach down.

Many people face difficulty with doing math in their heads because they just can't hold so many different numbers at once. As soon as the number 293 comes up, the number 143 gets lost. It may be helpful to ask for a sheet of paper to jot down numbers as you go.

Another trick that may help you is to keep your notes well structured. You might be periodically pulling from the wrong number on the page, causing you to wind up with a wildly inaccurate number.

Finally, memorizing common arithmetic "equations" can be useful. You probably have the multiplication tables up through 12 times 12 memorized, but you should also memorize up through 20 times 20. Make sure you really, really know them—it's an easy way to improve your results.

The Great Unknown

I recently interviewed with Twitter for a product management position and I was asked what I would do if I were CEO of Twitter. I feel like this is an unfair question. I can't possibly have access to the same information that the CEO or even the interviewer does. I told the interviewer the issue and she agreed to change the question, but I feel like she probably didn't like my reaction.

Your instinct is correct; she probably didn't like your reaction. While I understand your objection to it—there *are* issues with questions like this—she very likely disagrees with your reasoning and she might even interpret your reaction as a fear of answering the question.

(*continued*)

(continued)

Additionally, this question might not be as inappropriate as you thought. Yes, you didn't have all the information someone internal would, but that would be taken into account by the interviewer. You'd be evaluated based on your reasoning *given* your comparative lack of information.

In the future, avoid objecting to the interviewer's question—unless you're willing to lose a job over this.

Additional Resources

Visit www.crackingthetechcareer.com for additional interview questions and resources.

12 The Programming Interview

If you're applying for a software development position, you've got a special set of skills to prepare. Yes, you'll be asked to code. No, you don't get a computer (usually)—just a whiteboard, or sometimes just a sheet of paper. Whiteboard and interviewing coding requires a special set of skills. Even the best coders can bomb coding questions.

A typical software development interview consists of a little bit of conversation at the beginning about your prior experience, and a little bit at the end about the company. The bulk of the interview is spent on coding and algorithm questions.

Coding questions can be very quick, but will often take up the full interview time. You're not expected to be a flawless coder. Most questions are tricky enough that even the best candidates make a few mistakes.

What's the Point?

Coding interviews are a sore spot for many job seekers. What's the point of coding on a whiteboard? Don't they know that you can code by looking at your prior experience? And why do they force you to use a whiteboard rather than a computer? After all, you can't possibly be expected to write correct code on a whiteboard.

When asking, employers will usually make one or more of the following points:

- By coding on a whiteboard, you're encouraged to have a conversation with your interviewer. This helps the interviewer understand how you're thinking.
- Coding on a whiteboard encourages you to focus on the meat of the algorithm and code, rather than getting caught up in the details. For example, on a computer, a candidate is likely to spend time getting the exact syntax for a sort method correct. This isn't the type of stuff interviewers care about.
- Because you're not worried about making all the little pieces work correctly, you can actually write more complex code. Need a helper function to find the smallest value in an array? No problem. Just pretend you have one.
- Coding on a whiteboard tests how well you reason about how code works. Do you just verify that your code works by running it? Or do you actually think conceptually about how it works?
- Whiteboard coding encourages you to write good, clean code from the beginning, because it's so much slower. When you have a computer, you can be a bit sloppier and clean it up later.

This is not said to absolutely defend these interviews, but rather to help you understand what the company's reasoning is.

What's Expected—And What's Not

You are not expected to write flawless whiteboard code. Having gone through the process themselves, interviewers know that writing perfect code isn't a reasonable expectation.

However, pseudocode is generally not acceptable. Your code should be in a specific language (Python, Java, C++, etc.), and you should aim for as close to correct code as possible. If you mix up little things—for example, using `list.add` instead of `list.append`—interviewers shouldn't care much about that.

Do what you can to demonstrate that you care about clean, beautiful code. Wrap your code in a method declaration; loose code looks sloppy and can be confusing. You generally do not need to write the class definition, unless it's particularly relevant to the problem at hand.

Modularize your code. This shows an eye for maintainability.

If you notice parts of your code that you can refactor or clean up afterward, just go ahead and make the changes. You want to demonstrate that you are the kind of person who cares about the beauty of code.

How They Differ: Microsoft, Facebook, Google, Amazon, Yahoo, and Apple

For the most part, the top tech companies are far more similar than different. There really aren't "Google interview questions" or "Microsoft interview questions." Each interviewer decides on his or her own questions, and almost any question asked at one company would fit in just as well at any of the other companies.

However, certain companies have minor slants toward particular types of questions:

- Google tends to emphasize questions on scalability more than other companies (for instance, "Design a web crawler"). Questions on bit manipulation are also quite common.
- Amazon loves object-oriented design questions. If you're going to interview at Amazon, make sure you study these problems. And, since Amazon is a web-based company, you'll also want to prepare for scalability questions.
- Microsoft is all over the map, which is to be expected since it has a pretty diverse set of projects. Its interviewers tend to ask more questions about C and C++. If you don't list these languages on your resume, you have nothing to fear. However, if you do list these languages, you'll want to make sure that you're comfortable coding in them. Additionally, Microsoft tends to emphasize testing and design skills more in developers than other companies do, so be prepared for these questions.
- Apple wants people who are really passionate about the company. Make sure you understand Apple's products, especially those of the team you are interviewing with. What would you improve about the product? Remember that Apple has a lot of smart people who haven't yet done what you're suggesting. Think about why they haven't.
- Facebook has specific roles for their interviewers to ensure a diversity of questions. They often prioritize being a good hacker; that is, can you get stuff done? Be prepared to talk about your prior experience.
- Yahoo has historically emphasized more terminology and knowledge-based questions, but has begun to transition more to typical algorithm and problem-solving questions.

A good rule of thumb is to look at the position and the company. If it's a web-based company, team, or role, you should expect some scalability questions. If it's a front-end position, expect some front-end questions. But for almost all companies, expect algorithm and problem-solving questions.

How to Prepare

When it comes to practicing interview questions, quality matters more than quantity. There are literally thousands of sample interview questions online for companies like Google, Microsoft, and Amazon. Don't try to memorize the answers. It's impossible and won't help you anyway.

Take your time solving problems, and try the following seven-step approach in practicing questions:

1. Implement the common data structures and algorithms from scratch, first by hand and then via a computer. A lot of interview questions require this knowledge, so it's essential that you are very comfortable with them. Derive the time complexity for these algorithms as well.
2. Practice with real interview questions. A book on algorithms or data structures might be useful, but it's often far beyond the knowledge that you need to know. Let interview questions be your guide for what you need to know.
3. Try to solve the problem on your own—*really* try to solve it. If you read a question and get stuck solving it, that's okay and normal. Questions are designed to be tough. Don't give up, though. Keep working through the problem.
4. Write the code for the algorithm on paper. You've been coding all your life on a computer, and you've gotten used to the many nice things about it: compilers, code completion, and so on. You won't have any of these in an interview, so you had better get used to that fact now. Implement the code the old-fashioned way, down to every last semicolon.
5. Test your code! By hand, that is. No cheating with a computer!
6. Type your code into a computer exactly as is. Rerun both the test cases you tried and some new ones.
7. Start a list of all the mistakes you made, and analyze what types of mistakes you make the most often. Are there specific mistakes?

You can find thousands of coding interview questions on CareerCup.com that candidates have gotten from Google, Microsoft, Amazon, and other major tech companies.

What If I Hear a Question I Know?

If you do lots of preparation, you'll likely be asked some interview questions that you know. If this happens, tell your interviewer, "I think I've heard this question before" or "I've heard a problem similar to this—would you like me to continue anyway?"

With complex algorithm questions, interviewers are looking to see how you solve the problem. If they don't see your problem-solving approach, then they can't think that you're a good problem solver.

Even worse: many interviewers feel that not admitting when you've heard a question before is a form of cheating, and they might reject you just for that.

However, if you are honest and say that you've heard the question before, you'll win major bonus points. Interviewers care about honesty, even if there's usually no way to test it directly.

Must-Know Data Structures, Algorithms, and Topics

Most interviewers won't ask you about specific algorithms for binary tree balancing or other complex algorithms. Frankly, they probably don't remember these algorithms either. (Yes, that means you can put down the fancy algorithms book.)

You're usually expected to know only the basics. Here's a list of essential topics. This is not, of course, an all-inclusive list. Questions may be asked on areas outside of these topics. This is merely an absolutely must-know list.

Data Structures	**Algorithms**	**Concepts**
Linked lists	Breadth-first search	Bit manipulation
Binary trees	Depth-first search	Recursion
Tries	Binary search	Memorization/dynamic programming
Stacks	Merge sort	Memory (stack vs. heap)
Queues	Quick sort	Big-O time
Dynamically resizing arrays	Tree insert/find/etc.	
Hash tables		
Heaps		
Graphs		

For each of the topics, make sure you understand how to implement and use them, and (where applicable) the space and time complexity.

Practice implementing the data structures and algorithms. You might be asked to implement them directly, or you might be asked to implement a modification of them. Either way, the more comfortable you are with the implementations, the better.

Memory Usage

As you're reviewing data structures, remember to practice computing the memory usage of a data structure or an algorithm. Your interviewer might ask you directly how much memory something takes, or you might need to compute this yourself if your problem involves large amounts of data.

- **Data structures.** Don't forget to include the pointers to other data. For example, a doubly linked list that holds 1,000 integers will often use about 12KB of memory (4 bytes for the data, 4 bytes for the previous pointer, and 4 bytes for the next pointer). This means that making a singly linked list into a doubly linked list can dramatically increase memory usage.
- **Algorithms.** A recursive algorithm often takes up dramatically more space than an iterative algorithm. Consider, for example, an algorithm to compute the *j*th to last element of a singly linked list. An approach that uses an array to sort each element may be no better than a recursive algorithm—both use O(*n*) memory! (The best solution involves using two pointers, where one starts off *j* spaces ahead.)

Many candidates think of their algorithms on only one dimension—time—but it's important to consider the space complexity as well. We must often make a trade-off between time and space, and sometimes we do sacrifice time efficiency to reduce memory usage.

Coding Questions

Interviews are supposed to be difficult. The norm is that you won't know how to solve a question as soon as you hear it. You will struggle through it, get a bit of help from the interviewer (or a lot of help, depending on the difficulty of the question), and arrive at a better solution than what you started with.

When you get a hard question, don't panic. Just start talking aloud about how you would solve it.

The following seven-step approach works well for many problems:

1. **Understand the question.** If there's anything you didn't understand, clarify it here. Pay special attention to any specific details provided in the question, such as that the input is sorted. You need all those details.
2. **Draw an example.** Solving questions in your head is very different; get up to the whiteboard and draw an example. It should be a *good* example, too. The example should be reasonably large (e.g., if it's a typical array problem, you probably want one with around eight elements) and not a special case. This is actually much easier said than done.
3. **Design a brute force algorithm.** If there's a brute force/naive approach, or even a solution that only partially works, explain it. It's a starting point, and ensures that your interviewer knows that you've gotten at least that far.
4. **Optimize the brute force.** Not always, but very often, there's a path from the brute force to the optimal solution.
5. **Understand the code.** Once you have an optimal algorithm, take a moment to really understand your algorithm. It's well worth it to not dive into code yet.
6. **Implement the code.** If you're comfortable with your process, go ahead and implement it. Don't be afraid to go back to your example, though, if you start to get confused.
7. **Test.** Flawless whiteboard coding is rare. If you find mistakes, that's okay. Analyze why you made the mistake and try to fix it.

And, remember: you're not done until the interviewer says that you're done! This goes for both the algorithm part and the code part. When you come up with an algorithm, start thinking about the problems accompanying it. When you write code, start trying to find bugs. The vast majority of candidates make mistakes.

Step 1: Understand the Question

Technical problems are more ambiguous than they might appear, so make sure to ask questions to resolve anything that might be unclear. You may eventually wind up with a very different—or much easier—problem than you had initially thought. In fact, some interviewers (especially at

Microsoft) will specifically test to see if you ask good questions. A question like "Design an algorithm to sort a list" might turn into "Sort a sequence of values between 1 and 10 that are stored in a linked list." This is a very different problem.

Additionally, it's important to make sure that you really remember all those details that the interviewer mentioned. If the interviewer mentioned that the data is sorted, then your optimal algorithm probably depends on that. Or, if the data set has all unique values, this is probably necessary information.

If you think you might have forgotten some details, you can always ask your interviewer to repeat the problem.

Step 2: Draw an Example

For some reason, most candidates have this instinct to stay in their chairs to solve the problem. Don't. Get up and go to the whiteboard! It's very difficult to solve a problem without an example.

Make sure your example is sufficiently interesting. This means that it should be not too small, but not overwhelmingly difficult, and also not a special case.

It's surprisingly common for candidates to use a special case example. The problem with special cases is that they can make you see patterns that don't exist, or make you *fail* to see patterns that do. It's hard to distinguish between "works for this problem" and "works in general."

Consider, for example, a problem to count the number of elements that two sorted and distinct arrays have in common. A typical example that a candidate might come up with is:

A: [1, 3, 8, 9]

B: [3, 4, 5, 10]

This is a bad example for two reasons. First, it's too small. Second, it's a special case: the arrays are the same length.

How is this for an example?

A: [1, 3, 8, 9]

B: [2, 3, 4, 5, 10]

This is a bit better, but it's still a special case. The arrays have only one element in common *and* that element is even at the same index in both arrays.

This is a pretty good example:

A: [1, 5, 9, 13, 14, 20, 21]

B: [1, 9, 10, 11, 13, 14, 15, 16, 21]

This example is fairly large (but not too cumbersome). It has multiple elements in common and they are dispersed throughout the array. We even have two overlapping elements (13 and 14) that are right next to each other.

Step 3: Design a Brute Force Algorithm

As soon as you hear an interview question, try to get a solution out there, even if it's imperfect. You can work with a brute force algorithm to optimize it.

If you're having trouble coming up with an algorithm, remember our approaches to algorithm problems (presented later in this chapter).

Also, when designing your algorithm, don't forget to think about:

- What are the space and time complexities?
- What happens if there is a lot of data?
- Does your design cause other issues? (That is, if you're creating a modified version of a binary search tree, did your design impact the time for insert/find/delete?)
- If there are other issues, did you make the right trade-offs?
- If the interviewer gave you specific data (e.g., mentioned that the data is ages, or in sorted order), have you leveraged that information? There's probably a reason that you're given it.

Even a bad solution is better than no solution. State your bad solution and then state the issues with it.

Step 4: Optimize the Brute Force

Once you have a solution out there, focus on making it better.

If you have a brute force algorithm, it often works well to run through the algorithm—by hand with your example, *not* by writing code—and look for areas to optimize. Specifically, look for the bottlenecks, unnecessary work, and duplicated work (BUD) areas:

- **Bottlenecks.** Is there one part of the code that's taking a long time? For example, if your algorithm has first step that's $O(N \log N)$ and a second step that's O(*N*), there's little sense in optimizing the second step. The first step will always be a bottleneck. A bottleneck could also be a particularly slow part of the code that is called repeatedly. That might be a good place on which to focus your optimizations.

- **Unnecessary work.** Is there anything you're doing that isn't really necessary? For example, perhaps you're searching for an element on both sides of the tree, when you should really have some clue why it would be on one side.
- **Duplicated work.** Is there anything you're doing over and over again? For example, if you're continuously searching for the same elements, this could constitute duplicated work and you could optimize it with a hash table.

Of course, if a really novel and unrelated approach comes to you, don't be afraid to start from scratch.

Step 5: Understand the Code

Interviewees spend too little time on this step and, unfortunately, it typically results in their writing sloppy and incorrect code.

It's a bad habit instilled in coders from using a computer. If the code is short enough, you're used to just typing it out and running it, then fixing up what doesn't work. This is okay on a computer: typing a short problem is pretty fast.

On a whiteboard, though, it's very slow to write code and even slower to test it. This is why it's important to make sure you really, really know what you're doing.

Run through your algorithm meticulously before coding. For example, imagine you're trying to merge two sorted arrays into a new sorted array. Many candidates start coding when they understand the basic gist: two pointers, move them through the array, copy the elements in order.

This probably isn't sufficient. You should instead understand it deeply. You need to understand what the variables are, when they update, and why. You should have logic like this formulated before you start coding:

1. Initialize two pointers, *p* and *q*, which point to the beginning of A and B, respectively.
2. Initialize *k* to an index at the start of the result array, *R*.
3. Compare the values at *p* and *q*.
4. If A[*p*] is smaller, insert A[*p*] into *R*[*k*]. Increment *p* and *k*.

5. If B[q] is smaller, insert B[q] into $R[k]$. Increment q and k.
6. Go to step 3.

You don't have to write this out by hand, but you do need to understand it at this level. Trying to skip a step and code before you're totally comfortable will only slow you down.

Step 6: Implement the Code

You don't need to rush through your code; in fact, this will most likely hurt you. Just go at a nice, slow, methodical pace, and remember this advice:

- **Use data structures generously.** Where relevant, use a good data structure or define your own. For example, if you're asked a problem involving finding the minimum age for a group of people, consider defining a data structure to represent a person. This shows your interviewer that you care about good object-oriented design.
- **Modularize your code first.** If there are discrete steps in your algorithm, move these into separate functions. In fact, this can actually help you get out of doing tedious work. Imagine, as part of a broader algorithm, you need to convert a letter from A to Z to a number from 0 to 26. This is a tedious thing to write. Just modularize it off to another function and you probably won't need to worry about ever writing it.
- **Don't crowd your code.** Many candidates will start writing their code in the middle of the whiteboard. This is fine for the first few lines, but whiteboards aren't that big.

If you feel yourself getting confused while coding, stop and go back to your example. You don't need to code straight through. It's far better that you take a break than write nonsensical code.

Step 7: Test

It is rare for a candidate to write flawless code. Not testing therefore suggests two problems. First, it leaves bugs in your code. Second, it suggests that you're the type of person who doesn't test their code well.

Therefore, it's very important to test your code.

To discover bugs the fastest, do the following five steps:

1. **Review your code conceptually.** What is the meaning of each line? Does it do what you think it should?

2. **Review error hot spots.** Is there anything in your code that looks funny (e.g., "int n = length – 2")? Do your boundary conditions look right? What about your base cases (if the code is recursive)?
3. **Test against a small example.** You want your example to create an algorithm to be big, but now you want a small one. An example that's too big will take a long time to run through. This is time-consuming, but it might also cause you to rush the testing and miss serious bugs.
4. **Pinpoint potential issues.** What sorts of test cases would test against specific potential issues? For example, you might sense that there could be a bug with one array that's much shorter than the other; test for this situation specifically.
5. **Test error cases.** Finally, test the true error conditions. What happens on a null string or negative values?

When you find a mistake (which you will), relax. Almost no one writes bug-free code; what's important is how you react to it. Point out the mistake, and carefully analyze why the bug is occurring. Is it really just when you pass in 0, or does it happen in other cases, too?

Bugs are not a big deal (bug-free code is very unusual). The important thing is that you think through how to fix issues you see rather than making a quick and dirty fix. A fix that works for that test case might not work for all test cases, so make sure it's the right one.

Algorithm Questions: Four Ways to Create an Algorithm

There's no surefire approach to solving a tricky algorithm problem, but the following approaches can be useful. Keep in mind that the more problems you practice, the easier it will be to identify which approach to use.

Also, remember that the four approaches can be mixed and matched. That is, once you've applied Simplify and Generalize, you may want to implement Pattern Matching next.

Approach 1: Pattern Matching

Pattern matching means to relate a problem to similar ones, and figure out if you can modify the solution to solve the new problem. This is one reason why practicing lots of problems is important: the more problems you do, the better you get.

Example: A sorted array has been rotated so that the elements might appear in the order 3 4 5 6 7 1 2. How would you find the minimum element?

This question is most similar to the following two well-known problems:

1. Find the minimum element in an unsorted array.
2. Find a specific element in an array (e.g., binary search).

Finding the minimum element in an unsorted array isn't a particularly interesting algorithm (you could just iterate through all the elements), nor does it use the information provided (that the array is sorted). It's unlikely to be useful here.

However, binary search is very applicable. You know that the array is sorted but rotated. So it must proceed in an increasing order, then reset and increase again. The minimum element is the reset point.

If you compare the first and middle elements (3 and 6), you know that the range is still increasing. This means that the reset point must be after the 6 (or 3 is the minimum element and the array was never rotated). We can continue to apply the lessons from binary search to pinpoint this reset point, by looking for ranges where LEFT > RIGHT. That is, for a particular point, if LEFT < RIGHT, then the range does not contain the reset. If LEFT > RIGHT, then it does.

Approach 2: Simplify and Generalize

In Simplify and Generalize, we change constraints (data type, size, etc.) to simplify the problem, and then try to solve the simplified problem. Once you have an algorithm for the simplified problem, you can generalize the problem back to its original form. Can you apply the new lessons?

Example: A ransom note can be formed by cutting words out of a magazine to form a new sentence. How would you figure out if a ransom note (string) can be formed from a given magazine (string)?

We can simplify the problem as follows: instead of solving the problem with words, solve it with characters. That is, imagine we are cutting characters out of a magazine to form a ransom note.

We can solve the simplified ransom note problem with characters by simply creating an array and counting the characters. Each spot in the array corresponds to one letter. First, we count the number of times each character in the ransom note appears, and then we go through the magazine to see if we have all of those characters.

When we generalize the algorithm, we do a very similar thing. This time, rather than creating an array with character counts, we create a hash table. Each word maps to the number of times the word appears.

Approach 3: Base Case and Build

Base Case and Build suggests that you solve the algorithm first for a base case (e.g., just one element). Then, try to solve it for elements 1 and 2, assuming that you have the answer for element 1. Then, try to solve it for elements 1, 2, and 3, assuming that you have the answer to elements 1 and 2.

You will notice that Base Case and Build algorithms often lead to natural recursive algorithms.

Example: Design an algorithm to print all permutations of a string. For simplicity, assume all characters are unique.

Consider the following string: abcdefg

- Case "a" → {a}
- Case "ab" → {ab, ba}
- Case "abc" → ?

This is the first interesting case. If we had the answer to permutations "ab," how could we generate permutations "abc"? Well, the additional letter is c, so we can just stick c in at every possible point. That is:

- merge(c, ab) → cab, acb, abc
- merge(c, ba) → cba, bca, bac

We can use a recursive algorithm to solve this problem. First, generate all permutations of a string by chopping off the last character and generating all permutations of $s[1 \ldots n-1]$. Then, insert $s[n]$ into every location of the permuted string.

Approach 4: Data Structure Brainstorm

The Data Structure Brainstorm approach admittedly feels somewhat hacky, but it often works. In this approach, we simply run through a list of data structures and try to apply each one. This approach works because many algorithms are quite straightforward once we find the right data structure.

A good tip-off that you might want to apply Data Structure Brainstorm is that the interviewer hasn't specified a data structure for the data. This means that you'll probably need to come up with a data structure, and that might be the key to the problem.

Example: You are building a class with two functions: addNumber(n) and getMedian(). The addNumber(n) method will be called periodically by some external function with an integer value. When getMedian() is called, you need to efficiently return the median of all prior numbers. (If you have an odd number of values, the median is the exact middle of the sorted values. If you have an even number of values, the median is the average between the two middle values.) How would you implement these two methods?

Let's go through the common data structures and see if using one of them would be helpful.

- **Linked list?** Probably not—linked lists tend not to do very well with accessing and sorting numbers.
- **Array?** Maybe, if we kept the elements sorted. But that's probably expensive. Let's hold off on this and return to it if it's needed.
- **Binary tree?** This is possible, since binary trees do fairly well with ordering. In fact, if the binary search tree is perfectly balanced, the top might be the median. But be careful—if there's an even number of elements, the median is actually the average of the middle two elements. The middle two elements can't both be at the top. There might be a workable algorithm, but let's come back to it.
- **Heap?** A heap is really good at basic ordering and keeping track of maxes and mins. This is actually interesting—if you had two heaps, you could keep track of the bigger half and the smaller half of the elements. The bigger half is kept in a min heap, such that the smallest element in the bigger half is at the root. The smaller half is kept in a max heap, such that the biggest element of the smaller half is at the root. Now, with these data structures, you have the potential median elements at the roots. If the heaps are no longer the same size, you can quickly rebalance the heaps by popping an element off one heap and pushing it onto the other.

Note that the more problems you do, the more developed your instinct on which data structure to apply will be. Hash tables, trees, tries, and heaps are some of the best data structures to solve problems.

Object-Oriented Design

Object-oriented design (OOD) questions come in two flavors: OOD for a piece of software and OOD for a real-world object. Despite the seemingly huge difference between these topics, they're approached much the same way:

- **What are your goals?** Imagine, for example, you are asked to design the classes for a generic deck of cards. What kind of cards? Are they standard playing cards, UNO cards, or some other kind? Just how generic is it supposed to be?
- What are the core objects? For example, if you're doing the OOD for a restaurant, your core objects might be Restaurant, Patron, Party, Host, Server, Busser, Table, and so on. Each of these will become a class.
- **How do the objects relate to each other?** There is probably only one Restaurant, so this can be a singleton class. Restaurant has many Servers, one Host, many Bussers, many Tables, many Parties, and many Patrons. (*Note:* This is just an assumption; talk to your interviewer about this.) Each Table has one Server and one Party. Look for and remove redundancies. For example, Restaurant may not need a list of Patrons, since it can get that from the list of Parties.
- **How do the objects interact?** Think about what the major actions that occur in the restaurant are. For example, a Party makes a Reservation with a Host. The Host sits the Party at a Table and assigns them a Server. Each of these actions should generally correspond to one or more methods. By walking through these methods, you may discover that you missed some objects or that your design isn't quite right. That's okay—now is a great time to add them!
- **Are there any tricky algorithms?** In some cases, there may be an algorithm that impacts the design. For example, implementing `findNextReservation(int partySize)` might require some changes to how the reservations are referenced. Discuss these details with your interviewer.

Remember that object-oriented design questions require a lot of communication with your interviewer about how flexible your design should be and how to balance certain trade-offs. There is no "right" answer to an object-oriented design question.

Scalability Questions

Scalability questions can be very intimidating for candidates, especially recent graduates or those who haven't done much big system design. You can be asked very broad questions, such as to design Google Maps. Or the questions might be more specific, like being asked to design a web crawler.

Fundamentally, these are *problem-solving* questions and can be approached as such. They are not tests of knowledge. For example, Google does not expect you to know Google technologies like MapReduce and BigTable.

Preparation

One of the best things you can do is read how real-world systems were implemented. What are the components involved in the design? Why did the designers make the choices that they made? What were the trade-offs?

These systems can be major products (e.g., Twitter, Google Maps) or components of existing products (e.g., MapReduce, BigTable).

The more analysis you've done on how other systems are designed, the better you'll be able to design a new system. Again, it's not about memorizing how these systems are designed. You need to analyze *why* they've been designed that way.

How to Approach

A general structure like the following four-step sequence works well:

1. **Scope the problem.** You can't build a system without knowing what it should do. While asking any questions you need to, make a list of the necessary algorithms or components. For example, if you're designing Google Maps, you might need to route people, display maps, gather traffic data, and so on.
2. **Structure the architecture.** Outline what the key components to the problem are. For example, you might have a data store, a crawler, a front-end piece to fetch data from the data structure, and so on. This is a great moment to get up and use the whiteboard. It will make your thought process clear and organized, for both you and the interviewer.
3. **Identify key issues.** Describe what the key problems are that the system will hit. Is the application read-heavy or write-heavy? What does that mean for it? What are the bottlenecks or critical resources? Do you need to distribute your database across multiple machines?
4. **Resolve the issues.** Now that you've identified challenges, it's time to solve them. If it's not clear which one you should discuss, then ask your interviewer what she'd like you to do.

While this structure is provided in a linear fashion, you don't need to absolutely stick to it. Identifying a key issue might cause a tweak in the core architecture, or you might have follow-up questions for your interviewer. Prioritize communication throughout this process.

Testing Interviews

Test-related jobs have many names and are easily confused, but can be bucketed into two areas:

1. **Quality assurance/software test engineer/tester.** People in these positions design and execute test plans. Not everything in a piece of software can be tested; there are just too many different configurations. Testers prioritize the most important aspects of the software to test, and then perform these tests.
2. **Software engineer in test/software design engineer in test.** People in these positions are coders—they write code all day—but instead of building features, they write automation code. For example, they might test Microsoft Word by automatically building a set of large files and then automating Word to open, process, and close the files repeatedly.

Don't rely on the job names just given entirely. At a specific company, a software engineer in test might be more on the manual testing side and less on the automated code testing side.

If a specific testing job requires coding (regardless of the job title), you might be asked coding questions. This means that you need to practice coding, algorithms, and data structures on top of all of the usual testing problems. If you're a tester, do yourself a favor and make sure to practice coding—it's an excellent way to set yourself apart.

In addition, you can expect testing questions that fall into the following three categories:

1. How would you test this real-world object?
2. Explain how you would test this piece of computer software.
3. Test a method (possibly one that you just wrote).

In some cases, developers can also be asked testing questions.

Testing a Real-World Object

What does testing paper clips and pens have to do with testing Office or Gmail? Perhaps not a ton, but your interviewer certainly thinks they do.

Your interviewer is using this question to test your ability to deal with ambiguity, to understand your ability to think about the expected and unexpected behavior, and, as always, to test your ability to structure and communicate your thoughts.

Let's work through this recommended six-step approach for an example problem: test a pen.

1. **Ask questions to understand what the object is.** A pen doesn't seem that ambiguous, but it is. A pen could be anything from a fountain pen to a child's marker with multiple colors or a pen for astronauts. Ask your interviewer questions to resolve this ambiguity.
2. **Who is using it, and what are they doing with it?** Small children with poor dexterity are drawing with it, so it probably needs to be nice and thick. They'll probably be drawing on paper on the floor, but this means that they might end up drawing on the floor itself a bit.
3. **What are the unexpected uses?** Eating it—kids will put anything in their mouths. Drawing on other children or the walls (as my mother once discovered at her friend's house when she interrupted my sister playing a fun game called "Can I draw a solid line through the entire upstairs?"). Stomping on it. Throwing it.
4. **Are there additional stress cases?** Think about hot weather, cold weather, and so on. Not all of these will be applicable in every problem.
5. **Can you fail gracefully?** Ideally, we want our pen never to break. But if it does, can we prevent it from exploding?
6. **What are the test cases?** At this point, we've discovered that we probably want to test for at least the following elements:
   - *Nontoxic.* Perhaps we discuss the ingredients with poison control, which might be able to offer more specific tests if necessary.
   - *Washable.* Test drawing on floors, walls, clothing, and skin.
   - *Thickness.* We'll probably want to conduct a series of tests to understand what widths are uncomfortable for children, in addition to live testing our prototype pen.
   - *Softness/lightness.* The material should be a lightweight plastic, so that it doesn't hurt too much it if hits you.
   - *Durability.* The pen should not break easily. We should discuss with our interviewer how much pressure it needs to withstand.
   - *Leakage.* If the pen does break, we want to make sure that the ink doesn't do damage.

You may notice how testing fits into design—this is to be expected. After all, testers need to analyze whether the object fits the design requirements.

Testing a Piece of Software

Now that we've gotten what many consider to be the hardest questions out of the way, testing a piece of software isn't terribly hard. In fact, you approach it much the same way as a real-world object question.

Example: Explain how you would test an e-mail client.

1. **Ask questions to resolve ambiguity.** Not all e-mail clients are the same. Is it a corporate e-mail client? A personal e-mail client? Is it a web-based e-mail client, or desktop?
2. **Who is the user?** A corporate user will have very different needs than a personal user has, in terms of security, storage, maintenance, and so on.
3. **What is the feature set?** Some features you can probably assume (check e-mail, send e-mail, etc.), but other features may take more of a conversation. Does the e-mail sit on a server? Is it encrypted?
4. **Are there unexpected uses or stress cases?** In the case of an e-mail client, this might mean a flood of e-mail, huge attachments, and the like.
5. **When there are failures, how can you fail gracefully?** If a file is too large to be handled by the e-mail client, you will want to make sure that it fails gracefully. That is, the client should at most reject the attachment, but should not permanently freeze.
6. **What can be automated, and what must be manually tested?** Of course, there is an almost endless set of things that you can test—after all, companies have full teams to do this. What's important is that you focus on the biggest (or most interesting) items and discuss how you might test them. What can be automated, and what must be manually tested?

Testing a Method

After writing code, you might be asked to test the code or perhaps just to generate the test cases. In your test cases, remember to consider the following.

Example: Test a method that sorts an array.

1. **Ask questions to resolve ambiguity.** Should the array be sorted in ascending or descending order? What are the expectations as far as time, memory usage, and the like are concerned? What data type is the array supposed to have?
2. **What do you need to test for?** Make a list of everything that needs to be checked. In many cases, this might be just the result (e.g., is the array sorted?), but in other cases you might want to check for additional side effects (e.g., memory usage, other data being changed, etc.).

3. **Write the expected cases.** This is the easy one: one of your test cases should simply be an unsorted array.
4. **Write the extreme cases.** Check for null, empty arrays; huge arrays; already sorted arrays; and so on.

Questions and Answers

Too Much Prep, Too Little Time

I've been working for a few years as a software programmer at a consulting company, but my work is boring and mostly code maintenance. The little code I write is in C—there is no object-oriented programming. I don't feel like I'm learning much, and I'm definitely not moving up.

My dream is to work for a big company like Microsoft. I feel that I would need months to prepare for these interviews. Should I quit now so that I can focus on preparing?

I'll be honest—I'm not crazy about the idea of quitting just to do interview prep. First, Microsoft and companies like it hire fewer than 5 percent of applicants. Even with a lot of prep, your chances are slim. Second, you might need to give interviewers an explanation for why you quit, and "To prepare for you" is not a good reason. Third, the value of intensive, long-term preparation really depends on what your weaknesses are. All you've mentioned is a lack of knowledge about objected-oriented programming, and you probably don't need months to learn that.

I'd recommend quitting only if the following three statements are true:

1. You know you can find a job just as good as your current one without any prep.
2. You can't prepare simultaneously with working.
3. It will take you a long time to prepare.

(*continued*)

(*continued*)

If you've decided to quit, I'd recommend doing something a bit more tangible with your time. Rather than focusing just on acing the interviews, spend your time creating what could be a company. Build a piece of software or a website, and use this as your primary tool to learn what you need to know (object-oriented programming, etc.).

The benefit of this is that when employers ask you what you've been doing since you quit, you can tell them that you wanted to try to start a company, but you realized it wasn't for you (you discovered that you prefer working with larger teams, etc.). And you'll have something tangible to list on your resume that will show experience and mask any gaps.

Know It All

In preparation for my Google interview, I've gone through the course work for all my prior computer science courses. I've spent the most time on algorithms, and specifically dynamic programming and tree balancing. I'm still not sure I'll be able to complete a problem like this during an interview.

How do successful candidates tackle these questions?

Let's take a step back and put ourselves in the minds of our interviewers. They want to know if we're smart and if we can code. Having specific knowledge is not important, unless it's either (1) necessary for performing well on the job or (2) so integral to a basic computer science education that you would likely know it.

Inserting an element in a tree falls into category 2. Trees are not actually used that often in industry, but they're so fundamental, how could you not know them?

Tree balancing, however, does not fall into this category. You should know that tree balancing exists, and you should know basically how it works (rotations when the sides get too uneven), but the little details are not that essential to know. Skip it.

The complex dynamic programming questions—the ones you read about in big algorithm books—are usually too complex for an interview. They can come up, but they tend not to make good questions.

However, *simple* dynamic programming questions—memorizing (or caching results between recursive calls)—can come up. It's worth it to spend a bit of time practicing those questions, but they aren't as complex as you might assume.

Remember, also, that code in an interview is relatively short. You usually don't write more than 20 lines. Between designing an algorithm, testing the code, and fixing mistakes, there just isn't enough time to write much more than that.

So relax. Focus on preparing for normal range questions—the kinds that you can tackle in 45 minutes.

Misleading Information

I interviewed with Microsoft and I was asked a tough question. I started to think of a brute force solution, and the interviewer said that brute force is fine. I began to write the code, and before I was even finished, the interviewer began to bombard me with questions. His questions then led me to a better solution. I also noticed later that I had some bugs and other mistakes in my code, but these seemed fairly minor.

I feel that he misled me in telling me that my initial brute force solution was fine, and I ended up getting a rejection as a result. Do I have any chance to put up an argument?

There's a lot going on in this question, so let me break this down.

(continued)

(continued)

1. Did your interviewer mislead you in telling you that brute force was fine (when it really wasn't)?

   It is possible you got a bad interviewer who didn't direct you properly. Bad interviewers do exist, even at the best companies. I suspect that your interviewer was probably looking for whether you would notice and look for a more optimal solution, or if you would be satisfied with a good enough solution. Depending on how far along you were in your interview, the interviewer may also have been thinking, "Okay, we don't have much time, and I want to make sure I see this candidate's code. Let me encourage him to just get on with it."
2. Did this cause you to be rejected?

   Again, it is very hard to say that this really caused the rejection. First, typically 50 to 75 percent of candidates are rejected at each stage, so it's almost like you have to do things really, really right to not get rejected. Second, it's unlikely to be any one issue that caused a rejection. As you noted, you had some bugs and other mistakes. I'd guess that your interviewer's thought was more like "Hmm, I liked this guy, but his solution wasn't very good, and he had some bugs in his code and a few other mistakes."
3. Can you put up an argument?

   I wouldn't recommend it. Whatever you say to your recruiter, he or she will almost certainly side with your interviewer. You're more likely to spoil your decent reputation at the company, and it's just not worth it.

   I'm sorry things didn't work out for you, but you're not alone. Interviews are hard and, unfortunately, very random. Most of my coworkers at Google admitted that they didn't think they'd pass the interviews the second time around. Luckily, most companies understand this and let you apply again in six months to a year.

Additional Resources

Visit www.crackingthetechcareer.com for additional resources, and www.careercup.com for thousands of potential interview questions and answers.

13 Getting into Gaming

Even among technology companies, gaming firms stand out for their high-energy, fun-loving environments. Super-sized arcade games, beers on tap at weekly happy hours, colorful offices, entire rooms dedicated to Ping-Pong—all are typical of gaming companies. In terms of culture, they've "out-teched" the tech companies. Their appeal to candidates is clear.

The Culture: Is It All Fun and Games?

Alessandra, from gaming recruiting firm VonChurch, suggests that the festive atmosphere is integral to the nature of the field: "Gaming means blending the creative with the techy. Technology firms are already young, fun-filled environments. When you mix in a highly creative workforce, this is what you get."

Her colleague Katy Haddix concurs, but cautions that it's a work hard/play hard atmosphere: "You are expected to be full-seat-in, working 10 to 12 hours per day, plus the weekends when necessary."

Long hours are a necessity in the casual gaming world. Casual games fly from conception to release in a mere two months. Finishing a project before a deadline is always a race, and in this industry, there is always a deadline looming. The work can't stop.

Moreover, your product is live 24 hours per day and may depend on another live and changing platform such as Facebook. Things could break at any time; someone needs to be watching it.

In the console gaming world, release cycles are longer, which reduces the stress level, but the hours can still be intense. The entire gaming industry is fiercely competitive.

It is an industry for those truly passionate about games. If you aren't prepared for long hours—complemented, of course, by happy hours and foosball tournaments—then this is not the field for you.

Job Positions: What Can You Do?

Game creation is performed by four core roles: developers, producers, artists, and designers. A handful of other positions, from marketing to quality assurance (QA), assist the game creation, release, and post-production responsibilities. In this section we will cover what background, skills, and traits you need to have for each of these roles.

Software Engineering

Software engineering hiring at gaming companies is similar to that of other technology companies. "Candidates should expect to be grilled just like they would at Microsoft or any other tech company. We're just like them—we need people who are smart and can code," notes PopCap producer Ben Ahroni.

Because gaming firms move so quickly, they often cannot afford to wait for candidates to get up to speed with their technologies. A candidate who is already well versed in the company's pet language will fare much better in the recruiting process.

Audra Aulabaugh, a recruiter for Big Fish Games, adds that college students interested in gaming enroll in some related courses: "We do hire straight out of college, even without a gaming background, but a proven interest and background in gaming will help set you apart."

Production

Producers fill much the same role as product managers do in a tech company. They manage the full production of the game, including the prerelease schedule and the postrelease performance. In addition, Ben Ahroni told me, "The producer must be a leader. When things get tough, you need to be there to raise team morale."

BJ Bigley from Big Kind Games puts it a bit more bluntly. "Producers are socialites. You need to be able to keep everyone happy while getting results. You are the ultimate diplomat."

Being able to write code is nice, but not strictly necessary. What's more important is that you are analytical and quantitative, and that can come from anything from engineering to economics. After the release of the game, the producer must crunch the numbers to understand what's working and what's not. What is the download conversion rate? How many credits do people purchase for each increase in level, and how does this affect their lifetime usage rate?

Producers are commonly recruited from these two positions:

1. **Quality assurance (QA)/testing.** Many producers start off in QA, and specifically in so-called smoke testing. These roles enable them to see the full gaming life cycle, which translates nicely to the production role. Producers may also come from automation testing, or even from core software development, but this tends to be rarer for the simple reason that coders tend to like to stay coders.
2. **Consulting.** Former consultants, particularly from top firms like McKinsey, Bain, and Boston Consulting Group (BCG), can make excellent producers. They may lack the gaming industry background, but they have acquired another useful set of skills in their prior jobs. Their jobs developed their analytical approach to problem solving, while also requiring them to interface with a diversity of people and to react quickly to issues.

If your resume lacks both of these positions but you dream of being a producer, don't fret. "Other metric- and data-driven roles, such as online advertising, can also be a natural fit," says Alessandra from VonChurch.

Art

Artists tend to come from traditional art backgrounds, sometimes directly hired from art institutes. Candidates should expect to supply a portfolio and are strongly encouraged to have this posted on their website.

Hiring can be extremely subjective. It's not always about who draws the best, but rather who draws the best for the team. Understanding what style of art your dream company uses may help you prove yourself. "If the team doesn't like the way that you draw a dragon tail, even if it's an amazing drawing, then you won't get hired," Jeff from VonChurch explains.

Artists who can write a bit of code are always in hot demand as well. The automation skills can come in handy for mock-ups and other tasks.

Design

As the name suggests, designers create the concept, story line, and rules of a game. The role can be broken down into a variety of subdisciplines, including world design, game writing, and level design. Once the core game components have been decided, some designers may double as engineers.

Designers are not necessarily expected to have an artistic background, but they are expected to be highly creative. Recruiters typically want people with some sort of development background, even if they won't be full-time coders. Many schools offer courses or programs in game design, from which companies recruit designers.

Other Roles

Though development, production, art, and design may handle game creation, a number of other key support roles exist. The following are some of the most popular:

- **Quality assurance.** QA can be broken down into three types: functional testing, certification testing, and automation testing. While automation testers usually need a computer science degree from a four-year university, the other two testing positions may require only a two-year degree. Testers need to have a high attention to detail, and testers-to-be should find a way to highlight this on their resumes. (*Note:* This would be an extremely bad time to make a spelling or grammar mistake.) Testers should understand the different permutations of a sequence of steps and should understand which ones to focus on in developing test cases. An understanding of software can be handy here. QA tends to be faced with high turnover, as it's a relatively easy way into a gaming firm but is a nice avenue to other roles.
- **Customer support.** Requirements for a customer support agent tend to be less focused on academic or professional qualifications and more focused on one's inherent skills. A college degree may not be necessary at many companies, but candidates should have excellent verbal and written communication skills and a high attention to detail.

Fluency in multiple languages is also highly desirable. Audra Aulabaugh from Big Fish Games advises candidates to see customer service roles as a way into a company: "We don't look for people to stay in this position forever. Come in, learn everything there is to know about our customer and our product, and then investigate other roles within the organization that are of long-term interest." A customer support agent can move on to roles like QA, partner relationships, and associate producer.

- **Marketing.** Marketing hires are divided across several disciplines requiring very different backgrounds. In-game marketers need to understand virality: how do games spread? What makes them popular? Successful candidates often have a quantitative background. Business development marketers build the partnerships that make games successful, and candidates often need an MBA to be considered for these positions. A background in mobile or online marketing is also useful.

College Candidates

If you love gaming and you're in college, don't assume that you can't break in so young. It is a competitive field, but college candidates are often prized. Many gaming companies have younger people as their target users, making college students and recent grads highly desirable.

Don't Be Afraid of Entering Low

Customer support may not be the most glamorous use of your economics degree, but it's a great way to break into a fast-growing company. Or an English major might consider entering as a copywriter, with hopes of transitioning later to a marketing role. Financially and professionally, the company can matter more than the position.

In fact, recent college graduates can do very well at a social gaming company. "New grads can be great in positions close to the user, since they're much closer in age to the target market than more experienced employees," Alessandra from VonChurch explains.

Joining a gaming company at any level will offer insight into the industry and help you establish contacts in the field. Then, when you want to move up to a new role, you'll have the credibility and relationships to do so.

Find Your Niche

While grads excited about gaming should join a company at any level they can get, they should try to develop a specialty as soon as possible. Jeff from VonChurch reminds candidates that "they shouldn't get stuck in a less than ideal position for too long. Use the low entry point to explore positions, find a position you want to transition to, and do it."

Those who develop specialties will fare better in the long run as well. "It's about self-branding," Jeff says. "You build a name for yourself, and companies want to hire you for your specialty. It doesn't mean that you can't switch later, but people do tend to stay in their niche."

Create a Portfolio Website

While almost everyone could benefit from a portfolio website, this is especially important for artists and developers. Your portfolio website should list your resume and projects you've done (including screen shots). A good portfolio will get your foot in the door, even without company experience.

Your resume should also provide a link to your portfolio website, and you should expect companies to check it.

Get Out There

Finally, because many smaller shops lack full college recruiting operations, it's especially important for such candidates to start building their names as soon as possible. Start networking. Join relevant Facebook and Meetup .com groups, and attend their sessions. Get an internship or take a part-time job. If you can't find a job for whatever reason, spend some time on your own, hacking together games.

Reaching Out and Getting In

"The best way in is if you have a contact," Jeff from VonChurch says simply. While this is true of any technology company, it is especially true of smaller gaming companies. Software companies like Microsoft, Google, and Facebook can afford to scatter large masses of recruiters across the country to attend career fairs and meet candidates locally; the comparatively small casual gaming companies usually cannot. The three avenues that tend to be the most effective for establishing the personal connections that are critical to landing your job are college and professional recruiting, online networks, and events.

College and Professional Recruiting

Some larger companies may do some college recruiting, especially at the top universities. Even if you don't attend one of these universities, you may be able to pop over to one for a career fair. Just because a company doesn't recruit at your school doesn't mean it's unwilling to consider you; it may just mean that the company lacks the resources to recruit everywhere.

Alternatively, candidates with a bit of professional experience can consider working with a professional recruiting firm. As many gaming companies are small, this can be a great way to discover opportunities that may have otherwise escaped your notice.

Online Networks

LinkedIn's discussion groups are a great avenue for recruiting, but Facebook should not be overlooked, either. Many, if not all, of the companies you're aiming for are social gaming companies that leverage the Facebook platform in various ways. Becoming active in Facebook discussion groups about games or on a company's own page is a good way to get noticed. Rather than just asking for a job, consider first proving your worth. Offering insight and feedback will put you a step in front of all the other candidates banging at the door.

Similarly, become active in game developers' websites and forums. If you are known as a person who helps others, you'll be seen as smart, skilled, and the kind of teammate everyone wants. Recruiters scour these forums for great candidates.

Events

Attending events in person can be one of the most effective ways to network. Recruiters will be able to see how you communicate and act, and to put a face to a name.

The Game Developers Conference is a great chance for you to learn about the industry, and perhaps an even better opportunity for you to network. Recruiters flood the conference, as it acts as a huge recruiting event. Come with your pitch and business card ready. The registration fee is hefty, but college students can get access at a significantly reduced rate.

Additionally, if you follow companies on Facebook and Twitter, you may discover that they are hosting upcoming open houses, mixers, and happy hours. These events can be a great way to learn more about the company, meet current employees, or even network with attendees who work for other gaming companies.

Personality Fit

Geeks everywhere will be thrilled to hear that their personality doesn't matter—too much. As long as you're not arrogant and teammates wouldn't despise you, you're probably good enough on the personality front. However, while sociability is not required, "any engineer that that can carry on a conversation will be in high demand," says Katy Haddix, a recruiter at VonChurch.

For other positions, a strong personality fit is much more critical. These positions require more interfacing with coworkers, partners, and users. And, unlike for development positions, companies can afford to focus on the personality fit. The following five personality traits are some of the most universal requirements that interviewers will attempt to evaluate.

Some other traits, such as honesty and adaptability, are equally important but more challenging for an interviewer to assess. Demonstrating that you lack either of those, however, can certainly bar you from an offer.

Young at Heart

"You're working with teenagers," VonChurch recruiter Jeff says. "Sure, they may be technically 40 years old, but they're still teenagers."

Indeed, the casual gaming industry is young, in terms of the trade itself as well as the employees. This youthfulness gives it a high-energy, let's-go-grab-a-drink environment.

Additionally, Audra Aulabaugh from Big Fish Games adds, "The output is casual games. We want people who like to have fun because they're the ones who'll be able to build something really fun." Your suit-and-tie employee won't cut it there.

Console gaming companies are a bit more aged, but still cling to the young-at-heart culture.

Likable

Employees at casual game companies work unusually closely with each other to push out their nearly monthly releases, and a so-called bad apple can be poisonous to a team environment. On top of this, you're often working long hours, and when you're not, you're going to the bar, happy hours, and the like. It's critical that you get along with your colleagues.

Confidence is good, but you need to check your ego at the door. There is nothing worse than a teammate who can't wait to tell you how superior he is. We've all met the type.

Creative/Imaginative

Even in roles that don't require an artistic flair, employees tend to be more creative and imaginative. This is reflected in everything from how they solve problems to their stereotypical love for fantasy and science fiction. Gaming companies will want to know that you arc imaginative, as it's creativity that fuels their games.

Work Ethic

It's nice to be able to regurgitate the old line "It doesn't matter how many hours you work, as long as you get your work done," but the problem is that the work is never really done. Gaming companies require that you have the work ethic to put in these extra hours.

For this reason, a passion and drive for gaming and for the specific company are critical. You need to be willing to commit that time.

Strong Communication Skills

Cross-functional collaboration in order to push out a game rapidly is critical, forcing companies to stress strong communication skills. Interviewers want to see that you can explain and defend a position clearly, while also listening to and understanding another person's perspective. They may not ask as pointed questions to assess your communication skills as they might your technical skills, but you can bet they'll be evaluating your communication skills in every response. This is especially true if you want to move into a lead or management role.

The Gaming Interview—Three Tips to Doing Well

While all the standard interview advice (be concise, create questions to ask, etc.) applies equally to gaming interview advice, some advice is more specific to this field. The following three tips are especially important in gaming interviews, though they may be more broadly applicable as well.

1. Play the Game

Perhaps the best part of interviewing with a gaming company—other than getting a crack at playing a giant version of the flagship games—is that your interview preparation is playing games. After all, you have to research any company before your interview. What better way to do that than to play its games?

While playing these games, be sure to think about the following questions:

- What are you impressed by?
- What makes the game fun?
- What would you change in the next version?

In your answers to these questions, pay particular attention to anything that's relevant to your job title. An artist, for example, would want to think about why the art was created the way it was.

2. Show Confidence (but Not Too Much)

Because game companies move so fast, it's important that a candidate understand her skill set, and understand how it can be applied. "A candidate should be able to say 'I've done A, B, and C, and I know that I can do D,'" says Katy Haddix, a VonChurch recruiter. You need enough self-confidence to know that you can do something new, but not so much that you turn off your teammates.

3. Be Likable

Long hours make likability an essential trait, and even the least chatty person can apply a few tricks to make herself more sociable:

- **Smile.** Even if it's a phone interview, smiling will come through in your voice. In fact, not only does smiling make you appear happier, but it actually makes you happier.
- **Laugh.** Laughing suggests to your interviewer that you like to have a good time and are fun to be around. Pay attention to how your interviewer acts, though. If he's more serious, then perhaps you should follow his lead.
- **Be agreeable.** Being a complete pushover won't help you in your interview, but you don't want to be argumentative, either. You should assert your opinions while making an effort to listen to your interviewer. Stubborn candidates should make a special effort to keep that trait under wraps.

However, while likability and sociability are important, that's no excuse for being unprofessional. Off-color comments have no place in an interview.

Questions and Answers

Making the Jump

I've been a back-end server programmer at Microsoft for several years now, and have no background in gaming. I really, really want to move to a gaming company, though. Will my lack of experience in gaming hurt me? What can I do?

Sure, it'll hurt you, at least in the sense that all else being equal you'd fare better with some game programming experience. But you do have relevant skills, and you shouldn't forget that. Casual

(*continued*)

(*continued*)
gaming companies do require server-side coding, and that just happens to be your specialty. Don't overlook that.

However, you'd stand a better shot if you did two things:

1. Learn the necessary languages. When you're applying to a company, it will probably list a preference of languages. If not, you can probably track down some information online about what languages the company uses. Learn them.
2. Build a game. Set aside a weekend or two to write a game. You'll get resume-building experience, demonstrate a passion for games, and learn skills that will aid you in the interview. Provide a link or information on your resume that the company can use to track down a copy of your game.

And you might as well kill two birds with one stone—write the game in the language your top-choice company uses.

Value Added

I've been attending some events hosted by gaming companies in order to start developing a network there, but I find I'm never getting what I want out of the events.

The problem is that I don't know what to say to people. It feels awkward to pitch myself, so no one even ends up discovering who I am and what I'm interested in.

How can I make better use of my time?

If it helps, try not thinking about the events as networking events. Try just approaching them as an opportunity to learn—the networking aspect will come.

Prepare questions to ask people you meet in the industry. Stress that you don't know much about the industry but you're interested in learning. When applicable, react to the questions by sharing some of your own experiences:

You: What's the release cycle like at your company?
Them: We try to ship about every six to eight weeks, but there are often delays. If we don't feel that the user experience is quite right, we're not afraid of pushing it back.
You: Oh, interesting. I work for Adobe, and we'll usually try to cut features if it will help us meet a deadline. I guess your approach makes more sense for the gaming industry, since you don't have contracts with businesses for specific deadlines. Since you ship so frequently, though, how do you deal with software updates? Do you just not do them since the issues will be fixed in the next version?

As the conversation goes on, your companion will begin to learn about what you do, and may even ask you for a mini-bio.

To solidify this connection, create a reason to follow up with the person ("I'd love to ask you some more questions about the industry. Could I get your contact information?")—and follow through on this. Empty promises won't help you much.

It's the Little Things That Count

When gaming companies ask me why I want to work there, I never know what to say. It sounds so trite to say something like "Because I love games."

What makes a good response to this question?

Your first answer actually isn't bad. Loving games is really important. You need to prove this, though.

The key is in the details, but let's take a step back first. Why do companies ask this question?

There are two primary reasons: (1) they want to see if you've done your research, and (2) they want to know that you're interested and committed. Your job, therefore, is to give an answer that communicates both of those things.

(*continued*)

(*continued*)

Let's look at your answer from that perspective. Does it show that you've done your research? Not at all. Does it show that you're interested and committed? Somewhat, but not much more so than the fact that you showed up.

So what would make a good answer? Something like this:

> I've always valued my creativity, so gaming is a natural fit for my creative side as well as my drive to build cool things. I'm specifically excited about your company because I love its approach to fusing learning opportunities with fun. I saw a really interesting TED talk given by your CEO about the impact that engagement has in children's learning, and that really rang true for me.

A great answer here is about showing both passion, research, and relevant skills.

14 Women in Tech

I've mostly avoided talking in the first person for this book because career and interview advice typically isn't personal. It's abstract, somewhat objective: resumes should be concise, you should prepare a solid pitch for your interview, and so on. I haven't made this book about me, because it's not about *me*.

This chapter will be a stark contrast to the rest of the book. I can't possibly talk about being a woman in tech without acknowledging that this group includes me. The advice and the stories are those that I've experienced, both firsthand and through those who have confided in me.

Any view on this topic tends to make tempers flare. There are many questions, but no easy answers. Any anecdote can be countered by another anecdote, and any story has an alternate interpretation.

I wade into this topic reluctantly and out of obligation to give solid advice. I will do my best to offer fair and balanced advice—presenting the other side when possible—but I encourage you to scrutinize my advice for what rings true to you. There is no "one size fits all" answer.

On Men and Allies

Before talking about being a woman in tech, I want to say a few things to my male readers.

First, while this chapter is "for" women, I encourage men to read it, too. You have female coworkers, managers, and direct reports. Deeper insight into their experiences is valuable—and some of the advice applies to men, too.

Second, nothing in this chapter should be construed as being anti-male, particularly the parts about sexism. The majority of men are extremely supportive of women in tech, with only a few who are not (consciously or subconsciously). The same could be said of women, though; women can also propagate sexism against women (and against men).

Third, I understand how difficult many men find having discussions about gender to be. You feel you're walking into a minefield and that it's easier to just avoid the topic entirely. I get that. But for those who wish to be allies—to be supportive of the challenges that people face, whether gender-based or not—your support is deeply appreciated and commendable.

The Harsh(ish) Reality of Being a Woman in Tech

Tech is a male-dominated industry. Women represent anywhere from 10 percent to 25 percent of the workforce, depending on the company and exact definition of "tech." While most positions (especially the most technical ones, such as software development) are male dominated, a few are female dominated.

The unfortunate but logical result of this is stereotyping. Despite the fact that there are probably more female engineers than female recruiters (since there are so many more engineers than recruiters overall), many people will be more surprised to learn that a woman is an engineer than that she is a recruiter.

However, there is relatively little flat-out rejection of a woman's ability to succeed in technology. Many younger women can recount a single instance of clear discrimination—losing a job, missing out on a promotion, or facing a substantial limitation at work. Older women can typically recount several more, as a result of their age (ageism is a related issue) and of simply having been in tech in an earlier time period. Things are changing, for the better.

But gender-based issues (including prejudice) are still an everyday reality. I talked to a number of women about the experiences they've had that are unique to women, whether those experiences are positive or negative. Many of the stories were along the following themes:

- **Standing out.** Some expressed concern about attending certain events or competitions because they will stand out too much. If they fail, they will fail very publicly. (However, the same people also noted that standing out can be a positive.)

- **Recognition for being a woman.** Some told stories of winning awards and being asked about what it's like to be a woman in tech, whereas the male award winners were asked about relevant accomplishments.
- **Competitiveness between women.** Some expressed frustration that some female coworkers seemed ultracompetitive with them, as though only one woman could win.
- **"You got that job only because you're a girl."** Many—most, in fact—have had close friends tell them, "You got that job only because you're a girl."
- **Self-doubt.** Some women acknowledged that they constantly doubted their own accomplishments. *Did* they get that job only because they were female?
- **Working harder.** Some explained that they felt they needed to work extra hard to demonstrate that they were technical, and that tech conferences could be exhausting for that reason.
- **Representing all women.** Some women expressed concern that any of their failures would be seen as representative of all women.
- **Hiding femininity.** Many expressed that they need to hide their femininity (interest in fashion, wearing makeup, wanting children, etc.) so as not to be lumped in with negative female stereotypes.
- **Locker room behavior.** Whether right or wrong, some guys will continue locker room behavior at work—sexual jokes, openly insulting each other, and so on. This behavior is often particularly pronounced in tech because the teams are younger. Tech practically prides itself on not being serious and corporate. The youthful culture can translate to a lack of professionalism.
- **Blunt feedback.** Some women described being caught off guard by brutally honest feedback. They were used to feedback being softened, and thus they would read more into the criticism than was really there. When feedback suddenly got brutally honest, they continued to read something worse. They adjusted, but it stung at first.
- **Alertness to sexual advances.** Some confided that they felt they needed to be on guard for coworkers expressing an interest, and that they struggled most with the ambiguity. When that teammate invited them out on Saturday to see a movie, was it platonic or not?
- **Being labeled as aggressive.** Some women struggled with the gray area between being a pushover and being aggressive. Men can be both, too, but were the women being unfairly labeled as one or the other because of their gender?
- **Presumed to be a "womanly" job function.** Many women working in nonstereotypical job functions felt they were frequently pegged as being in a more commonly female role, such as recruiting.

If these women were staffing conference booths, some people assumed they were so-called booth babes.

This list looks long, but remember that no one cited all of these issues. This is just an overview of the types of challenges women mentioned facing.

At the same time, all women I spoke with were careful to say that, while they faced some disadvantages because of being female, they still loved being in tech. Being female even had its perks, they said. They talked about having special programs (scholarships, clubs, etc.) open only to women. Many felt that they were able to access additional mentorship opportunities and that senior women were often especially open to helping them. While they were frustrated sometimes at always standing out for their gender, it was easier for them to be known within their industry or company.

It should also be noted that this is only a broad generalization. Few people would say that they face all of these issues, and some would say that they face none.

Variation Across the Industry

Anecdotally, many women felt that gender-related issues were more pronounced as they got more experience. They admitted, though, that it was difficult to tell whether it was a result of advancing in their career or it was that they just became more attuned to the subtleties.

"In college and for the next few years, I brushed off the so-called sexism in tech stories," Heather explains. "Such conversations bugged me because I felt they made women look weak. I thought these issues were wildly overblown. Now, 10 years into my tech career, I've had a change of heart. Some of it is exaggerated still, but there's a lot of truth to it."

Many other women I spoke with felt that the big tech companies (Google, Microsoft, Facebook, etc.) tended to be comparatively insulated from sexism. But when they explored start-ups or left Silicon Valley, it became more pronounced.

Advice for Women from Women (and Allies)

Whether or not women face *more* challenges than men, one's gender certainly impacts one's experience. If nothing else, women typically face a relative lack of higher-ups and coworkers of the same gender. This leads to some special advice for women.

Mentors and Support Networks

Mentors are valuable for most people, and women will often benefit from a female mentor. The challenges or questions you face might have been faced by her, or at least someone close to her.

Look for someone you can identify with, too.

Ann from Microsoft recalls, "I got re-orged to a team that was mostly men, so I asked my manager to find me a woman-mentor who was senior, seen as a leader, effective, a good collaborator but who specifically wasn't bitchy. I wanted someone I could get good career and PM-specific advice from but who was also not afraid to be a girl and girl-talk over coffee with me a bit as well. She was great and she recommended great training for me to take to help be a better PM."

Ann's mentor had the personal traits she aspired to have, and was also someone whom she felt comfortable confiding in. This sort of support network is invaluable.

Your support network is broader than this, though. If you find yourself facing gender-related challenges (which, again, not all women do), surround yourself with supportive women *and men* who will listen without judgment.

Look for people in more senior positions, too. Not only will they be in a better position to help you, but they've also been around longer and seen more.

You can build this network through formal mentorship relationships, through networking events, or through your social network.

It's Okay to Be You

It's tempting to want to mirror the behavior of your male colleagues by being extra assertive, by hiding your interest in stereotypically female things, and by shunning behaviors that seem "girly." Advice on this is mixed, though.

On one hand, in certain professions, women can be stereotyped as less technical and less competent, and this stereotype can be especially strong for women who come off as ultrafeminine. Some women have found more success by masking, to a small or large extent, attributes that make them seem "girly." They say it helps them disassociate themselves from negative female stereotypes and to be accepted as "one of the guys."

However, just as many women argue the opposite. They caution that some women go too far—being extra assertive in order to "act like a guy," and end up being just rude. You might also lack the authenticity and vulnerability that helps people connect with you, and draw a particularly large wedge between you and other women.

There is no easy answer here. Be aware of the arguments on both sides, and do what feels right to you.

It Has a Name: Imposter Syndrome

Have you ever had that feeling that you're a fraud? That people who recognize you as an expert will soon figure out you've just been lucky? That you really aren't that good?

This is called "imposter syndrome," and it's incredibly common, especially among women. The first step to dealing with it is to recognize that *feeling* like you're not good enough doesn't mean that you *are* not good enough. Most people feel this way.

Fight the Battles You Want

While some women duck from conflict and avoid speaking up about each inequity, others do the opposite. They fight each issue because they feel like they *must.*

"When I first joined the tech industry," Cindy explains, "I spoke up whenever there was an issue. I don't regret this, especially since I was often doing so to support other women and minorities. But it was exhausting and it actually strained my relationships with coworkers. I think it even made it harder to fight the issues that did really matter."

It's admirable to fight for what's right, particularly when you're trying to help others, but it's also okay to let some issues go. It's a personal choice.

Ask for Help

It's okay to ask for help and it's okay to ask for more help. "I don't ask for help, because I don't want people to assume I can't do it." Does that sound familiar?

Asking for help is valuable. It's how you learn. You can ask for help too much, of course, but many people ask for too little help for fear of being "exposed."

Ask for More

There is a lot of debate around the pay gap—is there one and is it significant?—but what we do know is that women are statistically less likely to negotiate. This issue is complicated, since many studies suggest that women are perceived more negatively than men are when they do negotiate.

If you're inclined to just accept the offer you're granted, double-check this inclination. Are you sure it's not worth it to ask for more?

If you're concerned about the potential backlash from negotiating, you can take a more subtle approach. Explain that you need time to think the offer over because the salary was a bit lower than you were expecting. This avoids the direct confrontation from asking for more, while still encouraging the company to bump up their offer.

Negotiating goes beyond just offers though. You should ask for better projects, bigger responsibilities, and more visibility. This is how you advance your career.

Find the Right Culture

Cultures vary across teams, and you'll perform best in a culture that matches your style.

"My first team wasn't a good match for me," Jessica told me. "I got along fine with my teammates, so it wasn't that. The culture didn't fit with my personality. The team got drinks regularly together and, honestly, that's not what I wanted. I value the separation between work and personal life."

Jessica switched to a team that didn't push what she felt was an overly chummy culture. Because everyone was keeping working relationships strictly professional, she didn't feel as disconnected from her team.

"If you don't feel you mesh well with your team, find one you will mesh with," she advised. "You don't have to fight to fix something that's not right. You can just find the one that fits you the best."

Leverage the Positive

Being in tech, you will likely be surrounded by negative articles about the challenges that women face. Even if you don't personally experience these challenges, hearing about them so much can be disheartening.

Focus on the positives. There are a lot of wonderful things about being in tech. It's a growing industry. There are a ton of opportunities. It's changing relatively quickly. It values smart and competent people.

There are advantages to being female as well, and you can leverage these. This doesn't mean that you should try to leverage sex appeal—that would be very inappropriate and likely counterproductive. But you can use what you have.

Vulnerability helps people connect with you, and many women feel more comfortable exposing emotional vulnerability. This might be something you can use to your advantage.

Women have special mentorship and networking opportunities. Take part in these.

People often assume that women have better communication skills. Hone this skill. You might find that you're perceived as more well-rounded than your male colleagues.

You stand out, purely for your gender. It can be easier to be known, as a result.

It's Friction, Not Obstacles

The issues surrounding gender in technology are incredibly complex. If you're like most women in tech (and maybe you're not!), you'll get roped into debates about how to get more women into tech. You'll hear frequent "benign" sexist comments. You'll face the occasional overly sexist situation.

For the most part, though, being female in tech adds friction in encounters as opposed to direct obstacles. This friction is surmountable—and there's even the occasional time when it facilitates something good.

There are no easy answers to how to handle any of this stuff, but remember that most of it isn't about you. You don't need to be a "woman in tech"—you can just be a person in tech who happens to be a woman. You can fight it when you want to, and you can also ignore it.

Do the best that you can with the situation in front of you. Focus on that—and on helping the other women (and men) around you.

Questions and Answers

Misleading Information

> ***As a woman, I want to work in a company that's supportive of women (obviously). Unfortunately, every company I've looked at has an abysmal gender ratio. How do I know if a company is receptive to women?***

This is a really difficult thing to assess. Companies can say one thing but actually do another. This is especially true since a single obnoxious or hostile person can turn your whole work experience negative. (Of course, this can be true for everyone, not just women.)

The gender ratio is one clue to a company's support of women, but it can also be very misleading. One company might recruit fewer women just because of the type of product it creates. This doesn't mean that the company is less receptive to women.

Instead, I would look at senior leadership and your direct management chain. Are there are lot of women represented there, or not many?

You can also have a conversation with future teammates and HR to understand what the company does to support women. What you're looking for here is not just *what* they say but also how they react to your broaching the subject. If this is a difficult conversation for them to have or if they can't offer something concrete, then they might not make this an active priority. That could be an issue for you.

Maternity Leave

> ***I'd like to enter tech, but I'm increasingly thinking that now isn't the best time. I plan to start a family soon. Would I be better off waiting until my children are older? I don't know if it would be good to start a job and need to take time off shortly thereafter. I'm also not sure if I can handle the longer hours while also juggling family responsibilities.***

Go for it now. I see no reason to wait.

In part because they are struggling to recruit women, tech companies tend to have pretty generous maternity leave policies (and decent paternity leave as well). Some companies, like Facebook and Google, offer four or more months fully paid. Tech is actually a great place to be.

The hours aren't so bad, either. Some people will complain about the long hours, but that's mostly an exaggeration. The hours in tech are pretty reasonable compared to other highly paid industries, such as finance.

If you're deeply worried about the time commitment, though, you can stick to bigger companies or at least larger start-ups. Some smaller start-ups can have intense hours, but they're typically pretty open about this.

15 The Offer

You've done it. You've poured years into your studies and your career, and potentially weeks or months into preparing for the interview. It's all culminated into this moment, when HR calls you and tells you that you have received an offer.

That's amazing. Congratulations!

But, before you whip out your pen to sign the offer, stop and consider. Is this what you want? Can you do better?

How to Evaluate an Offer

Offers are complex. They include a salary, bonus, raises, vacation days, health care, and so on—and that's just the financial side. You also must consider your career direction, the company culture, your future teammates, and potentially even the feelings of a spouse or significant other. Then, to really muddy the waters, you rarely have all the information. How many hours will you be working? What are annual raises like? Even if you get answers to these questions, you can't really be sure that you're getting the unvarnished truth.

The complexities of an offer usually can be broken down into the following categories:

- **Career development.** Is this the right decision for your career? Will the job look good on your resume? Will it help you progress in your career?
- **Financial package.** How much are they paying you? What are the perks (health care, stock, etc.) worth?

- **Happiness.** Will you enjoy the job? Will you get along with your teammates? Is the location where you want to live?

Some applicants wind up debating the first two so much that they forget about the happiness factor. Happiness matters—not only to your well-being, but also to your financial and career success.

Your Career Development

New candidate, same story:

> I accepted a job with [Insert Company Name Here] and I thought it was a great opportunity. And it was! At first, anyway. But then, five years later, I was still at the same job, and I couldn't help but think—where had the prior year gotten me? I could have done something new or different, but instead I stayed at my job doing the same old stuff.

Technology companies are filled with people like this. They can be such great places to work that you lose sight of where you're going—and it's even easier to not want to jump ship. That's why it's important to assess, prior to accepting a job, if it offers what you want in terms of career development.

Talk to your future coworkers, your peers at other companies, and your future manager to assess

- What are the typical "next steps" for people in your role?
- How long do people typically stay in your role before moving on to something new?
- Can you transition to other roles within the company? What is the process to do that?
- Can you transition to other teams within the company? What is the process to do that?
- What are the skills that make people successful at your job? What are the skills that make them *exceptional?*

It's very valuable to talk to people outside of the company, as well as within the company. These conversations will allow you to see a contrast between what this company excels in and what other companies excel in.

As much as possible, push for concrete examples. Ask them to tell you about the people they know who were successful. What made those individuals so successful? Getting specific examples will push people to actually think about what really worked, rather than regurgitating the same stories about success. Concrete examples will also be more memorable to you.

Learning and Development

Many companies have some sort of continuing education or tuition reimbursement program, but the kind of learning and development we're talking about here is much deeper.

- **What is the process for onboarding new employees?** Many companies have new employee education programs. Google, for example, has "noogler" training, which teaches employees in many roles about the basics of their role. Facebook sends its developers (and sometimes other roles) through a six-week boot camp. Programs like these demonstrate a commitment to employee development.
- **How easy is it to switch roles or teams?** Employees tend to learn the most within their first year on the job. If the company is supportive of switching teams or roles, then you will often learn a lot more. Discover what the process is for switching roles (do you need to interview or not?) and what's considered a reasonable length of time to stay on a team.
- **How much exposure do you have to other roles and to more senior people?** People in more senior roles and in other functions have a wealth of knowledge to learn from. Working closely with them will help you improve your own skill set.

Tuition reimbursement and continuing education programs can be useful as well. However, realistically, few employees take advantage of these offers.

Responsibilities and Decision Making

As valuable as formal education is, you usually learn the most by doing. A position where you are given substantial responsibilities and are given the freedom to make mistakes will enable you to learn more powerful and relevant lessons.

In Peter's first two years as a software engineer at Google, he was given the opportunity to manage an intern, prepare design documents for key features, participate in planning and strategy discussions, and help shape the direction of the team. And all this was in addition to his regular responsibilities as a coder. When he left Google to join a start-up, he had no problems getting interviews for software engineering or program management positions. He had developed not only the technical skills necessary, but also the communication and planning skills.

To position yourself in the best possible way, look for teams that will give you responsibilities beyond your actual job description, and even beyond your level of responsibility. If you want to be a manager one day, find teams that will let you mentor or manage someone—even if it's just an intern. If you want to move from testing to development, find a position that will let you write code automation and do periodic bug fixes.

Additionally, you should make sure you understand how decisions get made. Many companies love to say, "Oh, we make them as a team," but that's rarely the case. Who drives the decision? What happens when there's conflict? What decisions will you be responsible for, and what decisions do you merely offer feedback on?

Promotions

While stability has its benefits, a company that's growing tends to offer the most opportunity for promotions. Growing companies mean rapid changes and new roles. Someone has to step into a senior role, and that might be you. It also means that, in a small amount of time, you are considered one of the more experienced employees.

Additionally, you'll want to consider *how* people are selected for promotions. A company that tends to promote from within will usually have more opportunities for advancement.

Resume and Prestige

For better or for worse, having a big name on your resume opens doors. It may not be the place where you would learn the most or have the most responsibilities (though it might be), but it offers credibility that you won't get at a lesser known firm. It's a stamp on your resume that says, "I am at least this good."

Therefore, in considering an offer, be sure to analyze

- **Company brand name.** How well known is the company? Remember that brand names are not universal. A company can have a strong brand within your field but not outside of your field, and vice versa. For example, working at the best advertising firm in the world may not help your resume stand out when it's being reviewed by recruiters unfamiliar with advertising.

- **Position and title.** Some companies inflate titles, some companies deflate them, and others give titles that just aren't quite descriptive or appropriate. I've talked to a number of candidates from smaller companies who were officially testers, but they actually spent their day writing production-level code. They can partially recover from this issue by listing both an official and unofficial title on their resume, but they certainly would have been better off had they been listed as developers from the start.

This does not mean that going to a big name is always the right thing to do. The credibility is merely an advantage; it could be offset by other disadvantages of a more mature company.

Company's Future and Stability

Candidates frequently ask me questions like, "Is Microsoft stable? Will they do layoffs again?" I always respond with this question: "Well, what if they do?" I find that most candidates overemphasize the stability of a company.

If you find yourself trying to analyze the stability of a company, ask yourself what the (realistic) worst case is. You probably won't find yourself unable to find a job, kicked out of your apartment, and sitting on the streets of San Francisco with a sign saying, "Will Code for Food." More likely, you'll walk out with a few months of severance pay and you'll find a new job before you've even used that up.

That said, job stability may be quite important in certain cases. If you require a visa or hope to apply for a green card, layoffs could disrupt this process. Alternatively, if you have very specific skills or requirements in a job, finding a new job that is a good match could prove challenging. Only you can decide how much of a disruption layoffs could pose to your lifestyle.

Location

Just as many candidates focus too much on stability, they often focus too little on location. Location matters for your happiness but also for your career growth.

In an ideal world, you'd want to select a location where you have room to grow at the company as well as where there are many opportunities externally.

- **Internal opportunities.** Being at a remote office for a company can often limit your opportunities, particularly if you are not a software developer. Most of the opportunities will be at the headquarters. You will also typically have fewer connections and relationships within the company, and that can limit your growth.
- **External opportunities.** Even if the company has lots of opportunities within your location, someday you'll probably want to look outside the company. The more options in your city the better.

San Francisco is by far the biggest tech hub, but there are other options. Seattle, New York, Austin, and Boston also have some small and large tech companies. However, in moving to one of these secondary tech hubs, you will still have fewer options and might find yourself pulled out to the San Francisco area eventually.

The Financial Package

Only you can decide the importance of money, but there are some general guidelines to consider about the financial implications behind an offer.

- **Divide one-time bonuses by number of years.** It's easy to get influenced by a big, fat signing bonus or stock grant, so you should instead thinking about one-time bonuses as being distributed by the number of years you expect to stay at a company. For example, if you expect to stay at a company for three years, then a $100,000 stock grant is roughly equivalent to $33,000 additional in salary. Thinking about bonuses this way will help you make a more direct comparison across offers.
- **Evaluate raises and other bonuses.** Raises and bonuses can vary substantially from company to company. Hopefully, your recruiter can tell you what a typical bonus and raise looks like, but if you can also obtain this information from employees, that's useful, too.
- **Adjust for location.** If all you care about is money, should you take a $90,000 offer from Amazon or a $115,000 offer from Twitter? Assuming these offers are from the headquarters, you're likely better off with the $90,000 offer from Amazon in Seattle. Seattle isn't cheap, but San Francisco is really expensive—after taxes and rent are considered.

Additionally, remember that the long-term career prospects of a job may make a bigger financial difference than any differences in salaries across offers. If a job pays well, but isn't a great career move, it will probably ultimately hurt you financially.

Evaluating Stock Compensation

With stock options, it's not the number of options that counts, but rather the percent of total shares. Therefore, you need to know the number of options you have *and* the total number of shares in the company (called the number of outstanding shares).

Note that the larger and older the number, the smaller your percentage ownership will be. Your potential upside should be *highest* when your risk is highest, which occurs as a newer company. Naturally, at a more stable company, your percent ownership will be smaller. This doesn't mean that you can't do very well with stock. Even people who joined Google and Facebook when the companies were well past their start-up days did quite well with stock.

If you join a start-up that goes through later rounds of funding, you might find your shares diluted. This means that the start-up offered additional shares to investors in exchange for money. If you imagine your percent ownership as an equation of (# your shares/# outstanding shares), the denominator just increased and therefore your percent decreased. Of course you would prefer to not be diluted, but this is normal and essentially unavoidable. Even the founders experience the same dilution.

Whether options or grants, stock compensation comes with a vesting period, usually of four years. A one-year cliff is typical, which means that 25 percent of the stock would vest at the one-year mark. If you leave after only 11 months, you would walk away with zero stock. After the one-year mark, your shares will usually vest evenly over each pay period.

The Happiness Factor

It's easy to look at a big, fat number in your offer letter and say, "Hey, I can stick it out a few years, right?" It's a lot harder to actually do that. Unhappy employees tend to work fewer hours, be less productive, and quit earlier.

The following factors are important to many people:

- **Manager.** Your relationship with your manager is a powerful influence on whether you enjoy your job. Make sure to have at least one conversation with your future manager and ask him questions like, what contributes to success at the company? What career paths have some of your prior employees taken? If possible, try to connect with these employees to discuss.
- **Teammates.** From credit stealers (people who take credit for other people's work) to outright nasty teammates, hostile coworkers are pervasive in many companies. They are almost always detrimental to your happiness—and why be miserable in a place where you spend half of your waking hours? Before accepting the offer, coordinate a time to grab lunch with your future team under the guise of asking questions. They don't need to know that you're actually evaluating them.
- **Culture and environment.** Every company loves to say that they just love to have fun or that they have a culture of innovation, but come on—those terms are relative and can't describe every company. Ask your future coworkers how they would describe the culture, and ask for examples of this. If people can't offer illustrative examples of the culture they describe, it's a good sign that they're just regurgitating the company line.
- **Hours.** Depending on your stage in life and your general priorities, you may or may not be okay with working long hours. Regardless, it's important to know what you're getting yourself into. Discuss with your manager and your teammates what time they usually arrive at work and leave, and in what situations they need to work nights and weekends. Is it just before a major release, or is it on a more regular basis?

Life is too short to have a job you hate. You'll be miserable, and it'll come back to bite you.

How Can You Negotiate an Offer?

You prepared thoroughly, you sweet-talked your way through resume blemishes, and you mastered all the hard balls they threw at you. Finally, the offer comes and your mouth drops; it's thousands of dollars lower than what you'd hoped for.

Or, perhaps you're actually quite thrilled with the offer, but you'd still like a bit more. Who wouldn't?

Should You Negotiate?

Perhaps the best thing you should know about negotiating is this: just do it.

Negotiating is a scary thing for many candidates. Some worry about the prospect of losing their job offer (which is extraordinarily unusual) and some worry about being perceived poorly, but most just don't like such direct confrontation. It's *easier* to just accept the offer if it's good enough.

Easier does not mean *better*, though. Typically, a company will at least throw you a little extra, just so that it doesn't have to tell you no. That extra $500 or $1,000 might not seem like much in comparison with a six-figure salary, but it's still a lot of money in absolute terms. Your time is probably not worth $500+ for a short conversation.

And that's the worst case. Often, a company will bump up your compensation by much more.

But What If the Company Hates Me for It?

If you're worried about a company having a grudge against you for negotiating, don't be. Few companies will hold it against you.

Richard, a recruiter for Facebook, tells you not to worry. "Once we've decided to hire you, we're going to do everything we can to do that. A little negotiating will not hurt you."

Plus, at a larger company, you'll usually be negotiating with the HR department. You will have little interaction with HR after being hired, so you shouldn't be too concerned with their feelings toward you. (Of course, this by no means excuses being rude!)

If you are concerned about this, Piaw Na, a salary consultant for tech hires, advises that you can approach negotiating more gently. "Explain to a company that you need sometime to consider their offer, as you are excited about the opportunity but it was a bit lower than some other offers. You're not directly asking for more money, but they will often respond by adjusting the offer."

What Can You Negotiate?

In theory, you can attempt to negotiate any part of an offer. Realistically, some aspects are much easier than others to negotiate. This is especially true as a company gets larger and more rigid with its policies.

- **Vacation time.** While many candidates want to negotiate this, it's usually quite difficult, particularly at a larger company. Additionally, even if you can, it might not be the wisest thing to fight for. What's the use of having four weeks of vacation if you, like many people, don't even use your full three weeks?
- **Stock.** If you're joining a fast-growing start-up, consider shooting for more stock options. Companies are often more flexible with this form of compensation as it's a powerful incentive to retain you later. Additionally, as new employee stock compensation must change with as the company grows, companies typically don't have rigid policies around this. Many candidates are able to double their stock compensation with just a bit of negotiating—something they could never have done with salary. If you get lucky, you can do very, very well on stock.
- **Salary.** There's usually a bit of wiggle room with salary, particularly as people get more experienced. Be aware that some companies, like Microsoft, have salary ranges that correspond to a particular level of employee. All Level 60 employees make essentially the same amount. In order to make bigger leaps in salary, you will need to prove that you should instead be slotted at a higher level. If this fails, you may need to fall back on getting a larger signing bonus or additional stock to compensate for the lower salary.

Sometimes it's not a matter of getting a better offer, but rather about getting an offer that's better for *you*. Many younger job seekers have found that they'd prefer to decline the "we pack and move your stuff for you" relocation package, and instead take a flat cash relocation bonus. It doesn't matter much to the company, but you walk away $5,000 richer.

Alternatively, you can also shift value between two items. For example, at a start-up, you could push to drop your salary a bit in exchange for substantially more equity.

Answering Questions about Your Current Salary

A recruiter might ask you about your current salary. Don't be alarmed if he does: he's not necessarily out to get you.

Often, a recruiter asks about your current salary because he wants to make sure that he's not wasting his time interviewing someone whose current salary is completely out of line with the company's range.

Imagine you have a financial analyst. That title can mean anything. If a financial analyst is making $60,000, she generally won't have the right experience for a $200,000 financial analyst job. The reverse is also true: someone making $200,000 is generally not open to a $60,000 job.

Rightly or wrongly, a salary can help a recruiter slot your experience and ensure that it's not a waste of time for either person.

If you get asked about your salary and you're worried it could cause them to peg you too low, you can try to dodge the question or decline to answer.

- "I'd prefer not to answer that if you don't mind. But it's my understanding that this job pays between $120,000 and $150,000. Is that in line with what you're thinking?"
- "Unfortunately I'm prohibited from disclosing it due to my company's NDA. But, I am comfortable with a range of $120,000 to $150,000."

If you get backed into a corner and need to answer the question, you have to shift your answer a bit to be higher or lower: give the *total* compensation not just your salary.

- If you're worried that your salary will peg you too low (causing a company to underpay you), then provide your total compensation: "My total compensation including stock, benefits and bonuses is $120,000."
- If you're worried that your salary will peg you too high (causing a company, such as a start-up with less cash, to think you're out of their reach), then explain that you're flexible: "My current salary is $90,000, but I'm open to a wider range depending on the stock versus salary compensation."

Do not try to argue that you're underpaid—or proceed carefully if you do. If your manager doesn't value you, that might make a recruiter wonder if you're really just underperforming.

Negotiating the Nonnegotiable

Sometimes, a recruiter might tell you that an offer is nonnegotiable. This can be just an unfortunate ploy to discourage you from negotiating. Many candidates have found success negotiating even in these cases.

If you wind up with an allegedly nonnegotiable offer, you can indirectly negotiate—or at least try.

> Hi Christine,
>
> I just wanted to reiterate my excitement about the opportunity at Dropbox. I'm sorry I haven't gotten back to you yet with a decision, but I am still thinking it through. The offer was a bit lower than some other offers I have (Google, for example, is offering me $120,000) and while Dropbox is my first choice, the salary difference makes this a difficult decision for me. I'll keep you informed, but if there does turn out to be any flexibility on the salary range, that would be very much appreciated.
>
> Thanks,
> Gayle

Technically, you haven't asked to negotiate. You're merely explaining the difficult position you're in. It's up to them to reconsider their inflexibility—and they just might.

How to Negotiate

Negotiating is scary to many candidates, but it's not so bad once you're actually in the midst of it. Take a deep breath, do your research, prepare for the discussion.

1. **Know your worth.** You need to know what you are worth. This can be established through your other offers, if you have any. If you don't, ask your friends. Figure out what other people are getting. You can also search online for stated salary ranges, but be aware that the data is often inaccurate.
2. **Have a viable alternative.** A company negotiates with you primarily because it feels it has to in order to get you to sign its offer. Therefore, the company essentially needs to worry that you won't take its offer. Ideally, your viable alternative is another offer, but it could even be starting your own company or staying at your current job.
3. **Compare the total package.** Money is fungible. It doesn't matter too much if it comes in the form of salary, stock, or a signing bonus. If a company isn't flexible with salary, it might have some flexibility on signing bonus or stock. You need to look at the total package to really understand it.
4. **Rehearse.** If negotiating is as scary to you as it is to most applicants, you'll want to rehearse. Figure out what exactly you'll say so that you're walking into the discussion calm and prepared.

5. **Ask.** Schedule a time with the recruiter to discuss the details of the offer. Remember that while the recruiter isn't totally on your side, she's also not your adversary. The recruiter wants to work with you to sign the offer. Treat her with respect and be relatively open about your concerns.

The complexity of offers is something you can leverage, too. If you're debating between Google and a start-up offer—Google is offering $10,000 more in salary, but the start-up offers a lot of equity—which is the better offer? It's a *personal choice.* That creates room for you to negotiate.

Tricky Issues: Deadlines, Extensions, and Declining Offers

How you communicate with your recruiter or manager is a sign of your professionalism. Are you cognizant of the time and effort they spend recruiting, or do you think that recruiting is all about you? By being open with your recruiter about your other pending offers and your feelings about the job, you can avoid catching her off guard. Recruiters just hate surprises—or at least they hate bad ones, anyway.

Deadlines and Extensions

If you're lucky, your recruiting time line will be lined up such that you'll receive all offers within a short time span. Most people aren't so lucky, though. Your deadline from one company might be days or weeks before another company will get back to you.

Unfortunately, companies need deadlines, too. They can't effectively interview candidates while holding open a position for you, nor do they want to drag out a decision for too long. Within reason, though, they will negotiate with you to extend the deadline.

If you need an extension, simply be up front with the recruiter. Explain to him why you need an extension, what your status is with other companies, and when you'll be able to have a decision ready.

> Hi Samantha,
>
> I noticed that you had given me a deadline for this offer of the 16th. I'm a bit concerned about my ability to meet that. While I'm very excited about Microsoft, I of course feel it's important to have all my

> options in front of me before making a decision. I'm sure you can understand that.
>
> I'm currently in the process of interviewing for Google, and I've asked my recruiting contact there to expedite the decision as much as possible. I will interview with Google on the 14th, and I hope to hear back by the 20th. I believe I'll be able to make a decision quickly thereafter.
>
> Could we push back the offer deadline until the 25th?
>
> Thank you,
> Gayle

Note that I didn't just say that I need an extension, but I also gave the recruiter my status with Google. The reason for this is that she may know much more about Google's process than I do. She may know, for example, that it's difficult for Google to make a decision within a week.

Likewise, I will communicate my status with Google:

> Hi Jason,
>
> I'm looking forward to meeting with your team on the 14th. I wanted to give you an update on my time line. I've just received an offer from Microsoft, with a request to respond by the 16th. I've asked to extend the deadline until the 25th, but if there's any way to expedite Google's process, that would be great.
>
> Thanks!
> Gayle

If the people at Google know the pressures you're under, they're much more likely to be able to accommodate your needs. In some cases, they might even move things around for you.

For example, one candidate, Lana, was flown directly out to Mountain View—bypassing the phone screen—after she informed Google she had an Amazon offer. The Amazon offer indicated to the Google recruiter that Lana was a relatively strong candidate, and the phone screen would just extend the process by another week.

Communicating openly with recruiters about your other offers will help these companies help you. It can also prove that you are a strong candidate and allow you at time to skip some earlier interviews.

In smaller companies or companies with very specific openings, extending a deadline substantially may be more difficult. Larger companies with many openings are more likely to be amendable to extensions.

Reneging

Reneging on offers is an explosive topic. Many people will vehemently argue that you should never, ever renege. They argue that it's not only unethical, but it will also hurt you in the end. The tech industry is not that big, people will find out what you did, and you will be forever banned.

While those points are reasonable, the experience of many candidates who have reneged shows a different story. None of these dire consequences actually happened. At most, the candidate was blacklisted from the company—and even that didn't always happen.

This is why my advice is a bit less rigid: consider the implications of reneging, but also consider the implications of *not* reneging. Typically, the consequences to *you* of passing up a substantially better career move exceed the consequences to a company of losing a soon-to-be employee. After all, large companies have employees quit every day. It's unfortunate and disappointing, but they manage.

This doesn't mean that it's okay to take an offer with the intention of reneging—even if the company is inflexible about their deadline. Think of it like agreeing to go to dinner with a friend while shopping around for better plans. That's not right. But if you agree to meet a friend and fully intend to do so, but you suddenly get tickets to see your favorite band, your friend should also understand—provided you handle the situation respectfully.

In fact, that's exactly what happened to me. Just before my last year of college, I interviewed for internship positions at Apple and IBM. Apple rejected me, so I accepted IBM's offer. I was just lukewarm toward IBM, but I didn't want to go back to Microsoft for a fourth summer, so I accepted IBM's offer. Three months later, Apple came back and offered me the position. Apparently, their number one candidate reneged, and I was number two.

Perhaps I should have turned it down and taken the high road, but I was just too excited about the position to do that. This was my dream offer. I took it.

My IBM recruiter was upset, but the company found a replacement—a student who apparently reneged on her offer with another company.

The guy who reneged on Apple (to go to Microsoft) took a much more honest approach: he told Apple about the Microsoft offer (which was apparently unusually high). Apple was actually *supportive* of him accepting the other offer because it recognized that this was the right thing for him.

Neither of us was blacklisted. Apple would have happily reinterviewed its first candidate the following year. Likewise, IBM tried to recruit me the following year. IBM either didn't know or didn't care that I had reneged.

Declining an Offer (and Building a Connection)

Turning down an offer does not mean severing contact; it should be viewed more as taking a rain check. Think of it this way: you liked the company enough to go through the full recruiting process, and the company liked you enough to give you an offer. This is a connection you definitely want to maintain.

You should turn down the offer in whatever medium you've been using for communication and with whomever you've been corresponding the most. That is, if the recruiter has been calling you regularly, you should decline the offer over the phone with him. Alternatively, if you've been e-mailing your manager the most, you should decline the offer first to the manager over e-mail. You should follow up these correspondences with short e-mails or phone calls to whoever else you've talked with frequently.

In your e-mail or phone call, use these tips to avoid burning bridges and to strengthen your relationship:

1. **Be polite and professional.** No matter how tense the prior negotiations have gotten, you should always address your recruiter in a nice and respectful way. Some people may be particularly upset about your declining the offer, after spending so much time and money on you, but don't let this bother you. Be open and understanding, but stand firm in your decision.
2. **Stay positive (and nonnegotiable).** Saying that the company is too bureaucratic is insulting, but saying that you would prefer a smaller company at this point in time is not. You should make sure that these reasons are not things the company could provide (such as a different location, if the company has only one location) or be prepared to reopen negotiations if it does. When declining over the phone, you should be prepared to say what offer you have accepted and why.
3. **Ask to stay in touch—and mean it.** Close your e-mail to the recruiter or manager with a note expressing a desire to stay in touch. You can follow up a day or two later with a LinkedIn connection. If you have friends or colleagues who might be interested in the position, ask the recruiter if he'd appreciate some referrals from strong candidates that you know. You'll probably be doing your

friend, and the recruiter, a favor. And it's a great way to stay in everyone's good graces!

4. **Reach out to everyone.** If you've been talking with multiple people, such as a recruiter and a hiring manager, inform everyone. Ideally you want the hiring manager to hear from you first, rather than being caught off guard by an e-mail from the recruiter saying that their offer was rejected. You might even queue up an e-mail to the hiring manager to send as soon as you get off the phone with the recruiter. If your primary point of contact has been the hiring manager, then inform him first and then e-mail your recruiter.

Declining an offer is an important step. You will likely be looking for another job within a few years. If you handle the situation well, you will have built valuable connections for your next job search.

Questions and Answers

Au Revoir, Vacation Days

I've been planning a three-week trip to Europe for over a year—dates set, flights booked, and so on. The issue is that I'm now applying for a new job and, if I get it, I'll be expected to start about six weeks before my trip. I obviously won't have built up enough vacation time by then to take this trip. How do I handle this?

The appropriate time to inform the company of your preplanned vacation is when you get the offer—not before, not after.

If you mention it before, you run the risk of the company's using this as an easy way to ding you in favor of another candidate.

If you mention this after you accept the offer, then you run the risk of the company's balking at your request and either refusing the vacation time or at the very least being nasty to you from day one.

Situations like this come up more than one might expect, and they're usually easily accommodated. Just before you accept, send your primary contact an e-mail explaining the situation as follows:

(*continued*)

(continued)

I'm really excited about joining your company.

Before I accept the offer, I do need to inform you of one potential complication. I've had a three-week trip to Europe (from DATE to DATE) planned for over a year. I recognize that this trip is at an inconvenient time—just six weeks after my proposed start date—but, unfortunately, the dates aren't flexible.

Is there some way to accommodate this? I'd be happy to do whatever you think is best—take unpaid time off, go negative on vacation days, and so on.

Thank you!

Most likely, the company will just have you go negative, and you'll have to be very conservative with vacation days to earn them back. Once you work things out with your primary contact and sign your offer letter, you should inform anyone else who needs to know. It would be an ugly surprise to your manager to discover this trip in your first few days.

In the event that the company refuses to accommodate your vacation time, you may be able to appeal to your secondary contact (if any).

Representative Representatives

People always say that you're interviewing the company just as much as the company's interviewing you, and that's where my question comes in.

I finished a full round of on-site interviews and enjoyed the experience as much as one could. The potential future coworkers seemed nice enough, smart enough, and so on. It was the HR people I didn't like.

My first phone screen was with a woman from HR whom I just didn't mesh with. She was basically reading off a script and seemed to barely register a lot of my responses. When she responded with anything other than an "okay," it was to argue with my answer. I guess I did well enough, though, to keep going.

When I came on-site, I met with a different person from HR—this time a man—and I again felt it was a somewhat hostile interaction. There was none of that friendliness that I'm used to seeing from recruiters. He talked with me for all of about 5 minutes when I came, and then made me sit in a chair outside his office for over 30 minutes until my first interviewer came to get me. When I asked him where I could get a drink of water, he actually seemed annoyed that I would disturb his precious time.

But it's a good job, and I liked my actual coworkers enough. Should I let this bother me?

I'd definitely look into the situation more. You have raised some valid red flags, but there are a few explanations.

1. You got unlucky. Maybe there are only two bad recruiters in the entire group of 30 recruiters, and you happened to get them.
2. It's symptomatic of a bad culture. You didn't say that you loved the people—just that they seemed fine. Maybe things really are bad under the hood.
3. The recruiters are too busy. The actions of both of your recruiters could be explained by a very understaffed HR department.
   - Reading off a script → tired
   - Not responding → preoccupied
   - Arguing → well, some arguing is okay
   - Making you wait for 30 minutes → busy

It could really be any of these, which means that you need to do some investigating.

Try to get to know your future team a bit better—join them for lunch or chat with them on the phone. Make sure to talk to multiple team members, as liking just one is far from representative. If you develop a particularly strong rapport with one, you could even delicately broach the subject. ("I've really enjoyed getting to know everyone here. I was a bit worried, to be honest,

(*continued*)

(*continued*)
because of some things that happened during the recruiting process, but I've had such positive interactions since then.") If they bite, then you could explain the situation. Stick to the facts and avoid blaming anyone.

Alternatively (or additionally), you could find some other sources. Check with your friends to see if anyone has a contact at the company. Or, if it's a big enough company, you might be able to find some information about the culture online. Remember, though, there's a vocal minority and it's usually negative. Take things with a grain of salt.

Big or Little

I need some career advice. I'm graduating from college, and I'm trying to decide between two offers. One is from my friend's start-up—I'd be employee number four—and the other is from Amazon. I keep going back and forth. What should I do?

Here is my humble advice: spend one year at Amazon, and then go to your friend's start-up—unless, of course, you think the start-up opportunity is a once-in-a-lifetime opportunity.

Let me explain.

Start-up opportunities will come by all the time. Trust me. Even if you have no interest in ever working at a start-up, you'll still have people banging on your door asking you to join them. You aren't giving up your chance to go to a start-up, you're just delaying it.

When you turn down Amazon's offer, you're giving up a lot. You're giving up the "you're good" nod people will give when they see your resume. You're giving up the opportunity to learn how real software development (with code reviews, style guidelines, and all that) works. And you're giving up the chance to get a freebie pass to quit a job after a short amount of time. No one will think it's funny that a college hire quit his Big Company job to go to Little Company after just a year. Joining Big Company for just a year a bit later in your career will look a bit odd.

However, my advice pertains specifically to what the right career move is for you. If you'll be unhappy at a big company, it's okay to make the worse move.

It's also not absolute advice that applies in all situations. If this start-up is on a trajectory to be wildly successful, getting in early might be a great move.

More likely than not though, the start-up will flounder a bit and then fail. That's why I advocate the big company move. Spend a year and then you can freely leave, with a prestigious company on your resume. That's usually, but not always, the best move.

16 Crafting Your Career

If it feels like the interview cycle never stops, that's because it doesn't. You need to start thinking about your next career jump on your first day at the current job. What will you do? When will you switch positions? Will you stay at your company or go to a new one?

Most new employees are extremely focused on creating great work, but that's only half the battle. To get promoted or get a nice, fat raise, you do (hopefully) need to execute on your responsibilities very well. But you also must build strong relationships, understand your weaknesses, and position yourself to make important accomplishments for the company.

Additionally, you need to know where you want to go to next. What's the point in slaving to become the best darn software engineer you can be if you want to become a product manager?

Define Your Career Path

The first year that Christine joined Amazon, she was thrilled. Great team. Great pay. And a company that most people would kill to work for. The second year was the same, as was the third and fourth year. She loved it there. Why would she leave? The dramatic rise of the stock price didn't hurt either.

By year five, she was finally ready for a change and started shopping her resume around. She realized then what far too many people do: she didn't really need those extra few years at Amazon. Had she left two years earlier, she would have been in *nearly* the same position. Oops.

It's easy to get sucked into a big company and let the years fly by blissfully unaware. This is why it's important to map out your career early and to check in on it often.

Plan Ahead

Defining your career path will ensure that you understand, up front, how long you intend to be at a company and what you believe you'll get out of it. Your plans may change, of course, either because you can actually move faster than you had originally thought or because your goals changed. In that case, simply redefine your career path.

Your career path will force you to rethink that extra year: Are you really going to get something new out of the job? It will also highlight what background you need to make the next jump.

Your plan should stretch at least 7 to 10 years in the future.

Depending on your manager and your field, you could consider sharing your desired path with your supervisors (or at least a tweaked one expressing interest in moving up at the company). Your supervisors will be in an excellent position to help you acquire the desired experience.

A Little Something on the Side

Side projects are valuable to finding a job, and this means that you should think about it *while* currently employed. A good side project can diversify your resume, teach you new skills, give you a more unique and interesting background, and broaden your network.

Although you're probably very busy with your work and personal life, try to set aside time regularly each month. If it's difficult to set aside regular time, then try to spend a weekend a few times a year to do something different. It doesn't take that much time to have something else to show for your experience.

Being Great

While politics and various other unfortunate issues do play a role in promotions and raises, the best employees still tend to move up the fastest. By far, the most important thing you can do is to actually be great in your job.

Be Great to Your Boss

In most companies, your boss will be the primary person responsible for your career. She'll be the one deciding if you get a raise, if you get that new title, or if you get put on that cool new project. She needs to really value you.

Be the solution to your boss's problems—and go above and beyond. Try, as much as possible, to anticipate these needs.

Know What the Criteria Are for Success

You should talk to your manager—and potentially even *his* manager—early and often to understand what the criteria are for success. What determines if you get that promotion? What were the key reasons why the last person got a promotion?

Ask specifically if there are any skills you'd need to acquire to move to this next level, and figure out how to get those.

Ask for Forgiveness, Not Permission

In most careers, managers consider that it's better to ask for forgiveness than permission. Initiative is valued because it relieves work from your manager. You will actually be performing better and doing more important work.

Additionally, initiative demonstrates that you're capable of taking on the next level of responsibilities. This is important for getting a promotion in the future.

With initiative comes the likelihood of making mistakes. Your manager should understand that. If she expects initiative and isn't reasonably understanding of mistakes, then this probably isn't a person you should work for.

Manage the Review Process

Many people have a love/hate relationship with the semiannual reviews. We understand that companies have to do them, and we may even look forward to them, as they're our chance to get promoted. But, still, we get slapped with so-called constructive criticism, and we have to write extensive comments about everything we've done over the past six months to a year.

Additionally, reviews are inevitably biased toward your most recent work since that's freshest in people's minds. To make the most of the review process, try the following tips.

1. Make Your Successes Known

No one likes a person who gloats about everything she's done, but at the same time, you won't advance if people don't know about your successes. Here are a few tactics to publicize your accomplishments without turning off your teammates:

- **Send your manager regular updates.** Keith from Google e-mails his manager an update before their regular one-on-one meetings. "I describe what I've accomplished in the past week and what problems I experienced doing so. This not only helps to make our meetings more efficient, but it also helps to create a record each week of what I've accomplished. This comes in handy during review time," Keith says.
- **Set team goals (and update them).** Encourage your team to set weekly goals, and send a weekly e mail with the team's progress. This will allow you to highlight your progress, in addition to that of the rest of your team.
- **Applaud your teammates.** Doing well does not mean your teammates have to do poorly. In fact, if you go out of your way to publicly praise your teammates, they are less likely to feel competitive or angry when you mention your successes.

The common theme is to have a reason to mention your progress. No one likes someone who shows off for no reason, and getting too close to this will inflame the competitive spirit of your teammates.

2. Track Your Accomplishments as You Go

If you've decided to e-mail your manager with your weekly progress, then great! You may not even need to do this at all. Otherwise, it may help to have an easily accessible file where you list your biggest accomplishments.

When one task is more or less wrapped up, write up your review-ready blurb right then and there. You'll be able to remember all the details, hardest parts, and lessons learned much better than you will after several months have passed.

If you've been storing this file on your work computer and you leave the company, consider taking this file with you. You'll want it for your resume or for your interview preparation.

3. Quantify the Results

Much like on your resume, you will also want to quantify your accomplishments for your review. The earlier you collect this information, the better. Imagine how much better a statement like "Implemented performance improvements, resulting in a 17 percent reduction in costs" sounds than a vague statement like "Implemented performance improvements." If you can't quantify the result, then you should at least record any impact or comments people had.

4. Ask Early for Feedback—and Get It in Writing

Feedback early and often is the key to continual improvement. It will help you know what your weaknesses are or what else your company is hoping from you.

Ask your manager for feedback on what you've been doing well, what you've been doing poorly, and what you could do better in the future. Are there any specific responsibilities or tasks he'd like to see you take on? How can you reach these goals?

This sort of conversation is usually best had in person, but follow up over e-mail to reiterate the conclusions. You want to create a written record of these conversations.

- It confirms that you and your manager have the same interpretation of the conversation.
- It gives you a record to refer to in the future, if you forget any details.
- It refreshes your manager's memory when your annual performance review comes around and encourages your manager to evaluate you from this.
- In the unlikely (though not terribly unusual) scenario that a serious management issue arises, it gives you, your manager, and HR a

document to refer to. If you feel that you haven't received much-deserved promotions, this document will be key to showing that you've been doing what you need to in order to progress.

Constant feedback will also enable you to correct issues early on, before they come up in your performance evaluation.

Play a Bit of Politics: Build Strong Relationships

We may hate the office politics, but what can you do? They're a fact of life. In order to get ahead, people need to like you or at least respect you. This is especially true if you hope to be promoted to a team lead or manager position.

Being well liked doesn't mean you need to be Mr. or Ms. Popular. It just means being a great team player. Make an effort to do the following:

- **Help others.** Chip in to help the new guy or discreetly help a struggling coworker. It'll earn the respect and appreciation of others.
- **Be supportive and positive.** Good moods are infectious. Keeping a smile on your face and being positive about changes in the team or company will make people want to be around you. Plus, no one will really want to bad-mouth the guy who's nice to everyone.
- **Give credit.** When a coworker does something impressive, be the one to shoot out an e-mail to the team congratulating her. Or if people praise you for something where the applause really should be shared, make a point of acknowledging your partner's help. You may be downgrading your own work to a small degree, but such kindness will easily be repaid. If you act as a champion for others, people will not only like you but they will also feel less threatened by you. This makes them more likely to champion your success.
- **Appeal to egos.** Everyone wants to feel important and valued; give your coworkers what they want here. Show them that you want to learn from them and that you think they're smart and insightful.
- **Shut up and listen.** Sometimes, we disagree with our coworkers so strongly that we want to scream. In these cases, the best thing you can do is to just listen. This will show them that you understand their perspective and that you value it. They'll likely return the favor by listening to you.

Those with strong relationships are not only perceived better, but they also tend to be more effective performers because they know how to get team support.

Identify a Mentor

A mentor is more than just someone who can teach you—she is also your advocate. Just like a parent wants to see his child succeed, a leader wants to see her protégé succeed. She will fight for you because your success is her success.

Seek out a mentor who has the following traits:

- **Successful.** While your peers can, of course, give you good advice as well, you'll generally get better advice from people who are 5 to 15 years ahead of you. Less than 5 years and they won't have too much wisdom; more than 15 years and they're likely to be out of touch with your issues.
- **Similar goals.** Advice from people who are successful in very different fields is likely to be unhelpful at best and detrimental at worst. What do you think the successful entrepreneur will tell you about your goal to be a VP at Microsoft? Probably something about bureaucracy and how you can't ever really affect change. Maybe he's right, maybe he's not, but that's hardly helpful if that's your goal. People with similar goals are likely to understand what did and didn't work for them, and will also be able to relate the experiences of their peers to you.
- **Similar background.** Your prior background will heavily affect your ability to accomplish your goals. Someone who went to a far stronger, or weaker, school is unlikely to be able to tell you how to leverage or handle your school's name. Seek out those with a similar education and career backgrounds, as their struggles will probably closely match yours.
- **Supportive, encouraging, and trustworthy.** Your mentor is not just there to offer advice; she is also there to encourage you. A good mentor will enable you to open up about your concerns and will help to ease them. She'll be supportive of you, whether you fail or succeed. And, of course, you need to be able to trust her to be honest with you when there's something negative you need to hear.
- **Has time for you.** Though this should be obvious, it's often overlooked. Your mentor needs to have the time for you. What's the point of a mentor if he's never there to chat or to connect you with the right resources?

If you read through the preceding five points, you'll note that what you're essentially looking for is someone who's just like you, only a few steps ahead. And that's a good thing, even if it's difficult for some people to find. If you can't find the perfect mentor, that's okay. There's no reason you can't have multiple mentors.

Your manager can certainly serve as a mentor in many ways, but you can't necessarily trust him to be unbiased. His first priority is to your company, not to you. If you're a star performer, will he really encourage you to leave, even if that's what's best for your career?

Promotions and Raises

Annual and semiannual reviews are not just a time to get feedback; they're also a time to get promoted or get a raise—or both. To position yourself effectively for these opportunities, you'll want to think ahead and carefully craft your own evaluation to make it clear that you deserve the boost.

How to Get Promoted

Many companies, including Microsoft and Google, have some system of career levels, enabling an employee to get promoted without a title or any other substantial change. Microsoft, for example, utilizes a universal level system, where employees enter at a level (usually between 58 and 65) depending on their prior experience and their new title. A promotion might constitute moving from a Level 60 to a 61. Moving from one title to the next may not change your work much if at all.

Such companies tend to have well-defined metrics for what attributes an employee at a particular level should exhibit. These may be written in a formal document, but if not, have a discussion with your manager.

By examining the attributes you need to have, you can make sure to acquire the relevant skills or just demonstrate that you have them. If the next level up requires being able to lead key feature design, then ask your manager to let you take on some of these responsibilities. The earlier you plan for promotion, the better.

And remember, it's usually easiest to get promoted when you show that you're already performing at that next level.

Figure Out What It Really *Takes*

Much as we'd love to believe that you just need to do a great job in your role to land a promotion, there's often a bit more to it than that. This is *especially* true at the larger tech companies. Sometimes it's about befriending a particularly senior person on your team. Sometimes it's about being successful in a particular way. Sometimes you need to be on the right projects.

Your manager will give you some insight here, but she might not give you the full story. Ex-employees and the cynical older employees can be a good resource to learn what it really takes.

How to Negotiate a Raise

In many ways, getting a raise is tougher than getting a promotion. At least a promotion, even if it includes a raise as well, involves your asking for something more in exchange for contributing more to the company. A raise, however, just means that the company is paying you a bit more and it gets little else additional out of it—except, of course, a reduced chance that you'll leave.

Companies understand that raises are a part of doing business, and by following a few suggestions, you can increase the chances that you'll get your much deserved raise.

Choose the Right Time

There are better times to request a raise, and in the middle of tough times for your company is probably not one of them. It may, in fact, have a detrimental effect, as it calls attention to just how much (or how little) you are worth.

The ideal time to ask for a raise is when things are going well for your company and its competitors. A company's primary motivation in giving you a raise is to ensure that you stick around. If the company can't afford your raise, or if there's little risk of your leaving, you're unlikely to get it.

Additionally, you should ask for a raise when it's convenient for your boss. After all, even if he wants to grant it to you, it may not be his decision. You need to ensure that he has the time and energy to go out and fight for you. If he's busy with other projects, or he's fighting for approval on other things (particularly things that increase your team's financial cost), he may not be a great advocate for you.

Do Your Homework

Because a company's primary motivation in giving a raise is to prevent you from leaving, you'll have a much better case if you can show that you're underpaid. Websites such as PayScale and Glassdoor can be useful tools in assessing how your pay compares with the industry pay. Be careful, however, in relying too heavily on these sites; the information is not totally accurate.

It may be more useful to ask your friends, or even very trustworthy coworkers, for their salary information. People are surprisingly open about their salary if they can trust you and if they understand why you're asking.

Interviewing about once a year with another company can also help you keep tabs on whether you're paid fairly. You might get a new exciting opportunity but even if not, it'll still give you a sense of your market worth.

Justify It

Your request for a raise should be backed up with solid reasons that include your accomplishments and what you've done for the company. If you can quantify your contributions in a dollar amount, that's even better. What company wouldn't fight to retain someone who was contributing millions to the company?

If you have coworkers who have been through this process and who you can confide in, you may want to consider asking them for their advice. They may be able to direct you on what people actually value or don't value. This may be different from what the company states publicly. For instance, many companies state that they value employees mentoring new employees. These companies likely recognize that mentorship is important in general, but this doesn't mean that it's strongly weighted during the performance evaluation process.

Overshoot

Much like in the offer negotiation process, you should shoot for more than what you can realistically expect. The company is more likely to meet you in the middle than to give you everything you ask for.

How to Handle Rejection

Your boss said no? Don't despair—that's common. Instead of just walking out of her office, ask her what would need to change to get the promotion or raise. Is it the company's financial situation? Do you need to take on more leadership responsibilities? What specifically would that entail?

Follow up this conversation with an e-mail summarizing this information. Then, the next time you ask for a promotion or raise, you can cite how you've done everything she's asked for.

If the issue is that the company simply can't afford it, consider alternative ways that the company could reward you. Perhaps it could let you work from home one day per week.

Finally, if your chances of getting a promotion or raise look poor for the foreseeable future, perhaps you should consider finding a new position—outside the company. What's the point of sticking around if there are no additional rewards for you?

How and When to Quit

Once upon a time, people got a job and stuck with it for nearly their entire lives. But now, much to the chagrin of the older generation, this fierce loyalty has been replaced by an expectation that you have at least two or three jobs by age 30. Stick around too long and you may be considered tainted by that company's culture.

Leave When It's Not Working

Successful people often don't want to give up; that's how they got to be successful in the first place. Thus, when their job isn't quite working out, they often want to try to fix things: develop a better relationship with a manager, find a different project, smooth things over with their coworker, or just stick it out until some point in the future.

Very frequently, that's the wrong move. There is an opportunity cost in sticking around in your job. Only in rare cases can the issue that's preventing you from loving your job be fixed totally. Instead, it typically just stays bad—a little better than it used to be, but still bad.

Think hard about if it's really worth it to stick around. There's a big opportunity cost in staying.

Leave When You Stop Growing

What have you learned in the past three months? If you aren't growing—if you haven't learned more—it's often a sign that you find something better. Your job should push you.

Leave When You Want to Quit

If you've got that itch to do something new, that's usually a pretty good indication that you should leave. After all, there's usually a reason you're thinking about it. Maybe you are unhappy at your job. Maybe you want something new. Maybe you just think you could get a better job elsewhere. Regardless, that *itch* is usually an indication you should consider looking for other options.

There is, of course, also value in sticking with the same company. If you want to make a big career change, you'll sometimes have an easier time doing that within your existing company where you've already proven yourself. When you transition roles within one firm, you have already built trust, and the firm understands your relevant skills at a great depth. Trying to change your role when moving to a new firm is much harder.

How Soon Is Too Soon to Quit?

Recruiters get concerned about hiring a frequent job hopper, but that's not necessarily a reason to stick it out at a company for a year or more. On the contrary, if you're unhappy in the first few weeks of a job, it's okay to quit. Yes, the company might be frustrated at your quitting so soon, but a year is a long time to wait it out. Additionally, if you leave early enough, you don't necessarily even need to list this job on your resume.

Most employers are usually pretty understanding of quitting a job early, as long as it doesn't become a pattern. They'll ask some questions about the quick switch but typically won't be overly concerned.

How to Not Burn Bridges

If you've ever had a job you hated, you've probably dreamed of quitting in some epic way. A public memo citing everything your boss did wrong. Spelling "I Quit" with spaghetti on the cafeteria floor. Borrowing the most annoying children of your friends to run wild around the office. It would be refreshing and—hopefully, I don't need to tell you this—incredibly stupid.

Even if you don't intend to have some massive blowout quitting ceremony, your departure is still likely to be a sensitive time, and it's all too easy to burn bridges. It's too small a world out there to do that; you may need your coworkers for references, or you might even end up working with them down the road.

To avoid leaving a foul taste in their mouths, do the following:

- **Give sufficient notice.** Two weeks is considered a bare minimum, but depending on the importance of your role and the situation, longer might be appropriate. At a small company, extra time might be appropriate due to the difficulty of finding someone to fill in.
- **Find an appropriate time.** Leaving halfway through a project or just before a deadline should be avoided, where possible. Ideally, you should leave as a project ends or even right when a project is beginning.
- **Voice concerns early.** If you're leaving because of specific things about the company you don't like, particularly if these are changeable, voice these concerns early. It's in your best interest to give your boss a chance to fix things.
- **Tell your manager first.** As tempting as it may be, don't tell anyone that you're leaving until your manager knows. It could get very ugly if he hears it from someone else first.
- **Leave on a positive note.** Work extra hard in your final days to make sure that your work is wrapped up or at least passed on to an appropriate person. You'll be remembered fondly for putting in the additional effort.

That said, be wary that waiting for the perfect time to leave isn't causing you to stay excessively long.

Should I Find a New Job First?

Many people advise that you should only search for a job while employed, and there's a lot of truth to this. It is easier to find a job while you're employed. Being unemployed can make you seem lazy or desperate—or make employers worry that you might have been fired. If you try to job search while unemployed, you might also feel pressured to take a job quickly.

However, looking for a job once you're unemployed has its perks:

- **Search openly.** Once you've left, you can publicly post to Facebook, Twitter, your blog, or wherever, that you're looking for a new job. There's no need to hide your job search from your friends, or even your (former) coworkers, and some might know about the perfect position for you.

- **Extended vacation.** No more worrying about using up your precious 15 days of paid time off. Now you can take that extended vacation to Europe.
- **Open scheduling.** Interviewing for a new position while holding down a current job is tricky. There are only so many doctor's appointment excuses you can use before your manager starts to think that you're suffering from some terminal illness.
- **Additional experience.** Your time off can be used not only to job search, but also to gather experience to improve your application. Perhaps you could take an online class on marketing, learn to code a bit, or volunteer at a local organization.

This is all predicated on being able to afford to take time off. If you can't afford to take at least three months off without breaking the bank, you probably do not want the pressure of unemployment. (Programmers, who have more job opportunities in the tech field, can probably get away with less time.)

Questions and Answers

Shakespeare Can Write

I started off college as a computer science major, but switched to English halfway through my sophomore year. My professors were bad, my classmates were antisocial, and the workload was way too much.

Now that I'm graduating—surprise, surprise—I'm finding that the job prospects for developers are substantially better than they are for writers.

I think I stand a chance at relearning the fundamentals enough to pass a round of Microsoft-esque interviews. But will they even consider me without a computer science major?

They might—with enough preparation—but the better question is, are you sure you want that? Remember you dropped out of

(*continued*)

(*continued*)
computer science for a reason and switched to a very different major. That's a pretty good sign that the programming life isn't right for you. Plus, it sounds like your primary motivation is money, and that motivation tends not to lead to the best coders.

Instead, you might consider career paths in the technology space that make better use of your dual interests. You'd be an excellent fit for technical writer, but a career path as a program manager may also be a nice match. There are a lot of options, in fact, for people who understand technology but can also write well.

If you do want to pursue this path still, you're going to need to really focus on developing each project and other practical experience. Put this as the primary focus for now. Realistically, you might have a better shot with a start-up since start-ups tend to be more flexible about hiring people without degrees.

In Name Only

My company recently had a round of layoffs, which included my own manager. His manager is now the direct manager of my teammates and me, and I've had to step up to take on most of my old manager's work. I'm now effectively the manager of the team, though without the title or the hire/fire responsibilities. I feel like I deserve a raise, if not a promotion. How do I convince the company?

You may deserve a raise, but it's not going to happen. Your company is going through some hard times and can't afford to give you a raise.

Instead, you should see this as an opportunity to get a lot more responsibility than you otherwise would have gotten. You get to acquire a bunch of new skills and prove that you have what it takes to truly fill your manager's responsibilities. Focus on that—learning things and demonstrating your worth.

When the purse strings loosen again, you'll be able to make a strong case for a raise. You can cite the prior additional responsibilities as evidence while noting that the company can now afford to compensate you more fairly for your performance.

If the company refuses, then this is an excellent sign to you to begin looking for other options. You're still in a better position than you were prelayoffs because your resume is that much more impressive.

Newbie Wants Out

I've been working at my new job for only five weeks, and I can already tell I want out. The company told me that I'd be working with customers, other departments, and so on, and that's just not true. At best, I work with people who work with customers. Moreover, the culture is just stifling. They say the hours are flexible, but people judge you if you're not there by 9 AM. This is just not the place for me. Is it too soon to leave?

Yes, leaving after five weeks will look bad. I'm not sure you have many other options, though. It doesn't sound like you want to stick it out for a year (the minimum length of time), and making it three or four months isn't much better. It's best to just bite the bullet and leave.

The question is, do you find a job while working or go ahead and quit? All else being equal, the more you can focus on the job search, the better.

(*continued*)

(*continued*)

There are strategies to minimize the damage to your career and your reputation.

If you can afford being asked to leave immediately, it's best to sit down with your manager and explain the situation: the company isn't the right fit for you, and you're going to start looking for a new position. You'd like to help the company make the smoothest transition possible, so you wanted to tell your manager earlier rather than later. This will be an uncomfortable conversation, but it's one you'll have eventually anyway.

As far as what to tell prospective employers, the best answer is the (softened) truth: that the position was very different than you were led to believe, and you decided that it's best just to move on immediately rather than drag things out.

If there's less than about a six-month gap, you don't need to list this short-lived position on your resume at all. You only need to explain the situation if asked.

17 On Luck, Leverage, and You

Success begets success. People who are successful at their job get stronger recommendations, get promoted faster, get cooler projects, broaden their network more, and get better opportunities across the board.

However, if you talk to successful people, they'll also point to a good amount of luck involved. They met just the right person, joined a company at just the right time, took some opportunity on a whim, or happened to stumble down a particularly lucrative path. How would they know where it would lead?

Most of us know that the truth lies in between these. It's luck, but it's also their work ethic, skills, intelligence, and other personal attributes.

There's another layer of complexity, though, and perhaps one of the best things you can do for your career: *saying yes*. These successful people said *yes* to opportunities.

Lucky opportunities pass you all the time. You won't and can't know that a coffee meeting, which you didn't really see the point of taking, will connect you to a to-be-pivotal person in your life. You won't and can't know that helping out your friend's company on the side will give you some skill that the next hot start-up will crave. You won't and can't know where many things will lead.

But what you can do is say *yes* to those little things that you normally wouldn't really feel like doing—because they just might be the stepping stone to something amazing.

Great careers are not linear so much as they are step functions. These lucky opportunities give you a few major boosts in life and make all the difference.

Say yes—and then leverage the heck out of the opportunity.
Create a killer resume showcasing your experience.
Prepare thoroughly for the interview.
Walk in with confidence and sophistication in your answers.
Negotiate for the things that matter to you.
Pick the offer that's the best match for your background.
Work hard and work smart.

You can't create your own luck, but you can leverage it. *Say yes.*

Index

PREPARE TO SAY *YES* TO A CAREER AT THE WORLD'S MOST EXCITING COMPANIES

Let's be real: preparing for a career at one of the world's most powerful companies can be incredibly challenging. But, if tech is the right place for you, it could be the most rewarding challenge of your life. In *Cracking the Tech Career,* Gayle Laakmann McDowell compiles countless insider tips on how to stand out from the hordes of applicants to land the most coveted jobs in the tech industry.

Google, Facebook, Microsoft, and other top tech firms are at the cutting edge when it comes to employment. But with perks like free organic food and shuttles to and from work, these companies can afford to be choosy. Successful candidates have to be special. *Cracking the Tech Career* walks you through the whole process.

This book is for any student or job seeker who ever wondered—*is tech right for me?* Even if you aren't a programmer, breaking into Silicon Valley takes some planning. In *Cracking the Tech Career*, you'll learn what it's *really* like to work for the big names and the small startups. Get the experience that they're looking for discover how to:

- Get your foot in the door with a knockout resume
- Nail the tricky coding, behavioral, and estimation questions
- Break into the exclusive world of game design
- *Get offered the job!*

With job offers from over 10 tech firms, Gayle Laakmann McDowell knows her stuff. Read *Cracking the Tech Career* to find out how she did it, and learn how you can, too!

GAYLE LAAKMANN MCDOWELL worked as a software engineer for Google, Microsoft, and Apple, and has received offers from ten other top tech firms. She was one of Google's most active interviewers and served on Google's hiring committee. As the founder/CEO of CareerCup.com, she now consults with tech companies on their hiring process and coaches candidates through the process.

Cover Design: Wiley
Cover Illustration: © iStock.com/min6939

BUSINESS & ECONOMICS/Careers/Job Hunting

$22.00 USA / $26.00 CAN

WILEY

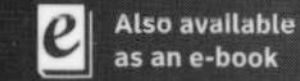